Curriculum Trends

A REFERENCE HANDBOOK

CONTEMPORARY EDUCATION ISSUES

Curriculum Trends

•◆ A REFERENCE HANDBOOK

Valerie J. Janesick

A B C 🞂 C L I O

Santa Barbara, California • Denver, Colorado • Oxford, England

Library of Congress Cataloging-in-Publication Data
Janesick, Valerie J.
  Curriculum trends : a reference handbook / Valerie J. Janesick.
    p. cm. — (Contemporary education issues)
Includes bibliographical references and index.
  ISBN 1-85109-461-X (hardcover : alk. paper); ISBN 1-85109-466-0 (e-book)
  1. Education—Curricula—United States. 2. Curriculum
planning—United States. 3. Education—Aims and objectives—United
States. I. Title. II. Series.
  LB1570.J33 2003
  375'.00975—dc21

                                                                      2003014242

08 07 06 05 04 03   10 9 8 7 6 5 4 3 2 1

This book is also available on the World Wide Web as an e-book.
Visit www.abc-clio.com for details.

ABC-CLIO, Inc.
130 Cremona Drive, P.O. Box 1911
Santa Barbara, California 93116-1911

This book is printed on acid-free paper.
Manufactured in the United States of America

❧ Contents

⚫◇ Series Editor's Preface

The Contemporary Education Issues series is dedicated to providing readers with an up-to-date exploration of the central issues in education today. Books in the series will examine such controversial topics as home schooling, charter schools, privatization of public schools, Native American education, African American education, literacy, curriculum development, and many others. The series is national in scope and is intended to encourage research by anyone interested in the field.

Because education is undergoing radical if not revolutionary change, the series is particularly concerned with how contemporary controversies in education affect both the organization of schools and the content and delivery of curriculum. Authors will endeavor to provide a balanced understanding of the issues and their effects on teachers, students, parents, administrators, and policymakers. The aim of the Contemporary Education Issues series is to publish excellent research on today's educational concerns by some of the finest scholar/practitioners in the field while pointing to new directions. The series promises to offer important analyses of some of the most controversial issues facing society today.

Danny Weil
Series Editor

◆◆ Preface

I have always loved to write. This book took shape because of my love of writing and the opportunity it provided to summarize my work as a professor of curriculum studies and research. For the past twenty years or so, I have been teaching courses in curriculum theory and inquiry, curriculum development, and curriculum improvement in the area of educational leadership. Thus, this book has been in the making for quite some time. The opportunity to pull together some major trends and help newcomers to the field understand a bit about curriculum trends was too good to pass up. This reference handbook evolved into an overview of trends in the United States from the late 1880s to the present. I wrote this text as an introduction to the field of curriculum studies by looking at the trends in the field. It is written for people who may be considering education as a career. It is also written for anyone who wants an introduction to trends in curriculum over time. In fact, the reader may see that there is nothing new under the sun. A careful reader may also see that certain trends pop up on a fairly regular basis in one form or another. The major idea I want to get across in this text is that curriculum trends are the result of contested ideas and the coming and going of money appropriated most often for some educational reform. In addition, the two key questions in the area of curriculum are:

1. What do we teach?
2. How best do we teach it?

These two questions permeate virtually every proposed educational reform activity. These questions, as basic as they are, still cause controversy in many quarters. Not everyone in a given community agrees about *what* should be taught, let alone *how* the topic or content should be taught. Furthermore, when you layer on the complexity of decisionmakers at the local, state, and national levels, you see how complicated any question in curriculum can be. Part of the strength of our democracy is evidenced when it comes to educational issues. For it is here that a great deal of dialogue, debate, propaganda, and politics get mixed together and eventually come to some resolution. The idea of a public school virtually ensures that whatever the educational issue of the day is, there will follow some level of controversy. One only has to read the newspaper to pick out the current controversy over high-stakes testing, poverty and schools, whether values should be taught in schools, and issues of multiculturalism, to name a few examples.

Because this text is a reference handbook, it is put together in a particular format following the long-established procedure of the publisher. Chapter One is about the big picture of the field, with the major themes and heart of curriculum trends. Chapter Two presents a time line of how the trends developed historically. Chapters Three and Four are a road map of resources. These chapters contain some major curriculum resources in print and nonprint media, such as books, journals, videos, web sites, and organizations related to curriculum trends. Of course, we live in an information age, and thus, certain sets of information may change even by the time this book goes to print. In any event, these resources are a good starting point for anyone interested in learning about our schools through curriculum trends. Chapter Five is focused on hopeful trends for the future. Those trends have been percolating for many decades and are coming to a recognizable shape and form in many schools today. They can only offer us hope for improving the quality of education for children. The appendixes offer many examples of the trends described throughout the text, as well as a glossary of terms in the field.

Obviously, when a topic as large as curriculum trends is to be explained, some trends will be omitted. It was in the interest of providing a comprehensive snapshot of the field that the key trends selected here were chosen. The three criteria that enabled me to further clarify trends and that guided this book included:

1. The trend must have been present in some form for five to ten years or longer.
2. The trend had to be of interest at federal, state, and local levels.
3. The trend had to resonate with teachers, curriculum leaders, and administrators, as evidenced by print or nonprint media.

The reader should know that I have a strong commitment to the field of curriculum studies, this being my lifework. I also appreciate the insights and contributions of my doctoral students and others who labor intensively in the front lines, bringing the issues raised in the text to fruition. They will never stop raising the questions that need to be raised, and they will never give up on schools and schooling. In the tradition of John Dewey, we draw hope and resilience from the recognition that by understanding the complexity of curriculum trends, we can help mold informed individuals who will be prepared for active and thought-ful participation in a democratic society.

Valerie J. Janesick
Chicago
January 2003

✦ Dedication and Acknowledgments

This book is dedicated to my students, former students, and colleagues who share an interest in curriculum trends. Special thanks go to Carolyn Stevenson and Lorna Elam, who, in addition to contributing their written work, helped track down references and the most difficult to find information. They are dedicated educators and continue this high level of professionalism in their respective careers. Additional and heartfelt gratitude goes to those educators who contributed their fine written work in the form of examples of autobiography, curriculum materials, and life experience recast. They are: Cheryl Buck, Brian Coleman, Lorna Elam, Suzanne Evenson, Beth Harris, Susan Hill, Ruth Anne Jepson, Susan Katz, Jennifer Kohnke-Moniuszko, Jan Mulqueeny, Nick Myers, Tim Podlewski, Barbara Schmitt, Eva C. Smith, John Steinhebel, Carolyn Stevenson, and Henry C. Thiele. I am indebted as well to the authors of all the texts referenced in this handbook. They led the way to a richer understanding of historical and current trends in the field of curriculum.

Curriculum Trends

A Reference Handbook

Chapter One

✎ Introduction and Framing the Field

INTRODUCTION

The field of curriculum can best be understood by viewing it in terms of trends. In this text, trends that took shape from the late 1800s to the present are described and explained. Three major categories of trends appeared in the field of curriculum studies. The three most sensible categories used for this text are: The traditionalists, the reconceptualists, and the postmodern writers. There are many subcategories, of course, in a field as wide as curriculum. For the purposes of this text, the three categories selected will enable the reader to get an overview of the field as well as an insight into particular moments in the history of curriculum that changed how we view schools, teachers, ourselves, and society. Many writers have used these or closely related terms. For this handbook, the three categories are wide enough to capture the complexity of curriculum trends.

In addition, this text represents my own journey through my career as a teacher, an educational leader, and a professor of curriculum and research courses. Schools and curriculum are reflections of our society. What happens politically, economically, and psychologically in daily life has some effect in the classroom. Likewise, schools also reflect our society. So there is no one way to view curriculum, nor is the complexity of curriculum issues lessening. In fact, one could argue that since the events of September 11, 2001, in New York, at the Pentagon, and in Pennsylvania, a spiritual and social-psychological curricular wake-up call has occurred. In the aftermath of September 11, we are more aware than ever before of the need to educate the whole person and go deeper into the meaning of curriculum. In other words, curriculum embraces the overt areas of learning, assessment, and the content of subjects but also pays attention to the inner needs of the learner. The spiritual center of an individual is as critical to develop as the external temporal components of learning. Thus, the key questions in the field

What do we teach?

How best do we teach?

are continually transformed to include the whole person.

In my own life as an educator and with a background in the arts and disciplined inquiry, curriculum studies was a natural career focus for me. In a sense, this book has been in preparation for two decades. In general, ever present is hope and optimism. Hope exists so that curriculum can be reshaped in many schools to allow learners to learn and teachers to teach effectively. Optimism exists so that within the context of curriculum, the education of the whole person will be a permanent fixture in curriculum trends. The result would be a critical reflective learner, participating actively in our democratic society.

CURRICULUM TRENDS AS A PAINTING

In an effort to understand curriculum, a helpful metaphor—the metaphor of painting—will be used. As trends in the field are described, think of a painting, in which each stroke of the brush and each color of paint brings us closer to understanding the current and latest portrayal of the subject that is curriculum trends. But all paintings begin somewhere on the canvas. The first stroke is about our history in the field of curriculum trends, or the traditional approach. The second stroke is about the reconceptualists, who challenged the nuts-and-bolts approach of the traditionalists and who revered science. The next stroke is the postmodern stroke. What the postmodernists questioned was our reckless adherence to logic and reason when so much else was going on in the learning process. They also wanted the learner as a person inserted into the educational equation. They disrupted the calm sea of the traditionalists and reconceptualists, so to speak. To complete the painting, the final strokes are about the future of curriculum as autobiographical text, curriculum as aesthetic text, and curriculum as ethical text. For the sake of clarity, this first section will focus on where we came from, or the traditional view of curriculum.

THE FIRST STROKE: THE TRADITIONALIST VIEW OF CURRICULUM TRENDS

As we look back over our history, recall that when the traditionalist writers began, they were the revolutionaries and the movers and shakers of their time. Now as we look back, it seems these writers portrayed a field that in fact did not exist. Nonetheless, they began the discussion and provided the points of departure for studying the field. Key texts on traditional curriculum views can be traced to as early as the 1880s and up to the 1970s, so strong is the voice of the traditionalist. Even in the early years, the politics of education was forcing and prompting some critique of these writings, although not overtly explained as such. Major events such as World War I shaped the thinking and writing of the time. Definitions, to be clear, were critical then as now. In fact, the word *curriculum* can be defined as, alternately and literally:

> The race to be run, from the Latin word *currerre*
> The racecourse
> A field of study
> The course the mind runs on
> All the experiences children have in school
> All learning opportunities
> A program for all experiences encountered by a learner

Obviously, the field is complex and complicated. But in a sense, each of these definitions adds to our understanding of curriculum trends. Now, let's continue with our painting.

What Did We Learn from the Traditional View?

The discussion of curriculum trends began as far back as the 1880s, and key educators in higher education met to proclaim the importance of curriculum in 1890. Yet it took fifty years to gel, and it was not until the 1940s that the educator Ralph Tyler wrote his now famous "Tyler Rationale." In 1949, Tyler wrote *Basic Principles of Curriculum and Instruction,* and our field of curriculum was on the way to many debates and new twists and turns; most likely, that work is responsible for today's reconceptualization of the field, especially in terms of the postmodern. Tyler's principles consist of four questions:

1. What educational purposes should schools seek to attain? (objectives)
2. What educational experiences can be provided that are likely to attain these purposes? (design)
3. How can these educational experiences be effectively organized? (scope and sequence)
4. How can we determine whether these purposes are attained? (evaluation)

But what was missing from the Tyler rationale was the person as learner and the teacher as public intellectual. Tyler assumed the teacher was like a banker, to use Brazilian educator Paulo Freire's term. When education is viewed as banking, the student comes in to the banker/teacher and makes a deposit or withdrawal. So Tyler in effect erased the human being. Of course, this would cause problems down the line in our history. In fact, Tyler created these questions, oddly enough, based on the work of the philosopher and educator John Dewey (1902) and the educator Franklin Bobbitt (1918). Both of these writers refocused the discussion on curriculum trends. It was Dewey who was to have extensive influence and results.

A Stroke of Dewey

Let me back up and explain the profound influence of the philosopher and activist John Dewey (1859–1952). Dewey is widely recognized as the most powerful influence on educational philosophy and practice. His pragmatism—that branch of philosophy that seeks to balance theory and practice, with an eye to social change—caused schooling to change and curriculum specialists to rejoice. Dewey began the Laboratory School at the University of Chicago in 1896 and ran it until 1904. He wanted to see theory in action and the importance of experience in education. Indeed, he claimed (and I agree) that we cannot know something without directly experiencing it. For example, you learn about painting a landscape through the actual engagement of paint and canvas, creative thought, and actually painting. Children at early ages learn mathematical principles by using manipulatives, or objects to work with. All of us who love literature love it because vicariously we experience the world of the writer and so on. Although Dewey historically falls in the time period of the traditionalists and reconceptualists, he foreshadowed and influenced the postmodern writers as well. Thus, any given writer may have elements of each of these traditions in his or her own work.

Dewey's groundbreaking work in the following texts helped to shape some of our schools then and now, in the United States and around the world. Of his voluminous writings, these texts in particular relate to curriculum trends:

"My Pedagogic Creed" (1897)
The School and Society (1899)
The Child and the Curriculum (1902)

How We Think (1910)
Democracy and Education (1916)
Art as Experience (1934)
Experience and Education (1938)

In addition to these dynamic resources, many texts have been written about Dewey's work. Still to this day, educators are actively attempting to put into practice his ideas, principles, and practices. Dewey was the first to argue for what would later be a major shift from control of subject matter by the teacher to control of learning by the student with student input regarding subject matter. In addition, he preferred at least a balance and a give-and-take posture between student and teacher. This was preferable to a technocratic, spoon-fed curriculum. Throughout Dewey's life and beyond, his writings influenced thinkers in philosophy, history, education, and the arts. In education, his most enduring legacy in terms of curriculum includes his focus on:

1. Experience as a key element in the educative process.
2. Child-centered activities for learning in the early years.
3. Democracy and education.
4. The significance of art as experience and a key component of education.
5. Awareness of the importance of the public school as a key element of educating the citizenry for a healthy democracy.
6. Pragmatism, or the balance between theory and practice.
7. Progressivism, or the movement to ensure experience-based education—a move away from technocratic approaches to curriculum—and dealing with the whole child. Not only that, progressivism had a goal of social improvement and change. For the first time, educators were looking to the school and society as never before.
8. The idea that a school must be a community. (It was this idea that the postmodernists took up and amplified.)

Although Dewey had many ideas that could be considered as rooted in traditionalist orientations, he certainly could also be perceived as a reconceptualist. His reconceptualist ideas would be those specifically centered on the person's need to experience something in order to learn it. This was congruent with other great thinkers worldwide, such as Jean Piaget (1898–1980), the Swiss psychologist, and Maria Montessori (1870–1952), the Italian medical doctor and educator. Furthermore, the

Austrian philosopher Rudolf Steiner (1861–1925) held these beliefs. Dewey's thought and writings and the Laboratory School most certainly affected many educators, many of whom we have come to call the reconceptualists. Likewise, the curriculum writer Franklin Bobbitt reinforced many ideas prevalent in Dewey's work and influenced the later work of Ralph Tyler. This is not to say that curriculum writers were one big, happy family. In fact, the criticisms of the traditional approach gave way to the next wave, the reconceptualists.

THE NEXT STROKE: THE RECONCEPTUALISTS

Although there are as many reconceptualists who helped to develop, improve, and, in some areas, negate the traditional approaches, the focus here is on some writers who stand out for the clarity of their contributions. Luckily, Elliot Eisner and Elizabeth Vallance (1974) listed five orientations to the reconceptualizing of the traditional approach to curriculum. Each of these can be found within the reconceptualists' writings. They are discussed in the following passages.

The Cognitive Process Orientation

This approach to curriculum focuses on cognitive skills that a learner applies to intellectual problems. The skills will endure after the content knowledge is forgotten or obsolete. This grouping would include developmentalist writers such as Jean Piaget, the Swiss psychologist, for example. For developmentalists, a learner learns in developmental stages that are age appropriate. At each stage, one retains characteristics of the previous stage but still continues development. For example, as adults, we might count on our fingers, an action most often associated with childhood. Yet we continue as adults to develop appropriately. Another such educator would be Maria Montessori, the Italian physician who created schools for children with physical and/or emotional problems and used concrete experiences to allow them to grow and develop into literate, well-rounded adults. One example of this approach can be seen in the recent discussion I had with one of my students. She happens to be taking a statistics course in the college of arts and sciences, and I asked her how it was going. She told me that she is doing well, oddly enough despite the fact that the class is totally based on one or more tests a week, no discussion of ideas, memorizing information, and decoding the textbook. Thus, she captured this orientation and its evolution in the postmodern time frame.

The Technological Orientation

In this approach to curriculum, technology may be involved but in the traditional "means to an end" focus. The problem is for the educational technologist to oversee the system so that goals can be achieved. In the field of curriculum, almost all textbooks smack of this orientation. Many rely on objectives, measuring, comparing scores, and the like. The technological orientation is almost totally traditional in origin. This is closely aligned with and follows from the traditionalists but adds the ever popular technology component. The problem is the way in which technology is viewed and how it is used or misused. An example of this orientation would be what currently goes on in most high schools. A student takes a course and learns how to do a Power Point presentation on a topic, and that supposedly satisfies as an understanding of technology. What is missing, a postmodernist might argue, is the critical eye toward the fact that there are race, class, and gender issues embedded in technology use. In fact, some students may not have the economic means to have a computer at home to practice even this basic exercise. Likewise, some minority members and women are excluded from the ownership, discourse, and use of any form of technology. Unfortunately, this continues presently in many schools and universities.

The Self-Actualization Orientation

In this approach, education and schooling are viewed as means to personal fulfillment, or self-actualization. Individuals find and discover their talents, skills, and abilities. Curriculum is thus enriching and valuable. This later was sometimes called the "personal success model." The psychologist Abraham Maslow was writing about self-actualization going through a hierarchy of levels and in effect sparked an interest in humanism sometimes associated with the traditionalists. However, recall that the traditionalist approach really erased the student and often the teacher from the learning process. An example of this approach would be the many alternative private schools that focus on developing the whole child, such as the Rudolf Steiner Waldorf Schools, the Montessori Schools, and experimental community schools based on the British experimental school Summerhill. In the 1970s, Summerhill, a model school, emphasized child-centered education for the purpose of self-realization. In addition, home schooling began to take shape as a viable alternative to public schools.

The Social Reconstructionist Orientation

Here, education and particularly curriculum are seen as tools for social change. Elements of equity, fairness, and social justice are considered. Education must be relevant to students' and society's needs. Curriculum is viewed as dynamic and active and eventually as having an effect on society. Writers such as Henry Giroux, Peter McClaren, and Michael Apple raised questions about the politics, economics, and purposes of education. They wanted to make accountable those educators who refused to deal with issues of poverty, hunger, and lack of wealth as serious flaws in education. They questioned the batching of poor and minority students into vocational education programs or special education, among other things. In effect, they raised many ethical concerns about schools and schooling.

An example of this approach can most readily be seen in the recent critiques of popular culture, such as Henry Giroux's dissection of the Disney Corporation products that students devour: the corporation's bombardment of advertising and its control of media empires in effect teach kids to be great little consumers. I myself saw this in my own niece's desire to have not only the *Pocahontas* video but also Pocahontas sheets, jewelry, clothing, toys, and school supplies. With a social reconstructionist approach, educators might use this kind of reality as an opportunity to critique this side of Disney. I call this the "Disneyfication" of society. This is not to say that Disney is not creative or magical or that Disney does not employ millions. It is to say, let's look at what this means for our children. All this was called into question most recently and most seriously in Giroux's text *The Mouse That Roared.*

The Academic Rationalist Approach

This approach seeks to have students learn and use the words and ideas of the Western world. In recent times, questions have arisen about the heavy emphasis on teaching about *only* Western writers. Movements to include Eastern philosophers, African writers, etc., still cause arguments on many college campuses. This orientation gave rise to our multicultural trend in curriculum studies eventually. It also laid the groundwork for the questions of the postmodern writers. In a way, this orientation was very traditional, on the one hand, and reconceptual, on the other, in that it included an awe of science and discovery.

As we look at these orientations, some may overlap in the actual classroom. They are handy tools with which to approach the topic of curriculum trends. If it were not for the reconceptualizing of the curriculum, we would not have come so far into the present postmodern moment. Ideas and questions about schools were percolating. The world was recovering from World War II. Science was supported without reservation, hence the nuclear bomb, for example. It was time for the intellectuals and educators to ask ethical questions again, and so we took the postmodern turn. A good example of this is the "great books approach" to literature, which, of course, features great Western writers. Perhaps the most well-known work on this subject is the writer Mortimer Adler's *Paideia Proposal* (1982). In this text, he argues persuasively for teaching the great books of the Western world.

ANOTHER STROKE: THE POSTMODERN TRENDS IN CURRICULUM

Postmodernism is often traced to post–World War II thought and action. After the bombing of Hiroshima and Nagasaki, we see a critical turning point in history. Many disciplines reassessed the meaning of life and their purposes and goals. Nowhere was this more evident than in education. For one thing, teachers began to see themselves as public intellectuals. In addition, postmodernism was a prompter for many educational researchers to actually look in classrooms, see what was happening, and interpret what was seen. Schools were viewed as cultures and entire social systems. Postmodern researchers looked to explain more of the puzzle of curriculum and schooling by viewing schools as entire systems. As a result, the writer/educator William Pinar and colleagues (1995) looked at schools with an eye to history and with a view toward the future. Their well-known schema considers the following categories:

Understanding curriculum as political text
Understanding curriculum as racial text
Understanding curriculum as gender text
Understanding curriculum as postmodern text
Understanding curriculum as aesthetic text
Understanding curriculum as autobiographical text
Understanding curriculum as spiritual, moral text
Understanding curriculum as international text
Understanding curriculum as emancipatory text

Curriculum as a site for multiple competing views of curriculum

In other words, postmodernists have forced educators to examine the complexities of race, class, gender, politics, spirituality, aesthetics, and all aspects of curriculum. They complete the current painting. The linear and technocratic stroke of the traditionalists gave us just that. Then, the questioning of why components were missing from discourse was layered on by the reconceptualists. Now, in our present day, the postmodernists have given texture to the painting of curriculum trends. Let us recall a bit about postmodernism.

Postmodernism: In Bold Strokes

Postmodernism is a theoretical framework and a form of critique that questions the following:

The primacy of Western reason and its social, political, economic, and educational effects so often idealized by the reconceptualist

Obligatory Western heroes, together with the supposed privilege for these heroes

Stories of expansionism, progress, and the success of science at the expense of working poor people who enable that expansionism, progress, and success

Western stories that critique other cultures without applying the same level of critical analysis to the Western ideology, mythos, and culture

Thus, you can see these issues alone are a challenge to the reconceptualists and the traditionalists.

Postmodernism and Applications for Curriculum Trends

If we take a postmodern view of schooling, one of the main concerns of the educator is to attempt to uncover ways that dominant schooling (1) serves to perpetuate the hopelessness of the oppressed, and (2) strives to treat people with equity. As a result, those who work in the field of curriculum would assert a framework that:

Recognizes the power of race, class, and gender differences and how these shape educational outcomes

Exposes the ways that power works to structure inequality

Promotes a narrative of hope, complexity, and multiple competing perceptions of social reality

Conceptualizes ways that promote a more human, hopeful way to approach school, work, parenting, play, etc.

States that all teachers are learners and all learners are teachers

Suggests that no one single vision of the world is enough to change the world

Suggests fairness as a guiding principle

Values critique, critical thinking, and critical pedagogy

Suggests that unraveling issues of race, class, and gender can sometimes be addressed legally to move the process forward

Suggests that we call into question any truth claims

Thus, postmodernism begins to question some of the basic beliefs and values of the traditionalists, and it also points out the weakness of the exclusionary reverence for science of the reconceptualists. Legal issues that arose on a regular basis seem to have been challenged in the courts during the postmodern era. This gave prominence to postmodern questions. Some of the key legal cases are indeed benchmarks for current and future trends in curriculum. Understanding some of these cases may illuminate curriculum trends.

LEGAL CASES THAT HAVE SHAPED CURRICULUM TRENDS

Obviously, cases related to educational issues and curriculum trends have to be tested in the courts. To help the reader understand the context and importance of the law and how the law affects curriculum, here are selected and seminal cases that relate to all the trends described in this chapter. Cases relating to curriculum issues such as race, class, gender, and diversity are described and most recently came into prominence in the postmodern era of curriculum trends. There is no intent to leave any one out; the goal here is to mention the most powerful and useful cases. They begin in the 1890s, the pretraditionalist era, and go to the present time.

Plessy v. Ferguson *(1896)*

This case set the precedents for racial segregation in public schools. The court upheld an 1890 Louisiana statute mandating racially segregated but equal railroad carriages, ruling that the equal protection clause of the Fourteenth Amendment to the U.S. Constitution dealt with political and not social equality. The case arose from resentment among black and Creole residents of New Orleans and was supported by the railroad companies, who felt it unnecessary to pay the cost of separate cars. Justice Henry Billings Brown wrote the majority opinion, stating that "separate but equal" laws did not imply the inferiority of one race to another. Justice John Harlan (1833–1911) dissented, arguing that the U.S. Constitution was color-blind. The decision provided constitutional sanction for the adoption throughout the South of a comprehensive series of Jim Crow laws, which were maintained until overruled in 1954 by *Brown v. Board of Education of Topeka, Kansas*. It had particular relevance to education, with Justice Brown drawing parallels between race segregation on trains and in educational facilities. It is critical to see the history here, for this case led to the next most famous groundbreaker, *Brown v. Board of Education of Topeka, Kansas*. These two cases brought to bear the issues of race and equal opportunity for education and curriculum trends.

Brown v. Board of Education of Topeka, Kansas *(1954)*

This case set the precedents for racial discrimination in schools. Linda Brown was denied admission to her local elementary school in Topeka because she was black. When, combined with several other cases, her suit reached the Supreme Court; that body, in an opinion by then recently appointed Chief Justice Earl Warren, broke with long tradition and unanimously overruled the "separate but equal" doctrine of *Plessy v. Ferguson,* holding for the first time that de jure (legally imposed) segregation in the public schools violated the principle of equal protection under the law guaranteed by the Fourteenth Amendment to the U.S. Constitution. Responding to legal and sociological arguments presented by lawyers from the National Association for the Advancement of Colored People (NAACP) led by Thurgood Marshall, the Court stressed that the "badge of inferiority" stamped on minority children by segregation hindered their full development, no matter how "equal" physical facilities might be. After hearing further arguments on implementation, the Court declared in 1955 that schools must be desegregated "with all deliberate speed." Restricted in application to de jure segregation, the *Brown* case was applied mainly to southern school systems. After strong resistance, which led to such incidents as the 1957 Little Rock, Arkansas, school crisis, integration spread slowly across the South, under Court orders and the threat of loss of federal funds for noncompliance. The *Brown* decision gave tremendous impetus to the civil rights movement of the 1950s and 1960s and hastened integration in public facilities and accommodations. This was a time of upheaval in the country, and many note this case as contributing strongly to the awareness of the need to clarify civil rights at this point in history. This case is the basis for many current cases that are still unresolved, such as the Kansas City, Missouri, desegregation case.

Lau v. Nichols *(414 U.S. 563) (1974)*

The failure of the San Francisco school system to provide English language instruction to approximately 1,800 students of Chinese ancestry who did not speak English—or to provide them with other adequate instructional procedures—denied them a meaningful opportunity to participate in the public educational program, said a group of parents. Thus, discrimination was alleged, based on race.

There were dissenting opinions, but basically, this case laid the groundwork for the upsurge in bilingual education and all resulting curricula, as well as programs that are called bilingual or language immersion or that give children who do not speak English the right to an equal education under the law. This and the *Brown v. Board of Education* are looked upon by educators as the two most critical legal cases that affect school curriculum.

Daniel v. State of California *(Los Angeles Superior Court) (1999)*

On July 27, 1999, the American Civil Liberties Union (ACLU) filed a suit on behalf of California high school students who were being denied equal and adequate access to advanced placement courses by their local school districts and the State of California. The defendants in this case were the State of California, the state superintendent of public instruction, the State Board of Education, the Inglewood Unified School District, and the superintendent of the Inglewood Unified School District. The named plaintiffs were African American and Latino high school students enrolled at Inglewood High School. The ACLU argued that the allocation of advanced placement courses was unequal across California, with low-income and minority students being denied equal access to these rigorous classes. As a result, these students were disproportionately disadvantaged in the quality of their high school curriculum and their opportunities to pursue and succeed in higher education.

In this case, the issues of race, class, and gender all came into play and were part of the postmodern trends described earlier. By litigants taking on the state with the largest population, great emphasis was given to their concerns, and a window of opportunity was opened for students who, by virtue of their race, class, and/or gender, were not able to avail themselves of educational options afforded others. This case opened the door for awareness that minority children were able to perform as well as anyone else.

Americans with Disabilities Act (ADA) (PL 101-336, enacted July 26, 1990)

The Americans with Disabilities Act, a U.S. civil rights law enacted in 1990, forbids discrimination of various sorts against persons with physical or mental handicaps. Its primary emphasis is on enabling these persons to enter the job market and remain employed, but it also outlaws most physical barriers in public accommodations, transportation, telecommunications, and government services. Among the protected class are persons with AIDS and substance abusers who are in treatment. Some 50 million current or potential workers are estimated to be covered by the law's provisions. This law is hailed as absolutely the most critical and powerful movement forward for persons with disabilities. It affected curriculum trends immediately by requiring that in practice in schools every day, the curriculum would be changed forever. It became the rule of thumb that every student classified as a special education student must have an individual education plan on file in the school. This added more paperwork for special educators and principals, on the one hand, but, on the other hand, it provided for all of us a model of what can be done to individualize the curriculum for those in need.

In schools, special educators had always done this due to excellent training and development in this area; however, what is groundbreaking is that individuals with disabilities had the power from that point on to challenge in the courts any occurrence in which they may have been wronged. Thus, the legal arena became more active, with many cases put forward under the aegis of this statute. Subsequently, this law went through many changes before assuming its current state. It is now called the Individuals with Disabilities Education Act (IDEA).

The Education of All Handicapped Children Act Amendments of 1990 (PL 101-476)

In 1990, PL 101-476 changed the title of the special education law to the Individuals with Disabilities Education Act, and this act became known as the "person first" law. The thinking was that we should speak of and write about people first, then their physical disabilities. Basically, the term *handicapped* was deleted entirely. In a sense, this is a postmodern interpretation for recognizing people as people. The measure is thought to be a major victory for persons with disabilities. In any event, the current IDEA follows from the original ADA.

Although each of these cases may seem like something we have always taken for granted, they actually reshaped how we think about schools and schooling. Particularly, they reiterated the importance of education as a civil right and emphasized that issues of race, class, and gender must be considered in schooling and that language issues are ever present in curriculum trends. In addition, the powerful notion that people with disabilities may not be discriminated against by virtue of their disabilities changed not only schools but also society. Thus, we can see how laws can help schools, students, and teachers to achieve educational goals. But where do we go from postmodernism in curriculum trends? How do we apply postmodernism in the classroom? One way is to use integrated thematic units, across content areas, to punctuate the notions of education of the whole child, experience-based education, linking concepts across disciplines, and allowing the learner to take responsibility for learning.

INTEGRATED THEMATIC UNITS

Educational reformers for many years have been trying to make connections between content areas to allow students to learn subject matter more effectively. This has been happening at all grade levels, K–12. In this next section, you will see two examples of how teachers have pulled together thematic units across disciplines, a postmodern trend. In the first example, you will see how first-grade students benefit from an integrated thematic unit. The bear unit was created by Ruth Anne Jepson and Suzanne Evenson.

Example 1: Bear Theme Study—Grade One

Day One: Kickoff to *The Three Bears*
Day Two: Sequencing of story events
Day Three: Transition words and tear bears
Day Four: Big, bigger, and biggest (comparing), serration in
    math, and begin *Beary Interesting Facts* flipbook
Day Five: Creative bear writing and flipbook
Day Six: "Story Soup"—elements of a story

Day Seven: Musical paper bag puppet art project and
 Teddy Gram story problems
Day Eight: Puppet show practice and bear paws math
Day Nine: Videotape puppet show presentations and
 addition game
Day Ten: Teddy bear celebration and "The Teddy Bear Tea Party"

Day One: Kickoff. Introduce *The Three Bears* big book.

Discuss how it is a folktale.
Talk about the cover, title, and author.
Take a picture walk.
Look for various punctuation marks throughout the book.
Do a shared reading—whole group.
Sing a song called "The Five W's and One H," written by Suzanne Evenson.
Following the song, use these words to ask comprehension questions
 about the story.

With the magnetic math bear, graph the following:
 Who was your favorite character?
 Papa Bear, Mama Bear, Baby Bear, or Goldilocks?

Talk about glyphs. It is a way to organize information. Students will make
 their own bear glyph (the glyph will be used for a math lesson in Day
 Two).
Start a K-W-L. What do you know about bears? What do you want to
 know about bears? Leave the L for the last day's unit celebration.

The Five W's and One H
by Suzanne Evenson
(sung to "Bingo" tune)

There are some words that make up questions
And mainly start with W's
Who, What, Where, When, Why,
Who, What, When, Where, Why,
Who, What, When, Where, Why,
And now and again it may be How!

Day Two.   Do a story retell with a finger puppet (we made ours with a garden-
ing glove, pom-pom balls, googly eyes, and felt).

Break into two small groups; retell the story by drawing the sequence of
events.
Bring it back into whole group and together retell the story with their
pictures.

Using the magnetic math bear, graph the following:
Did Goldilocks learn her lesson? Yes or no?

Introduce the Venn diagram.
Talk about differences and similarities.
Lay out two hula hoops into a Venn diagram and get out those great bear
glyphs.
Now give the students the following prompts and have them place their
bears accordingly on the Venn diagram.
Ideas to use for the Venn diagram (have these written out on notecards
to make it easier):

I liked Goldilocks best/I liked the Three Bears best.
I always sleep with a bear/I sometimes sleep with a bear.
My favorite meal is breakfast/My favorite meal is lunch.

Continue this process with other questions you create.
On an overhead projector, put up the *All about Bears* fact sheet.
Using highlighters, have students follow along, only highlighting the
"most important" facts.
After highlighting, have the students fill in this sentence: The most inter-
esting thing I learned was . . .
(Save these for their portfolios.)

Day Two: All about Bears
There are many kinds of bears: polar bears, black bears, brown bears,
and grizzly bears are just some of them. The koala is not really a bear,
even though it is sometimes called a bear. Bears live in many parts of the
world. There are no bears that live in Africa or Australia. Bears are large
animals. They have thick fur that protects them from the cold. Their
paws are large with long claws. Bears have a good sense of smell but poor
eyesight. They are very fast. The grizzly bear can run up to about forty
miles per hour. People cannot run as fast as a bear. Bears can also swim.
Polar bears are the best swimmers. Bears are also excellent fishermen. A
male bear is called a boar, a female bear is called a sow, and a baby bear
is called a cub. Cubs are very small when they are born. They stay with
their mother until they are about two years old. Then, the mother bear
chases her cubs away, and they have to live on their own. Bears live fif-

teen to thirty years. They eat all kinds of foods, such as fish, meat, leaves, fruits, nuts, and berries. The bear's greatest enemies are people. People hunt bears and destroy the forests where they live.

Day Three. Read a different version of *The Three Bears.*

Discuss the transition words: *first, then, next,* and *last.*

Revisit the students' sequence of pictures. Ask individual students to come up and place transition words in order in the pocket chart. Complete the pocket chart by adding sentences to match up with the transition words while retelling the Three Little Bears story.

Make a large bear paw using brown construction paper—this will be used for a sequencing activity. Use the "Transition Words Paw" page to organize information on the large brown paw.

With the magnetic math bear, graph the following question:
What is your "beary" favorite meal of the day?
Breakfast, lunch, or dinner?

Make tear bears.

To introduce the activity, you will tell the students, "Today, we are going to make bears using different shapes."

Head—circle
Body—rectangle
Front and back paws—ovals
Nose—triangle
Ears—little circles
Eyes—circles

Carefully tear these shapes from the construction paper.
Brainstorm a list of characteristics of mammals.
Discuss why bears are mammals.
Sing the "Mammal Song," written by Suzanne Evenson.
Review the directions north, south, east, and west. Discuss the saying "*N*ever *E*at *S*limy *W*orms."
Students will complete the worksheet called "Directional Bears."

Day Three: Planned Activities

Day Four. Do a minilesson on the short *i.* Sing the "Word Family Song," written by Ruth Anne Jepson. Use the *ig* chunk for the song today.

Read the book *Pig, Pigger, and Piggest,* by Rick Walton.

Now make big, bigger, and biggest flipbooks.

Students can illustrate their work by using any example they want (apples, pumpkins, bears, etc.).

Using the magnetic math bear, graph the following question:
> A bear is a mammal—true or false?

For today in math, work on the concept of serration.

Students are to place their tear bears (from the previous day) into one of three hula hoops labeled "big," "bigger," or "biggest."

Beginning with the bears in the "big" hula hoop, invite the class to start comparing the size of each bear in the hoop to determine if the bear was placed in the correct hoop according to its size. If not, the students as a class need to determine where it should be placed.

Once the bears are sorted into the three hula hoops, each group will work together to sequence their bears by size, from largest to smallest, within their group. Then, turn these three groups into a whole-class group. Now, sequence them from smallest to largest as a whole group. It will be awesome to see the group stretch across the classroom! Wow! What a powerful sequence example this demonstrates! The kids love it!

Start the *Beary Interesting Facts* flipbook.

Read pages 5 to 9 in *Bears,* by Lynn M. Stone.

Discuss different kinds of bears and where they live.

Today, you will have the students write their names on the cover page and illustrate page 1 in the *Beary Interesting* Facts flipbook.

Day Four: "Word Family Song"

Day Five.   Students will write about the tear bear they made on Day Three.

They will answer the following questions:

My bear's name is _____.

If I could have a bear over to play, this is what we would do all day

_____.

Attach this writing activity to the bottom of the tear bears.

Hang these up around the room.

Using the magnetic math bear, graph the following question:
> Do you like honey? Yes or no?

For math today, do the "Teddy Bear Fraction Game."

This is an outdoor math activity.

Die-cut four different colored bears: red, yellow, blue, and green.

Each child will need to have one die-cut bear.

You will also need a dry-erase board for every "den." A den will consist of two, three, or four bears. Outside, place the dry-erase boards and markers here and there around the area where you will be playing the game.

Yell "Hungry bears!" The students will scatter. Then call out "Bears in the den!"

At this point in the game, students will form groups at each dry-erase board—a den. Each group may have two, three, or four bears.

Now, yell out a color. The students with the called color need to sit in their den.

As a cooperative group, each den of bears will create a fraction to represent their den. Total bears in the group will be the denominator, and the sitting bears will be the numerator. Each den is then responsible for writing their fraction on the dry-erase board and holding it up to be checked. After all groups are checked, yell "Hungry bears!" The students will scatter and repeat the preceding process.

Continue the *Beary Interesting Facts* flipbook.

Read pages 11 to 14 in *Bears,* by Lynn M. Stone.

Discuss bear characteristics and places for bears to live.

Read and illustrate page 2 in the *Beary Interesting Facts* flipbook.

Day Six.   Introduce "Story Soup" (recipe is in graphic file for Day Six). You will be stirring up the great story of the Three Bears today! This is a perfect introduction to the elements of a story. Mix together all the ingredients. When you are finished, pull the book out of the pot (it was hidden in there before making the "soup") and read it to your class!

Make it extradramatic by wearing a chef's hat and pretending you are the head chef of the Story Soup Café.

Using the magnetic math bear, graph the following question:
Do you like oatmeal, cream of wheat, or neither?

For math today, revisit fractions.

The students will do the "Bear Fraction Worksheet."

They will color the fractions to represent each set of bears.

Continue the *Beary Interesting Facts* flipbook.

Read page 16 in *Bears,* by Lynn M. Stone.

Discuss bear cubs.

Read and illustrate page 3 in the *Beary Interesting Facts* flipbook.

Day Six: Story Soup and Bear Fractions

Day Seven. Today, students will make paper bag puppets to represent the characters from the Three Bears story. Each student will make one character. Label each bag with the name of one of the four characters from the story (e.g., Papa Bear). Pass out brown paper bags. Students will form four groups according to what bag they received. All Papa Bears will be one group, all Mama Bears will form another group, Baby Bears another, and students with Goldilocks bags will form the last group. Discuss ways they can be "clever" and "creative" in making their character puppets very unique! Make sure you have plenty of supplies in a tub at each table (for example, yarn, fabric, felt, googly eyes, glue, scissors, and markers). Children are to add to the character puppet that lies in front of them. Turn on the boom box with some fun music and let them go! Once all the puppets are finished, have the class form a large circle. Start the music again, and students will begin to pass the puppets to the right in time with the music.

> When the music stops, the rotation is final: whomever they end up with will be the character they will be playing in the upcoming days during the puppet show. Stay tuned for the details. See Days Eight and Nine.

> Using the magnetic math bear, graph the following question:
> Have you ever broken something like Goldilocks broke the chair?
> Yes or no?

Day Seven: Story Problems with Teddy Grams
Introduce the idea of subtraction by using Teddy Grams to let students
   eat their way through subtraction.
Have a variety of story problems written out on chart paper.
Read the story problems out loud and have the students actually eat the
   take-away part to discover the difference.
Continue to practice by having them eat their way through math.
Continue the *Beary Interesting Facts* flipbook.
Read page 19 in *Bears*, by Lynn M. Stone.
Discuss bear eating habits.
Read and illustrate page 4 in the *Beary Interesting Facts* flipbook.

Day Eight. Using the puppets from the previous day, students will practice their own retelling of the Three Bears story. Then, as a cast, they will create their own scenery to be used the next day at the puppet show.

Using the magnetic math bear, graph the following question: What's your favorite bear—a polar bear, a black bear, or a grizzly bear?

Today, you will teach "How Many Ways to Get to Five?"
Cut out bear paws.
Paste paws onto a 12-x-18 sheet of construction paper.
With bear paper counters, manipulate bears to create as many addition number sentences as have the sum of five.
Record their work.
Circle one number sentence to illustrate on the paws.
Glue paper counters to represent the number sentence that was circled.
Continue the *Beary Interesting Facts* flipbook.
Read pages 20 to 23 in *Bears*, by Lynn M. Stone.
Discuss how people interact with bears. Also, discuss bears becoming extinct.
Read and illustrate page 5 in the *Beary Interesting Facts* flipbook.

Day Eight: Ways to Make Five and Bear Paws

Day Nine. Have a good time! It's time to put on the puppet shows.

Videotape them so you can show them to the students at the Teddy Bear Celebration.

Using the magnetic math bear, graph the following question: Would the Three Bears rather eat at McDonald's, Wendy's, or Taco Bell?

Using the bear spinner, play a game called "Bear Math."
Each group will need one spinner, the recording sheet, and a pencil. Students can make a spinner using a pencil and a paper clip. Put the pencil point down in the middle of the bear spinner and through one end of a paper clip. Then spin the paper clip!
Taking turns, students will spin the spinner. Each student needs to spin two times in order to create a number sentence. Where the spinner lands will determine the value. Now, the student will use the values to create a number sentence. Students will use the "Bear Math" recording sheet to record their number sentences.
Values of the numbers on the spinner can be changed to increase or decrease the difficulty of the number sentence.
Watch a video on bears. Check one out from your school library.

Day Nine: Planned Activities

Day Ten. Teddy Bear Celebration. Children will bring in their favorite stuffed animal bear from home, hidden in a brown paper sack.

Read the book *The Best Loved Bear,* by Diana Noonan.

Teach the students the "Adjectives" song, written by Ruth Anne Jepson.

On the "Adjective Bear" sheet, students will come up with three sentences to describe their bears. Each sentence will contain an adjective to describe something about their bears (for example, "My bear has brown fur").

Now, dump all of the bears in the center of a circle. Each student will be given a chance to read his or her clues. The rest of the students will be trying to decide which is the correct bear that fits the description. Continue the process until each student has a turn.

Now it is time to start the "Teddy Bear Tea Party."

Hold a two-room center rotation:

In room one, students are molding bear biscuits and getting them ready for the oven.

In room two, students are making special necklaces for their bears, with their own names on them. This will be a special touch at the tea party.

While biscuits are baking, you are graphing the stuffed bears on a huge floor mat graph by color, size, sitting position, standing position, etc.

Have the tables decorated for the tea party, ready with apple juice, Teddy Grams, and the hot cinnamon buttered biscuits. Yum yum! The students have a special tea party accompanied by their special "stuffed" guests.

Now, it is time to revisit the K-W, which was created on Day One, and do the L part of the chart. Ask the students what they have learned about bears. Fill this in on the chart paper.

Get together with book buddies and have the students share their *Beary Interesting Facts* flipbooks (save these for their portfolios). Now comes the *grande finale* to the unit. Watch the tape of the puppet shows that were recorded on Day Eight.

Day Ten: Planned Activities and Wrap-Up

What Can We Learn from This Example? In this example, with selected information with a broader integrated unit following the theme of learning about bears in first grade, the teachers have shown evidence of the postmodern trend toward making connections—a holistic approach to learning—and allowing students to take control of the experience involved each day in the learning process. This unit spans a ten-day period; however, the teachers would certainly return to and recall material from this unit, as it may apply to others in the future.

Now, take a look at this second example from middle school teachers. This unit is about "Another World" and is a study of African cultures. Middle school consists of grades seven, eight, and nine. These teachers from Michigan have created the following integrated thematic unit.

Example 2: Another World Theme—Middle School (Grades Seven, Eight, and Nine)

Here is an example of an integrated thematic unit compiled by three teachers in Michigan. The teachers are John Steinhebel, Tim Podlewski, and Beth Harris. This is an example of postmodern curriculum trends in that:

1. It is a critical approach to the topic.
2. It is an attempt to integrate prior knowledge and new knowledge.
3. It shows that students experience, by way of activity, hands-on learning.
4. It is an attempt to carry the theme "Another World" across content areas involving history, current events, anatomy, nutrition, cultural awareness, art, math, and diversity.
5. It allows learners to take care of their goals and learning process.
6. It allows students to be part of the evaluation process.

Another World Theme—Cultures

Table of Contents
Another World?
CURR 622: Integrative Unit Requirements (green pages)

Prefatory Address of Planning Questions
Unit Rationale
Concept Map
Unit Goals

Objectives from Unit Lessons
Prior Knowledge Assumptions
Skills Incorporated in This Unit
Cognitive Outcomes
Unit Calendar
Summary of Culminating Event
Culminating Event Student Guidelines
Culminating Event Rubric

*Some lessons may combine content areas

Language Arts (purple pages)

Lesson #1   Friendly Letters and E-mail
Lesson #2   Introduction to Interviews
Interview Critique Sheet
Interview Self-Critique Sheet
Learning Contract
Lesson #3   Preparing for Interviews
Interview Check-List
Lesson #4   Ypsilanti Historical Research
Lesson #5   Ypsilanti Historical Walking Tour
Lesson #6   Senior Citizen Interview

Social Studies (blue pages)

Lesson #1   Current Events
Current Events Document
Lesson #2   A Focus on African Current Events
A Focus on African Current Events Document
Lesson #3   Africa Map Projects
Map Project Criteria Form
Map Project Grading Scale
Lesson #4   African Region Articles
African Region Article Team Assignment Document
African Region Article Scoring Sheet

Science (yellow pages)

Lesson #1   Planning a Healthy Meal
Copy of the Food Pyramid
Notes on the Food Pyramid
Journal Checklist
Meal Recording Sheet

Table 1.1   Integrated Thematic Unit: Another World—Concepts

Culminating Activity—Students will utilize various presentation formats to make a cultural comparison between Ypsilanti and the region they studied. Presentations will be given during a dinner/social prepared by the students.

Science	*Math*	*Art*	*Social Studies*	*Technology*	*Language Arts*
Skeletal system	Calculating tax and discounts	Portrait interpretation	Research and interpret current events	Utilize desktop publishing	Expository writing skills
Health & nutrition	Ratios and proportions	Self-portraits	Cartography	Formatting magazine articles	Letter writing
Muscular system	Money management	Flat student	Cultural diversity		Interviews
	Measurements		Geography		

Lesson #2   Discovering Bones and Muscles
    Discovering Bones and Muscles Document
Lesson #3   Introduction to the Skeletal and Muscular Systems
Lesson #4   Muscle Fatigue
    Muscle Fatigue Document including result recording sheet
    Graph for Charting Results
Lesson #5   Skeletal and Muscular Systems—Relationships
    Task Cards
    Frog Dissection Resource Document

Unit Rationale

    Seventh Grade.   Early adolescents have many concerns and interests as they move from childhood to adulthood. They have concerns about their bodies, their image, their choices, their society, and their world. This unit attempts to address many of the concerns of young adolescents by looking at various aspects of culture. The unit will address psychological, intellectual, cultural, and physical questions and concerns. Students will explore themselves as individuals as well as parts of a particular culture. They will be asked to look at similarities and differences between cultures of age and region. Further, the unit will address several state standards and benchmarks while teaching students to be respectful of others and themselves, to take responsibility for those who are in need and to "see" the world from a variety of perspectives.

Unit Goals

1. Students will interact with elders in their community and people from other regions of the world in order to examine the similarities and differences in their cultures.
2. Students will explore the ways in which geographic location, age, natural resources, economy, etc., affect culture.

Unit Objectives

Cognitive: The Student Will Be Able To …

- Recognize the difference between open-ended and closed ("yes/no") questions
- Develop open-ended questions
- Determine characteristics of interviews and interview questions
- Write biographical articles about an elderly person in the community based on a personal interview
- Use friendly letter format to write a pen pal in one of four regions in Africa
- Properly address an envelope
- Research the history of their community in order to develop interview questions
- Identify parts of a friendly letter
- Identify parts of an E-mail message
- Use editing and proofreading skills to prepare a magazine article for publication
- Properly format a variety of magazine articles for publication
- Through writing, examine the differences between adolescent concerns in different regions in the United States as well as in different regions in Africa
- Identify the parts of the skeletal and muscular systems
- Describe how the parts of the skeletal and muscular systems work together
- Identify the muscles in the frog's leg
- Describe how the muscles of the leg work together in unison
- Plan a healthy menu according to the basic food groups
- Plan and manage a budget for a meal
- Explain the relation between the size of items and their cost
- Demonstrate understanding of world events by locating articles in magazines, newspapers, and the internet and sharing with the class
- Identify the characteristics of various maps
- Explain the functions of important muscles and bones in the body
- Cite resources used in research in the form of a proper bibliography

- Summarize current events articles
- Demonstrate understanding of the relationship between scale and size

Affective: The Student Will Be Able To ...

- Communicate effectively in a group
- Interact properly with peers by being supportive of others, raising a hand during discussion, and offering constructive criticism
- Show appreciation of other people and cultures through writing and asking questions
- Work collaboratively with peers in order to develop well-written interview questions
- Critique and offer constructive criticism to others
- Accept and utilize constructive criticism given by others
- Interact appropriately with lab partner
- Collaborate with students to create a meal
- Demonstrate effective listening skills in several situations
- Self-critique mock interview performances
- Offer appropriate criticism to classmates regarding interviews
- Express their feelings about the experiences they have had in class
- Share and reflect on current events
- Work effectively with a small group to create a magazine article about an African region
- Demonstrate appropriate behavior by respecting the property of others, listening to a tour guide, and asking relevant questions
- Draw conclusions about the relationship between muscle endurance and physical activity

Psychomotor: The Student Will Be Able To ...

- Dissect a frog
- Use a computer to dissect a frog
- Use push pins to label the parts of a frog leg
- Follow a procedure in frog dissection
- Engage in an interview with a senior "friend"
- Participate in mock interviews with a partner
- Present final products to community, family, and staff members
- Formulate appropriate questions
- Prepare for an interview by making a phone call or writing a letter
- Use nonverbal and verbal communication effectively
- Engage in activities to develop an understanding of the functions of bones and muscles and the relationship between the two systems

- Create a map of a specific region in Africa using the grid expansion technique
- Record information gathered through interviews, in-class instructions, and science labs
- Graph data
- Use computer programs and the internet to prepare a presentation
- Play "Current Events Bingo" with classmates
- Participate in small and large group discussions
- Participate in cooperative learning groups
- Find and cut out current events articles in newspapers and magazines
- Utilize E-mail as a form of communication with pen pals
- Prepare a healthy dish to share
- Write a magazine article
- Use a video camera to record presentations

**Table 1.2 Integrated Thematic Unit: Another World—
Prior Knowledge Assumptions**

Language Arts	Science	Social Studies
1. Writing Process	1. The Four Basic Food Groups	1. Basic Map Reading Skills
2. Paragraph Construction	2. General Knowledge of the Human Body	2. Preconceived Ideas of African Culture
3. Basic Grammar Rules	3. Basic Math Computational skills	3. A Basic Understanding of Cultural Diversity
4. Basic Word Processing Skills	4. Use of the Scientific Method	4. An Understanding of Current Events
5. Interpersonal Skills	5. Basic Lab Safety Procedures	5. Knowledge of How to Use and Interpret Periodicals
6. Proofreading Marks	6. Rubric Scoring	6. An Understanding of How to Search the Internet for Information
7. Basic R7eading Skills		7. Rubric Scoring
8. Familiarity with Different Poetic Styles		8. A Basic Understanding of Geographic Locations
9. Oral Presentation		
10. Rubric Scoring		

Table 1.3 Integrated Thematic Unit: Another World—Skills Incorporated in This Unit

Study Skills	*Higher Level Thinking Skills*
1. Taking Notes	1. Analyzing Data
2. Organization of Current Work and Research	2. Making Predictions
3. Recording Auditory Information	3. Looking for Patterns
4. Synthesizing Notes	4. Applying Knowledge to Real-World Contexts
5. Paraphrasing	5. Reflecting on Conclusions
6. Studying for Quizzes	6. Drawing Conclusions
7. Practice Reciting Interview Questions	7. Synthesizing Information
8. Completing Homework Assignments	8. Comparing and Contrasting Past and Present
9. Brainstorming	9. Translating Thoughts into Writing
10. Practicing Oral Presentations	10. Evaluating Outcomes
11. Using Library and Reference Materials Wisely	11. Justify a Position
12. Using the Internet and Other Computer Programs as Resource Tools	12. Varying Writing Techniques
13. Setting Goals	13. Constructing Interview Questions
14. Organizing Tasks	14. Critiquing Self and Others
15. Budgeting Time	15. Creating a Writing Piece Based upon Research
16. Editing Notes	16. Reorganizing Data
17. Being Physically Nourished into a Particular Writing Style	17. Organizing and Integrating Research
18. Getting Help from Teachers or Parents	
19. Utilizing Research to Form Questions	
20. Using Charts to Organize Data	

Table 1.4 Integrated Thematic Unit: Another World—Cognitive and Affective Outcomes

Content-Specific Knowledge	Skills and Attitudes
1. Natural Resources and Economical Land Use Based upon Geographic Location	1. Develop Sensitivity to Diverse Backgrounds
2. The Effects of Geographic Locations on Culture	2. Find an Appreciation for Historical Events and Places in Ypsilanti
3. Cultural Effects on Diet and Nutrition	3. Understanding the Effect of Nutrition and Exercise on the Human Body
4. The Effects Natural Resources and Economics Have on Culture	4. View Technology as a Tool for Research
5. Use of Multi-Media as a Form of Communication	5. Demonstrate Interview Skills
6. World Geography	6. Engage in Social Interactions with Peers and Adults
	7. Develop an Appreciation of Cultural Diversity
	8. Develop an Appreciation of the Value of Communication with Senior Citizens
	9. Understand the Relationship between Culture and Events That Affect That Culture

Table 1.5 Integrated Thematic Unit: Another World—
Culture, Unit Calendar

WEEK 1

Monday
Language Arts (#1)/Social Studies
  • Use information from Current Event Articles to write letters to pen pals
  • Parts of a Friendly Letter Activity
Science (#1)
  • Introduction of the Food Pyramid
  • Work on Journal Checklist Assignment
Computer Technology
  • Introduction to PowerPoint
Social Studies (#2)
  • Ongoing Current Events Activity focusing on one region in Africa
  • Students will take an interest inventory as a pre-assessment tool
Art
  • Introduction to Self-Portraits

Tuesday
Language Arts (#2)
  • Viewing a television interview and writing a critique
  • Discussion of good interviewing techniques
Science (#2)
  • Discovery of the Skeletal and Muscular System
  • Students will share conclusions
Computer Technology
  • Continue PowerPoint and reinforce research techniques throughout the remainder of the unit
Social Studies (#3)
  • Introduction to Africa Map Projects
  • Sort teams for the Cumulative Activity
  • Teacher will assign students to Culminating Activity teams
  • Students will decide on the type of map they will design
Art
  • Continue Self-Portrait lesson through week 1

Wednesday
Language Arts (#2)
  • Continue from yesterday
Social Studies (#3)
  • Students will go to the media center to gather research for the Map Projects
Science (#3)
  • Introduction to the Skeletal System
  • Review of the Skeletal and Muscular System Diagram
  • Put together the Skeleton Assignment

Thursday
Language Arts (#2)
- Continue from yesterday

Science (#3)
- Focus on the muscular system
- Flexercise
- Microscope investigation

Social Studies (#2 and #3)
- Students will complete their research in the media center
- Share African Current Events
- Play Current Events Bingo

Friday
Language Arts (#3)
- Whole day field trip (Walking Tour of Ypsilanti)
- Respond to tour through drawing and writing

WEEK 2

Monday
Language Arts (#4)
- Students will be in the media center researching the history of Ypsilanti
- Use information to formulate questions for interview

Science (#3)
- Demonstration Knot a Bone
- Name That Bone Game

Social Studies (#3)/Math
- Combining math and social studies, the students will use grids to expand their map drawings
- Students will use class time to complete maps, any remaining work will be completed at home

Tuesday
Language Arts (#4)
- Continue from Monday

Science (#3)
- The class will work on the How Muscles Move Bones Activity
- Review for Skeletal and Muscular Systems Quiz on Wednesday

Social Studies (#3)
- Students will prepare 3"x5" cards for their map presentations
- Review the components of a good speech
- Students will begin their Map Project presentations
- All presentations will be videotaped

Wednesday
Language Arts (#5)
- Role-playing the setting up of interviews
- Confirm time, date, and location of the Senior Friend Interview

Table 1.5 (*continued*)

Social Studies (#3)
- Continue Africa Map Project presentations
- Begin watching taped presentations during Core Explore for reflection purposes

Science (#3)
- Skeletal and Muscular System Quiz

Thursday

Language Arts (#6)
- Team field trip to Bortz Health Center to conduct Senior Friend Interview

Social Studies (#2 and #3)
- Complete Africa Map Project presentations
- Share Current Events
- Play Current Events Bingo
- Map Project video reflections will continue during Core Explore until completion; Core Explore will focus on reinforcing proper speech techniques Friday

Friday

Language Arts (#6)
- Senior Friend Interview learning contract

Science (#4)
- Begin Muscle Fatigue Lab

Social Studies (#4)
- Introduction to African Region Articles
- Using the Africa Article Assignment Sheet, students will decide upon responsibilities
- Review and discuss Africa Article Scoring Sheet

WEEK 3

Monday

Language Arts (#6)
- Continue working on learning contracts

Social Studies (#4)
- To the media center to begin research for African Region Articles

Science (#4)
- Complete Muscle Fatigue Lab

Tuesday

Language Arts (#6)
- Continue working on learning contracts

Social Studies (#4)
- Continue from Monday

Science (#5)
- Begin Skeletal and Muscular Relationships System Lab

Wednesday
Language Arts (#6)
- Complete learning contracts
Science (#3)
- Continue lesson from Tuesday
Social Studies (#4)
- Final day of research in the media center

Thursday
Language Arts
- Introduction of the Culminating Activity
Science
- Class will be used to work on the Culminating Activity, or the class will move on to a new unit
Social Studies (#2 and #4)
- Students will work on the layout of their magazines
- Students will prepare their presentations for their classmates
- Share Current Events & play Current Events Bingo

Friday
Language Arts
- Work on Culminating Activity through Thursday
- Time can also be used for science and social studies lessons if necessary
Social Studies
- Begin African Culture Article Presentations

WEEK 4

Monday
Language Arts
- Continuation from Friday
Social Studies
- Continue presentations

Tuesday
Culminating Activity to present their prepared meal and their Cultural Comparison Project to their senior citizen pals, parents, friends, etc.

Wednesday

Thursday
Social Studies (#2)
- Final sharing of African Culture Current Events
- Play Current Events Bingo

Friday

Summary of Culminating Activity

This activity will be the final result of many activities that have been developed in several classes. Students will have the opportunity to share their multitude of experiences through a multi-media event that will be shared with families, senior friends, community members, and school and administrative staff. Students will be in charge of preparing a nutritious meal based on what they have learned in science class, setting up and decorating for the event, choosing music, and sending out invitations. They will present their projects to the members of the audience and explain their understanding of various cultures. They will answer questions and discuss their findings with all who are interested. At this time, they will present their senior friends with the final product of their interview and have a chance to introduce their senior friend to their parent(s)/guardian(s).

Another World Theme: Cultures Content Area—
Social Studies, Lesson #1, Current Events

Objectives

TSWBAT:

- Find and summarize current events
- Include Who?, What?, When?, and Where? as components of their story summaries
- Use newspapers, TV, or the Internet to find their events
- Write a bibliography to cite the sources of the two articles they elaborated on
- Share one of his or her stories with the class
- Play current events bingo
- Interact appropriately while sharing events

Time Needed

30 minutes in class per week to share events.
Approximately 1–2 hours per week to find and record events

Materials Needed

- Resources to learn about weekly events (TV, Newspapers, Internet, etc.)
- Pen/pencil, or computer
- Sheet to record events
- Bingo chips in order to play on Thursdays
- Candy (or other rewards) as Bingo prizes

Vocabulary

- Bibliography
- Periodicals

Table 1.6 Integrated Thematic Unit: Another World— Culture, Cultural Comparisons Project—Scoring Rubric

Criteria	Scoring				Points
	Poor (1)	Fair (2)	Good (3)	Excellent (4)	
Compare ✓ Describe similarities between Ypsilanti and your region in Africa ✓ Information is accurate	1–2 comparisons	3–4 comparisons	5–6 comparisons	7–8 comparisons	___ × 5 (20)
Contrast ✓ Describe differences between Ypsilanti and your region in Africa ✓ Information is accurate	1–2 differences	3–4 differences	5–6 differences	7–8 differences	___ × 5 (20)
Personal Experiences ✓ Experiences from your senior friend's life are included ✓ Information gained from your pen pal is included	2 experiences	4 experiences	6 experiences	8 experiences	___ × 5 (20)
Creativity ✓ Demonstrates time and thought ✓ Eye catching ✓ Organized ✓ Unique	Few requirements met	Some requirements met	Most requirements met	All requirements met	___ × 5 (20)
Visul Aids ✓ Map of African region ✓ Map of Ypsilanti ✓ Colorful ✓ Neat ✓ Accurate	Few requirements met	Some requirements met	Most requirements met	All requirements met	___ × 5 (20)
					TOTAL ___

Activities/Procedures

*This assignment will be given during the first week of school, and will be repeated weekly throughout the year.

1. The students will be given background information on how to find and properly summarize weekly current events. Including Who? What? When? And Where? Special emphasis will be placed on the requirement of students to use their own words.
2. I [the teacher] will indicate television news programs, newspapers, and current event or news web-sites as good sources to find events.
3. Students will be given a form that has a 3 x 3 grid on the front. This is where they will record summaries of nine events that occur each week.
4. On the reverse side of the form students will be advised as to how to elaborate on their two favorite stories from the front.
5. Students will be given examples and shown how to cite the sources of the two articles they elaborated on.
6. Students may either fill in the form I have [the teacher has] provided, or they may generate a similar form in order to type their events on a computer.
7. Every Thursday, each student will share one of their nine events with their classmates.
8. Students will be given a short time period in order to reflect upon each of the shared events.
9. Students will write the event they shared on a small piece of paper that will be collected once all students have had the opportunity to share.
10. Those collected events will then be used to play Bingo (events do not have to be identical, they just need to be based upon the same story). The first five winners will receive prizes.
11. Each week the theme of the current events can be altered to enhance a lesson being taught that week.

Assessment

Students will be assessed through the accuracy and proper writing techniques that were used in writing their events.

Homework

This assignment will be given out each Thursday and will be due the following Thursday for sharing.

Another World Theme: Cultures Content Area—
Science, Lesson #2, Introduction to the Skeletal and Muscular Systems

Objectives
TSWBAT:

- Identify the parts of the skeletal and muscular systems
- Explain the function of important muscles and bones
- Understand the importance of stretching
- See how the parts of the skeletal and muscular systems work together so we can move

Time Needed
This lesson will last for five days

Materials Needed
Diagrams of the skeletal and muscular systems
The skeleton activity
"How Muscles Move Bones" activity
Skeletal and muscular quiz

Vocabulary
The parts of the muscular system
The parts of the skeletal system
Tendons
Ligaments
Muscles

Activities/Procedures

1. The students will receive diagrams of the skeletal and muscular system.
2. The teacher will give a short lecture on the skeletal and muscular systems using a skeleton and the handouts. The students will take notes.
3. The students will put together the skeletal system using the attached material (the Skeleton). Students must follow the directions on the worksheets.
4. (Day 2) The teacher will lead the class through some stretching exercises.
5. The students with one partner will go through the flexercise to check their level of flexibility.
6. The students and one partner will look at a piece of steak or chicken under a microscope (see lab procedure). The students will draw a picture of what they see.

7. (Day 3) The teacher will start off the day with a demonstration (Knot a Bone).
8. The class will work on the "How Muscles Move Bones" activity.
9. (Day 4) Divide the class into teams of 4 or 5 kids to play the game "Name That Bone."
10. Play the game until all the major bones are identified. Give the teams one point for identifying the bone and another to identify its function.
11. (Day 5) The students will take the test.

Assessment
The students will be graded on the test. The grade the students receive will help place them in a readiness group for lesson 5. The students will be assessed on the "Skeleton" and "How Muscles Move Bones."

Homework
Study the parts of the skeletal and muscular systems.

Another World Theme: Cultures Content Area—
Social Studies, Lesson #4, African Region Articles
   Objectives
   TSWBAT:
   - Develop an "article" that studies different aspects of the region that they are learning about.
   - Work in cooperative groups to develop series of articles and pictures that highlight specific topics of student interest.
   - Develop cooperative learning skills as they divide the responsibilities necessary to complete the project. Some of the roles include (1) editor, (2) photographer, (3) research manager, and (4) layout manager.
   - Use the library and the Internet to research information for their articles.
   - Combine their articles and their photographs to create a "Magazine" or other representation of the accumulated information.
   - Present their information to their classmates.
   - View the videotape and assess their presentations.
   - Reflect on their presentations as preparation for the culminating activity presentation.

   Time Needed
   Three days of Social Studies/Language Arts class period

   Materials Needed
   - Maps that show the regions that are being studied
   - Library for use of resource materials

- Computers for internet access
- Pen/pencil
- Paper
- Possibly a scanner for photographs
- Access to presentation programs such as "PowerPoint"

Vocabulary
None

Activities/Procedures
1. Students will develop an "article" that studies different aspects of the region that they are learning about.
2. Students will work in cooperative groups to develop a series of articles and pictures that highlight specific topics of student interest.
3. Each student will choose a topic that they will research based upon the African region they are studying.
4. Each student will develop an article based upon his or her research topic.
5. Each team will divide up responsibilities required to develop the final product.
6. Some of the responsibilities include: 1) Editor, 2) Photographer, 3) Research Manager, 4) Layout Manager.
7. Students will use the library and the Internet to research information for their articles.
8. Students will combine their articles and their photographs to create a "Magazine" or other representation of the accumulated information.
9. Students will be encouraged to use a variety of strategies to present their information. EX. (PowerPoint, video presentations, etc.)
10. Students will then present their information to their classmates.
11. The presentations will be videotaped.
12. Students will view the videotapes and assess their presentations.
13. Students will reflect on their presentations as preparation for the culminating activity presentation.

Assessment
Students will be assessed through their final projects and presentations. Students will be given a grading rubric prior to starting the project.

Homework
Students will be given a minimum of three hours in the media center. Any additional work needed to complete the assignment must be finished at home. The media center will be encouraged and accessible each day after school for the duration of the project.

What Do the Units Teach Us about the Curriculum Process?

As we review these examples, what immediately pops out is the clear attempt to connect together more than one subject (such as math, social studies, reading, language arts, and history) to assist students with a holistic approach to learning. This is definitely traced to the postmodern trend. This type of curriculum work leads students to see learning as part of an ongoing process. Rather than presenting each subject area as separate and fragmented, the approach ensures a smoother and more balanced view of the learning process

THE NEXT STROKES: CURRICULUM AS ETHICAL, AESTHETIC, AND AUTOBIOGRAPHICAL WORK

Although longer discussions will be devoted to these three approaches to the curriculum trends of our day later in this text, these themes are a natural evolution in our society. What with the events of September 11, 2001, and the current greed and corruption scandals of big business, how could we not look at ethical issues? How could we not examine our goals and values? How could we not look to the arts for instruction and unity, as Dewey once suggested? Historically, the ground is fertile with ideas on aesthetics and ethics from the work of John Dewey, ethics with the work of Nel Noddings, and autobiography with the work of William Pinar and Patrick Slattery. More will be described and explained on these three trends in a later chapter. However, let us review some examples of educators' work on curriculum as autobiographical text. It was a natural development that people would go inward to question their basic assumptions about why they were teaching, why they do what they do.

Autobiography as a Natural Evolution in Curriculum

The current curriculum trend of autobiography to inform what is being done in the educational process is a natural evolution. This trend evolved to react to the strict technocratic approaches of the traditionalists. The opening up of approaches to curriculum from the reconceptualists was the perfect beginning for a postmodern step toward autobiography as curriculum text and procedure. Basically, autobiography allows curriculum workers such as teachers, administrators, parents, and school community personnel to reflect on their own educational work. As new teachers and administrators are educated in their profes-

Figure 1.1 Schema of Curriculum Trends

Key Questions: What do we teach? How do we teach?

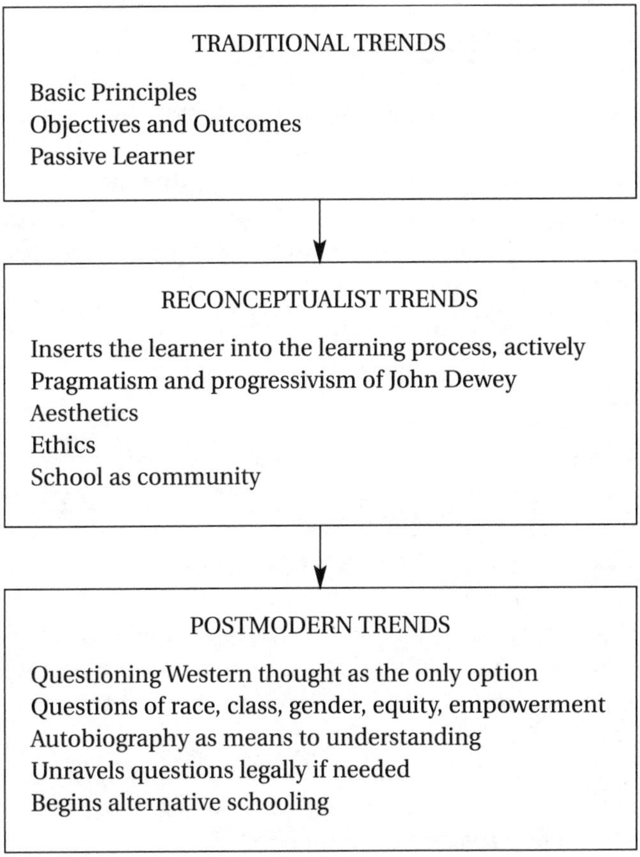

TRADITIONAL TRENDS

Basic Principles
Objectives and Outcomes
Passive Learner

RECONCEPTUALIST TRENDS

Inserts the learner into the learning process, actively
Pragmatism and progressivism of John Dewey
Aesthetics
Ethics
School as community

POSTMODERN TRENDS

Questioning Western thought as the only option
Questions of race, class, gender, equity, empowerment
Autobiography as means to understanding
Unravels questions legally if needed
Begins alternative schooling

sions, reflection is a major requirement. Writing one's own educational autobiography provides a hands-on, experience-based opportunity to reflect, reformulate ideas, and make meaningful one's autobiography. Thus, autobiography offers a vehicle for reflection in action.

Often at the university level, curriculum workers are criticized if they are too theoretical. One practical application of theory is definitely autobiography. It makes understandable to the general reader what it means to be an educator. For too long, we have relied only on numbers and some sort of reporting to explain the educational process. Now, in this present moment, through autobiographical writing we have the human face of education. Autobiography provides us with a story. This story is reflective, teaches us about a real person involved in educating, and may provide a model for others who wish to be educators. Because the educational endeavor is complex, multilayered, and problematic, autobiography allows individuals to tell a story to multiple audiences, such as students, parents, community workers, and curriculum workers. At this juncture of postmodern trends in curriculum, the richness and complexity of the educator's life may be a healthy alternative to prescribed curriculum approaches, on the one hand, and expensive experiments for wealthy individuals, on the other. Additionally, autobiography forces reflection on personal values, spiritual and ethical issues, imagination, and social facets of the curriculum. To understand these concepts, look at the following examples of education autobiography. Recall that *currere*, meaning to run the course, is a verb.

Case Example A: Reflecting on My Educational Self
by Jan Mulqueeny

As I near completion of my doctoral studies, my focus shifts from course work to research: researching my future. I know that my immediate future includes completing a dissertation, but beyond that point, I am myopic. When I began graduate school in January 2000, I had a definite plan in mind. For most people, having a plan would not be unusual. I, however, have done little career planning over the past 25 years. How have the events of the past two and a half years clouded my formerly clear vision? This "research" will necessitate a look backwards before I move forward.

A quick glance behind me finds me physically in the same place I was two summers ago when I first attempted using autobiography as a way to sort through my present situation. I feel a quiet uneasiness as I read through the opening paragraph, and realize just how similar my life has remained, but how significantly it has changed . . .

> As I sit in my office, staring out the window, I wonder what to do. While I look through the job section of *Ed Week*, I try to pinpoint why I feel a sense of urgency, a need to move on. How is it I have arrived at this place? Why am I anxious to move forward? I know that much of my professional journey has been unplanned, a meandering walk down lovely paths. They weren't uncharted, I am just not the type of person who consults a map! As I would come to a junction, I would decide which path to take, not based on reaching any specific destination. What called to me from each new chosen path, I do not know. As I

reflect on my career goals, I am unsure of exactly which road I should choose next. I hope this walk through my past will help me plan ahead for my future.

Then, as now, I was waiting to become better acquainted with a new immediate supervisor, or boss, the Assistant Superintendent of Elementary Education. Then I was anxious, having been unsuccessful in obtaining the position for myself, now I am simply curious. When Pete (the departing assistant superintendent) announced he was leaving the district for a superintendency out of state, I contemplated applying for the vacancy for less than a minute. Although it would be a logical next step in my career path, I have learned a lot about my school district as an organization, and realize that the only way to work and successfully complete a dissertation is to remain in my present position as an elementary school principal. The longer I've thought about it, the less sure I am about my "next step." However, I must return to my immediate future, which involves cutting the grass prior to a trip down to Illinois State to pick my son up from band camp.

As I begin the forced solitude of mowing the lawn, I return to my thoughts of "what's next" and try to recall events that led me down the previous paths in my personal and professional lives. I look carefully behind me as I take my first step back, and think about the series of events that led me into administration. In the fall of 1990, I was working as a program consultant and parent-infant educator, serving children who were deaf-blind. I was (and continue to be) married with a five year old son in kindergarten. I was balancing a full time job with family responsibilities and taking graduate courses to complete a Master's degree in Early Childhood Education. I was well respected professionally, felt I was being a good wife and mother, and I was very happy with my life.

One evening in late November, my husband, Jim, came home from work complaining of a sore shoulder. He had been working outside on an "L" platform all day completing a customer satisfaction survey. Not accustomed to working outside in the cold, we assumed the pain was from the cold and holding a clipboard all day. Some aspirin and a hot shower should alleviate the pain. When he awoke the next morning, the ache was gone. At lunchtime I got a call from Jim, who was clearly worried. As he was using his computer keyboard, he realized that his left hand was numb. Initially, he didn't think much of it, assuming it would pass in a minute or two. An hour later he still didn't have any feeling in his left hand, arm or shoulder. He couldn't tell for sure, but he didn't feel like he could move his fingers very well when he was typing. We talked for a few minutes, hypothesizing a pinched nerve or some other simple, but annoying malady. I told him he should call for a doctor's appointment.

When we arrived at the doctor's office the next day, Jim's numbness spread throughout the left side of his body, and his right side was beginning to tingle. Jim thought the doctor was reassuring, however, I was able to overhear her as she called a neurologist and Rush-Presbyterian St. Luke's Hospital to arrange for his admittance. The mysterious condition worsened over the next couple of days to the point where left-sided voluntary movement was severely compromised. The tingling on the right side of his body made it difficult for him to get any type of proprioceptive input, and thus be aware of where his body was in space. I cannot begin to describe my fears and emotions as the doctors tried to diagnose this ailment. They would not share the list of maladies they were trying to "rule out." A week, a course of anabolic steroids and many inconclusive tests later, Jim came home. Within three weeks he was physically recovered enough to return to work. Exactly what had occurred was still a mystery. The doctors were not giving any odds on if (or when) Jim might experience another flare-up.

Though I was grumbling as I started cutting the grass, complaining to myself about the heat, I realized that I was using the time productively. My mind wandered ahead to the college visits my son has planned in the next few weeks, and then it hit me. I always knew that my move to administration had been in response to an offer by my superintendent who also became a mentor and my concern over my husband's health. The opportunity to take a position that would provide greater earning potential was my safety net. What I had failed to notice up until now is how various health-related situations had influenced many facets of my life: both in my day-to-day outlook on things and in the choices I made at the forks in my path.

My own life began as a preemie; born almost eight weeks early and weighing just under three and a half pounds. I spent several weeks in an "incubator," the most high-tech equipment of the time. As a toddler I remember frequent trips to the eye doctor to make sure that I didn't have any residual damage to my retinas as a result of the oxygen I received. No lasting impact, at least from my vantage point. I am the oldest of four girls, and my parents had to face several dilemmas with their two youngest. Karen, the youngest, joined our family in 1965. Although there was nothing remarkable about her birth, within a few months, our family doctor thought something didn't seem quite right. He really couldn't (wouldn't?) explain his concern, but referred my parents to a specialist at Children's Memorial. My parents learned that my sister was an achondroplasic dwarf, and that she had hydrocephalus.

I was in fourth grade, and remember waking up at night, over-hearing my parents' conversations. The exact words have escaped my memory, but I remember the timbre of fear in their voices as they tried to decide if they should allow my sister to have surgery to put a shunt in that would relieve the excess cerebral-spinal fluid. Should they do it, how would they pay for it, what if something went wrong? These were the fears and questions that circled around our kitchen late at night. How they made the final decision to proceed, I will never know. Totally successful, my sister came through the surgery without complication. Later, I did learn that the neurosurgeon had never done this surgery before and that my sister had one of the first shunt surgeries performed at Children's. Other surgeries followed, but none had quite the same impact on my family.

My second sister, Darlene, had her share of health problems. Frequent ear infections that continued into elementary school age sent her to an otolaryngologist (ENT) for further evaluation. The doctor noted enlarged adenoids that he thought might be responsible. Surgery solved that problem, but the ear problems persisted. A mastoid was removed from near Darlene's right auditory nerve. That left her with a moderate hearing loss. Between semiannual trips to the ENT, one ear infection ruptured her left eardrum. I wonder now how she stood the pain . . . and if any adult (like my parents or the doctor) ever asked her about her silence when it occurred. Now with a bilateral hearing loss, Darlene used hearing aides without complaint. Two attempts were made to surgically repair her ruptured eardrum, but neither was successful. As she continued through high school, she failed to tell anyone that her residual hearing was deteriorating, fearing additional surgeries. She needn't have worried. Her bilateral, progressive sensory-neural hearing loss has left her completely deaf and, at that time, there were no surgical remedies in sight. As her residual hearing deteriorated, completing her job responsibilities at work, even with someone's help making phone calls was becoming difficult. A bright young woman, Darlene sought a tutor to teach her sign language with an eye on returning to school. After a year of lessons she enrolled as a college student, living on the hearing impaired floor of the dorm. She became comfortable in the deaf culture and did well in school and is now married (to a hearing man) and a mother of two.

I think that watching my parents handle these difficult situations gave me the opportunity to see how to take control where you can and when you can't control it, roll with the situation, rather than let it rock you. In my personal life, that philosophy has helped me cope with the neonatal intensive care unit where my son, born 10 weeks prematurely, spent his first six weeks of life looking like an alien hooked up to venti-lators, IVs and monitors with their colorful wires and electrodes. It has kept me centered through my husband's diagnosis of multiple sclerosis and the (thankfully) minor ups and downs of his health.

I believe that I took that philosophy with me into my teaching, al-ways looking to capitalize on a student's strength while minimizing his/her weakness. That strategy was at the root of many heated discus-sions with my deficit-focused, medical model, special education col-leagues. I have spent the past ten years as an administrator working with students from preschool through eighth grade, their parents, and teach-ers in two suburban school district communities. I have had the oppor-tunity to work with some truly exceptional leaders who mentored and shaped my growth as a leader. Inspired by the two women who were su-perintendents during my eight year tenure in Skokie, I felt that I would like to pursue a central office position as an assistant superintendent or superintendent. That was what I was thinking as I began looking into doctoral programs. Now, I am not so sure. I have achieved a level of fi-nancial stability that will allow my family to maintain our middle class lifestyle should my husband's health worsen. My remaining profes-sional goal is really quite simple; I want to make a positive difference in the lives of the people around me.

Spending four years in a large, suburban unit school system has given me a different perspective than I had as an administrator in a small, elementary district. Both are inherently political, but I have come to realize that there are few children's faces driving the decisions made in the large central office with five assistant superintendents, directors and departments filled with people each doing well-defined jobs. This does not mean that what is best for kids does not drive the thinking of the Board and the administrators, it just means they are much more re-moved from our students.

As I moved to open a new elementary school four years ago, I wanted to see if I could make a difference in a large arena. My experience in an extremely diverse elementary district would be beneficial in my new principalship. The faces of the children in the classrooms were changing. As the diversity of the district has increased over the past sev-eral years, there have been few different voices speaking and even fewer heard. I have been able to model respect for the various cultures and eth-nic groups represented among my school's families. My beliefs about the value of diversity have influenced our PTA, the teachers, and ultimately the students. I have served on a committee to give a voice to our high school students and begin a parents' advisory that will serve as a resource in sharing culture as well as assist in recruiting minority teachers and staff members. In four years I realize that I have made a positive difference, every day, in the lives of 500 children and their families. I have worked hard to share my experience and my beliefs to make a positive difference at a district level. My own voice is small, but combined with others working to better empower our nonmajority families, we have begun to make a difference. My circle of influence beyond my own school building does not ripple out as far as I would like; some of the obstacles blocking the path are visible, while others are submerged below the surface. I am not sure I have the energy or desire to remove the barriers.

Is it enough to be the type of building principal I can be proud of? I look around me at my colleagues with their sights locked on to managing minutia, getting through the day or week, with no articulated vision for the future (except for those who are anxiously anticipating retirement). I know that if I stay here, I will either have to fight so that I won't be pulled down to that level, or have to isolate myself to avoid contamination. If I decide to remain in a principalship, I cannot imagine leaving a school that I have been able to form since its opening. Can I find a position as an assistant superintendent or superintendent in a district where others share my vision and values? Although I am cognizant of the years I have paid into the Teachers Retirement System, I still have a good 10 years ahead of me for full pension benefits, but I want to be open to other opportunities that might arise.

My current circle of influence is primarily populated by children. I hope that the opportunities my students have in elementary school to learn from their classmates and neighbors who have different religions, traditions or skin tones (although I am not confident) will carry them through adolescence. I do know that I have made a difference in the way many members of my faculty and PTA approach each student and family with respect as they try to pronounce their last name or understand their particular dietary restrictions. A parent or child who needs to use alternative forms of communication encounters patience as the message is conveyed through gesture, writing or sign language. Families are treated and respected as partners in our school.

I need to remain true to my personal goal of making a positive difference. Although I would like to widen my circle of influence, I am pleased with the impact I have had thus far. As I look at future professional opportunities, I need to look back on my meandering path and avoid unproductive side roads. The path ahead of me is still foggy, but I believe that if I keep my eyes open to all the possibilities, I will be able to see more clearly if the fog lifts.

What Can We Learn from Autobiography as a Curriculum Trend?

As you read through Jan's reflection, it is hard to escape her thoughtfulness, her touching on ethical issues, and her view of herself as an educator. Let us review still another example before interpreting the importance of autobiographical work as curriculum.

Case Example B: A History Teacher's Thoughts on Curriculum by Nick Myers

The texts assigned for both courses presented this semester, 2002, have struck a sound chord with me as both an administrator and former history teacher. Indeed, my desire to enter into the field of education was deeply rooted in the belief that educators must expose students to what some writers refer to as the "hidden" and "null" curriculum. As an undergraduate student at the University of Nebraska, I was fortunate to work with innovative methods instructors who encouraged me to further explore the null and hidden curriculum. I became increasingly aware that a fundamental reason why more teachers, particularly at the secondary level, resisted teaching such interesting and vital topics as labor unrest, gender conflicts, and conflict between ethnic groups was due to their own ignorance of the truth of America's history. Teachers, themselves educated in a system riddled with bias, lack a true understanding of the conflicts that have shaped the development of our nation. It is clear that teacher-training programs must expose students to sources such as Howard Zinn's *A People's History of the United States* and *Lies My Teacher Told Me* by James W. Loewen if changes are to be made in the way curriculum is presented to young people. Both of these texts offer engaging and eye-opening accounts of history and the way it might be presented to young people.

Other challenges exist that make it difficult for educators to teach the null or hidden curriculum. I would agree with Pinar's assertion that our current approach to curriculum effectively serves to indoctrinate students into accepting or ignoring social injustice. I would assert that the strongest messages about injustice many teachers send to students come from the lack of attention paid to historical examples of injustice that have taken place in the United States. By deleting portions of the curriculum dealing with the struggle for equality due to time constraints or overt prejudice on the part of the teacher, students are done an extreme disservice. In examining the textbook utilized for teaching American History in my own school district, I was saddened to find that while 28 pages were devoted to the Civil War, 27 to World War I, 29 to World

War II, only 3.5 pages were given to what the text discussed as "The Conflict in Viet Nam." In fact, this portion of the text was embedded in a 25-page chapter that accounted for the sole discussion of all of the events of the late 1960s including the Civil Rights Movement, Viet Nam, Kennedy, Johnson's Great Society, and the space race. Absent were the stories of Malcolm X and the women's movement as well as any photographs or stories that neared the point of controversy. In essence, the text has taken out all controversial, and interesting, elements leaving students with a less than accurate or enlightened view of the era.

It is critical for educational leaders to examine this issue closely. Current approaches to curriculum development involve an overreliance on texts written from an extremely narrow perspective. It is clear, as pointed out in the readings, that schools also face political challenges from the communities in which they are located. The approach to curriculum advocated by Pinar is certain to elicit response from conservative elements in the field that wish to present curriculum study in simpler, less complex terms. In my current role as an administrator, I relish the opportunity to present these ideas to my staff for open discussion. I can already anticipate significant resistance on the part of educators who like the status quo, unaware that they are perpetuating myths and supporting flaws in the existing social structure in the process.

Combining Elements of the Autobiographical, the Ethical, and the Aesthetic

As you can see from this example as well as Jan's, in a postmodern world it is difficult to separate the ethical from the aesthetic and the autobiographical. Both writers, as they reveal aspects of why they are in education to begin with, uncover ethical questions and in an aesthetic way. They punctuate the importance of understanding the person in the process of teaching, learning, and curriculum trends. Let us continue with another example. I ask all my students to create a portfolio of their work, beginning with their professional goals. The questions are prompts for their reaction.

Continuing Thoughts on My Life in Education
by Nick Myers

What are your professional career interests and even goals?

Education is at once a challenging and rewarding field that demands a firm commitment on the part of all who strive to improve instruction for the betterment of students and our society as a whole. My professional career interests and goals are closely tied to the Interstate School Leaders Licensure Consortium's standards for school leaders including:

- Promote the success of all students by facilitating the development, articulation, implementation, and stewardship of a vision of learning that is shared and supported by the school community.
- Promote the success of all students by advocating, nurturing, and sustaining a school culture and instructional program conducive to student learning and staff professional growth.
- Promote the success of all students by ensuring management of the organization, operations, and resources for a safe, efficient, and effective learning environment.
- Promote the success of all students by collaborating with families and community members, responding to diverse community interests and needs, and mobilizing community resources.
- Promote the success of all students by acting with integrity, fairness, and in an ethical manner.
- Promote the success of all students by understanding, responding to, and influencing the larger political, social, economic, legal, and cultural context.

What are your professional experiences to this time including those which may not be related directly to your career interests and goals?

I entered teaching as a ninth grade, integrated social studies teacher at North Platte High School in North Platte, Nebraska. As a member of an interdisciplinary curriculum team, I worked with talented educators to create and deliver thematic units of instruction that broke down the barriers between disciplines. This experience would provide me with valuable knowledge as I moved on to Cary Junior High School where I taught eighth grade U.S. History along a thematic path. My approach was postmodern constructivist as I reorganized the curriculum into the following thematic units:

- Conflict Between Races and Ethnic Groups
- Gender Conflict
- Conflicts Between Nations
- Economic and Political Conflict
- Conflict With The Natural Environment

•• Ideological Conflict

Seeking to have a greater influence on teaching and learning in schools, I entered school administration as an assistant principal at Cary Junior High School before moving to Deer Path Elementary School in August of 2000. As an assistant principal, my primary responsibility has been the improvement of instruction and I have focused on the following areas the past three years:

- •• Multicultural Education
- •• Improving Writing Across the Content Areas
- •• Conflict Resolution

What are your reasons for pursuing this doctoral program?

Learning is a life-long journey and continued growth and development only occurs when individuals stay active and informed of best practices in the field. Pursuing a doctoral degree is a personal choice I have made based on my desire to remain on the cutting-edge of research. As I have continued in my education, I have only come across more questions I wish to find answers to and more areas of focus I wish to delve into more deeply. Education remains with us forever and it is my sincere desire to make my journey an enlightened one, enriched by the process of participating in advanced study.

Where do you see yourself in 5 years?

This past summer, I was honored to become the principal of Deer Path Elementary School in Cary School District 26. As a new principal of an ECE–4th grade building, I have made a firm commitment to my teachers, students, and parents to remain in my role for a sustained period of time. In five years I see myself continuing to serve the community of Cary as principal of Deer Path School. I do intend to have completed work on my doctorate in 5 years and will consider my options for movement at this time. Several possibilities intrigue me including serving as a superintendent or teaching at the college level in a teacher preparation program.

What are some issues that you have a passion for?

My initial motivation for entering the field of education was related to my belief that traditional approaches to schooling fail to empower students to solve some the problems inherent in our system of democracy. As a result, many of the issues I am passionate about involve trying to promote a sense of social justice and true equality for a wide range of student learners. Specific areas of focus include:

- Multicultural Education
- Special Education
- Improving instruction for students identified as ESL
- Meaningful staff development for educators

Philosophy of Education Statement:
All students can learn when encouraged to utilize their unique talents to solve problems in highly creative ways.

Reactions

Here, as in the previous two vignettes, I hope you will see the contents in the autobiographical sketches as those that include many aspects of the postmodern trend in a curriculum. They include statements that:

Deal with ethical issues
Go beyond the surface curriculum
Raise questions about community, diversity, and gender
Raise questions about empowerment
Reflect a critical thinking posture

Thus, as we move into an era where more writing is done of an autobiographical nature, ethical issues arise. Further, the actual ability to write so clearly is aesthetic in itself.

All examples selected here and included in the appendixes reveal what I call the postmodern turn in curriculum trends. Look at the following example of curriculum as ethical or theological text.

Some Thoughts on Curriculum as Ethical Text
by Brian Coleman

The postmodern curriculum theme of interdependence and connectedness is examined by some as theological text. Curriculum as a theological text seeks to provide students with opportunities to explore divine reality, cosmic meaning, and mystical nature. One section in particular addresses the relationship between the past, present, and the future. Both contemporary theology and Reconceptualization of curriculum support the view that past experiences are an integral part of present reality. The postmodernist also sees the present as an opportunity to transform the future and inspire global awareness and responsibility.

Slattery in his book *Curriculum Development in the Postmodern Era* suggests that the focus of the postmodern curriculum should be ecological sustainability and holistic models of teaching. Instead of the traditional isolated and mechanical approach, the postmodernist's curriculum views the world as an interconnected organism. The work or nonwork of one part of the organism affects the whole organism in its function and even in its survival. As the past affects the present, and the present defines the future, these durations of time become interconnected. What happens in one time, affects the others. The postmodernist suggests that these time durations are inseparable and interrelated. Slattery sees the future as a direct product of the present. According to Pinar, this connectiveness of time and of individuals to each other, and the world, is essential for social transformation and the survival of the global society.

There is some indication that this postmodern approach to the curriculum is emerging in the classroom setting. Instead of teaching separate and isolated subject areas, themes are developed by teachers and a concerted effort is made to connect different content areas to each other. Current teaching strategies like constructivism and problem-based learning both provide opportunities for students to explore their world and pursue connections that build upon their own knowledge-base and solve real life problems, most relating to some ecological crisis. Both strategies move from the teacher being the holder and giver of all knowledge to a classroom in which the teacher is a guide and a mentor that orchestrates self-reflective learning experiences. The learner's situation and the learning context are no longer separated from the curriculum. It is very apparent in the postmodern curriculum that the classroom environment and interconnectedness of experiences remain a central priority in the holistic approach to teaching and learning.

As an administrator, this reflective and building-knowledge approach to teaching is more prominent at the graduate level with adult learning. With adult learning it makes sense to have students be more responsible for their own knowledge and learning with the instructor being more of an advisor and guide that orchestrates learning experiences. This becomes a little more difficult at the primary level where the teacher is the primary giver of information and knowledge. At the primary level students appear to have less ownership of their learning, being very dependent on the classroom teacher. Problem-based learning and cooperative groupings do provide some constructivist experiences for students that allow them the opportunity to interact with each other and their surrounding. They can build and connect knowledge, but it becomes more teacher-directed than student-directed. One advantage to the constructivist's approach is the attachment of meaning to what students are learning. Context plays an important role when students learn new information. The ability to attach meaning to what you are learning furthers your ability to retain the knowledge and retrieve it. Anyway we can improve our ability as educators to connect meaning to what we are teaching, it is worth pursuing.

Comments

Note that all of these reflections bear the characteristics of postmodernism and carry strong characteristics of John Dewey. Most noticeable is the connection to the practice of the writer. Another trend that is related to postmodernism but began in the reconceptualist era was that of alternative schooling approaches. Alternative approaches include all the private schools, charter schools, and, of course, home schooling. The brief descriptions of the major alternative approaches included in the following segment focus on home schooling, the Waldorf Schools, and the Montessori Schools. Parochial and religious-based schools may be a topic for another author at another time. However, the three approaches to alternative schooling are important to understand, if only to realize how some educational reform models actually work. Indeed, public school personnel may learn a great deal from any of these models.

Home Schooling as an Alternative Curriculum Trend

Home schooling has historical roots prior to the industrialization of the nineteenth century. Then, most American families were centered on the daily home-based activities of their agrarian lifestyle. In addition to teaching their children how to grow crops and tend to livestock, parents sometimes taught their youngsters how to read, write, and do arithmetic. In 1852, Massachusetts enacted the first compulsory school attendance law. At about that same time, the first child labor laws were also being passed, as the United States shifted from being an agrarian society to an industrialized nation. Public schools gained popularity. And by the end of the nineteenth century, American children were becoming accustomed to government-sponsored compulsory education.

The origins of the contemporary home-schooling movement can be linked to the outcry for school reform from the 1960s until the present day. In the 1960s, educational reformers began challenging school methodology and criticizing academic outcomes. Among those who called for reform were Paul Goodman, who wrote *Compulsory Miseducation* (1962), John Holt, who wrote *How Children Fail* (1964), Charles E. Silberman, who wrote *Crisis in the Classroom: The Remaking of American Education* (1970), and Ivan Illich, who wrote *Deschooling Society* (1971). Subsequently, Raymond and Dorothy Moore, authors of *Home Grown Kids: A Practical Handbook for Teaching Your Children at Home* (1981), began encouraging home schooling among members of the religious right. And by the mid-1980s, increasing numbers of home-schooling proponents were pressuring state legislators to rewrite compulsory school attendance statutes (Farenga 1999). In fact, as a result, all fifty states, Puerto Rico, and other territories have rules about home schooling.

Today, it is estimated that up to about 800,000 students attend home schools in the United States. What began as part of a religious movement for a small group has gained popularity among mainstream Americans. Although laws vary from state to state, home schooling is a legal alternative in all fifty states, the District of Columbia, and in the U.S. territories (Home School Legal Defense Association 2002). Reasons for educating their children at home can vary considerably among parents. Many claim that schooling their children at home offers better: (1) safety, (2) security, (3) morality, (4) discipline, and (5) educational quality. And according to proponents, "the flexibility of curriculum and schedule, the closeness and emotional unity of the home, and the security possible in the home environment enhance educational learning and growth" (Lines 1995). Yet home schooling has developed in the past decades to offer more than comfort and safety and security. Currently, guidebooks, textbooks, and other teaching materials much like those in public schools are available for home schoolers. Thus, the criticism that the home-school movement was content-free can no longer make sense.

Although home schooling may work for some, there have been continuing criticisms of the movement since it was originally an idea of the fundamentalist Christian right. Proponents of the movement wanted to use home schooling as a tool to take their children out of the public schools due to violence, values, and other concerns. As a result, the movement was severely criticized, since many home schoolers were without texts, teachers, and so on and in fact were doing something like an informal Bible study. Thus, reformers who really saw value in home schooling began to work with educators, state department of education personnel, and parents to revise how home schooling might take shape, and they were helpful in changing a potentially small group of eccentric approaches to a formal, organized, content-rich curriculum. All indicators in the literature suggest that home schooling is growing due to the allure and increasing success of some aspects of this model.

The Maria Montessori Model:
Schooling and Curriculum

The noted educator, physician, and activist Maria Montessori (1870–1952) discovered that children who were orphaned, disabled, and abandoned could be educated with a caring approach to education. The Montessori method includes direct hands-on experience, learning by doing, and education of the whole child. Montessori believed that children learn best when they are exploring as scientists performing experiments, rather than passively accepting the ideas. In the Montessori School environment, children initiate learning and socialization voluntarily. Teachers, meanwhile, permit the children to interact with their planned environment and with each other without expectations or scrutiny. The rationale of Montessori education is based on the philosophy that: (1) children are to be respected as individuals and as being different from adults, (2) children possess a special sensitivity and an unusual intellectual ability to absorb and learn from their environment, and (3) the first six years are the most important years of children's development. And as such, Montessori Schools are geared for elementary-age children.

Montessori educators design and direct the learning environment by preparing it in advance to be a positive and safe social atmosphere. They provide children with copious educational materials that emphasize concrete versus abstract learning. According to proponents, the children work for the joy of learning and discovery. There often is a three-year age span of children in the classroom, with older children teaching the younger ones. This in itself often helps with development. Beyond maintaining certain rules for safety and mutual respect, teachers play a relatively unobtrusive role in the classroom, like facilitators. However, they control the environment by manipulating what learning materials are available for the children, and they serve as resource persons and role models in the classroom.

Today, there are thousands of Montessori Schools worldwide. In the United States, there are approximately 5,000 Montessori Schools. Although some opponents argue that Montessori Schools are too rigid, others claim that they permit children to run around doing whatever they will (Ruenzel 1997). Indeed, the Montessori method is geared to providing experiences from which children will learn. Many of the classroom activities focus on the development of social skills and physical coordination. Yet the Montessori classroom takes a relatively holistic approach to curriculum by permitting children to learn through their natural curiosity. Similar to home schooling, the focus is on safety, caring, experimenting, and communication. A third model of schooling and one with similar characteristics is the Rudolf Steiner Waldorf School model.

Rudolf Steiner and the Waldorf Schools

The first of the Waldorf Schools opened in 1919 in Stuttgart, Germany, for factory workers' children. Rudolf Steiner ran the school based on his questioning of the purposes of schooling in the modern era. It was called the Waldorf School due to the fact that the factory where the school was placed was the Waldorf-Astoria cigarette factory. By 1928, the first Waldorf School opened in New York City, and others followed in North America. Today, worldwide, there are around 700 schools in 40 countries. Steiner emphasized intuition, creativity, movement, dance, the arts, and thinking as required for children to grow and develop. Due to World War I, he was taken with questions about creating a better society. He wondered about building a free society with ethics and responsibility. A Waldorf School balances academics, the arts, character development, and a sense of community responsibility. Because students stay with the same teacher for up to eight years, a true learning community is constantly developing. Steiner wrote numerous books and articles on how children learn and develop and about his method.

Steiner coined the term *anthroposophy,* which he defined as a spiritual movement for education of the whole person. Obviously, this all ran counter to the norms of the day, which followed a traditional approach to education. In addition, another term, *eurythmy,* is a key term for the Waldorf Schools. This is defined as speaking and singing through movement and gestures for the purpose of getting children in touch with their own rhythms and the world around them. It was believed to be therapeutic as well. By including this in the curriculum, Steiner envisioned this as a way for children to acknowledge and name their own feelings. Research on this topic after Steiner's schools were created shows that eurythmy can increase one's ability to communicate. To learn more about the Waldorf Schools and to read more on this creative approach to curriculum, the Anthroposophic Press is a good resource. Waldorf Schools and their goals are about head, heart, and hands in order to develop individuals who are able to impart meaning to their lives.

In Appendix A, a more detailed summary of Waldorf curriculum is described.

Writing across the Curriculum (WAC) and Journal Writing as Postmodern Trends

What Is Writing across the Curriculum?

The trend in curriculum studies called writing across the curriculum, or WAC, began in the mid-1970s and continues to the present day. This educational reform movement began when leaders in business and industry began asking the question, "Why can't Johnny read?" Business leaders noticed that many workers could not write effectively. In fact, many workers out of high school and college could not communicate basic facts in a written memorandum. Neither could they write a complete paragraph. As a result, educators at all levels—K–12, junior college, college, and university—began to think of ways to address this state of affairs. Research undertaken on composition from the 1970s to the present has pointed to the many ways learners can write as well as the differences in writing in various disciplines. Nonetheless, all agree that writing can help learners to understand course content. Today, many schools across the country use WAC, and many universities have entire Web sites devoted to it.

How Does WAC Work?

We all can see that in our field of curriculum studies, critical literacy is a major goal. Critical literacy includes the ability to think, to read, and to write with a critical eye. In terms of WAC, writing is used across disciplines and within a given discipline to sharpen thinking skills and develop creativity. In order to achieve those ends, faculty members have to agree on the importance of writing. Once a majority of faculty agree, the next task is to implement WAC. Some techniques of WAC include:

- ⇥ Journal writing—for example, keeping a reflective journal on a class and what you are learning
- ⇥ Letter writing—for example, writing a letter to the president
- ⇥ Idea papers—for example, writing about two ideas that changed your life
- ⇥ Descriptive essays or papers on world events or personal events—for example, describing your views on September 11
- ⇥ Position papers on a controversial topic—for example, argu-

ing whether the rapper Eminem incites critical thinking or violence

The list could go on, but one can see that this approach is rooted in both the reconceptualist and postmodern eras. It always involves the learner, so direct experience is required by the learner. Remember, WAC is about writing in *all* courses, not just in writing or English classes. A postmodernist might say that in this approach, writing is not added on to a content area. Instead, learning the content comes through writing about that content. WAC ensures that students learn to:

- Think clearly about a topic
- Ask effective questions
- Summarize and evaluate information
- Pose and critique arguments
- Understand how to provide evidence for claims and opinions
- Know how to find and cite references
- Clearly state a position
- Give and receive constructive criticism
- Articulate, understand, and describe complex issues and problems
- Agree or disagree in writing with another person's ideas

Thus, WAC provides all learners a vehicle for developing critical thinking, reading, writing, and reflection skills. In addition, it puts responsibility on the learner to learn. Since writing is across disciplines, the learner benefits from improving content knowledge and writing performance. Many universities use WAC to help students succeed in their various areas of study. Here is a partial list, as of this writing, of universities that use WAC:

Indiana University, Bloomington
The Citadel
University of Missouri, Columbia
Boise State University
University of Hawaii
George Mason University
Harvard University
Georgia State University
University of Toledo

University of Richmond
Northern Illinois University
Colorado State University

In addition, many universities have a WAC Web site or link, as, for example:

WAC at Arizona State University
WAC at Chesapeake College
WAC by the Daedalus Group, University of Texas, Austin
WAC at Eastern Washington University
WAC at Georgia State
WAC at University of Hawaii
WAC at University of Idaho
WAC at Indiana University
WAC at Longview University
WAC at University of Massachusetts, Amherst
WAC at National University
WAC at University of Richmond
WAC at State University of New York, Cortland
WAC at University of Toledo
WAC at Tufts University
WAC at Weber State University
WAC at Wright State University
University of Minnesota Writing Support Network

In any event, the universities are trying to address a serious condition among young people—the problem of poor writing. They accept a class of freshmen each year, hoping that they possess the skill set to succeed at college-level work. If that is not the case, WAC is one useful tool for improving the learner's skill set. Another tool and a major trend today in schools is the use of journal writing not only to teach writing but to improve critical thinking skills in all subjects.

Journal Writing as an Ongoing Curriculum Trend

Teachers have found that the best way to teach students to be critical thinkers is to model those skills that will help them in their quest to be critical thinkers. One such skill is journal writing to develop critical thinking skills. By keeping a journal, either in a notebook or on the computer in an electronic file, anyone can sharpen his or her critical thinking skills. For example, many teachers focus on keeping a classroom journal. A classroom journal is a journal that individual learners, as well as the teacher, construct and create on a daily basis. For a teacher, keeping a classroom journal as a tool for deepening critical thinking about classroom practice is a most provocative practice.

A Brief Historical Overview

Journal writing has a lengthy history in the arts and humanities, as well as various moments in the sciences. It is not by accident that artists, writers, dancers, musicians, physicians, poets, architects, saints, scientists, therapists, and educators use journal writing in their lives. Virtually in every field, one can find exemplars who kept detailed and lengthy journals regarding their everyday lives and their lifework. Keeping a classroom journal may help to illuminate and refine thinking skills at all levels. In addition, keeping a journal may be viewed as an interactive tool of communication between the teacher and the learner.

As we begin this journey of describing and explaining journal writing, it is important to realize the lengthy and significant history of journal writing. Although individuals have probably kept journals throughout recorded history for various reasons, some of the first known journals were written in Greek and Roman times. Indeed, St. Augustine and Blaise Pascal kept journals to chronicle moments in their own lives as they tried to find out more about how the mind works. In the tenth century, ladies of the Japanese court wrote precise and candid descriptions of everyday life and the inner workings of their beliefs and feelings. Often, these writers hid their journals under their pillows, and so the journals became known as "pillow diaries." These documents went beyond the daily recording of life; they were texts that recorded dreams, hopes, visions, fantasies, feelings, and innermost thoughts. Next, the rebirth and awakening of the Renaissance brought with it an era of almost required journal and diary writing. There was a general sense that one should chronicle the spirit of rebirth and living in personal terms, case by case.

The 1660s brought us Samuel Pepys, who for nine years described exactly and in astounding detail the people, politics, sorrows, and joys of life in London. His thick description of the problems of the Church of England, the monarchy, the navy in which he served, various wars of the day, the great fire, and the plague are brilliant and illuminative records of literature and history. As luck would have it, the first published versions of his diary did not appear until 1825, followed by reissues and new editions well into the late 1890s. It was at this time that the Victorians focused on both letter writing and journals.

Prior to the Victorian era, a number of spiritual and some religious groups kept spiritual journals. The Quakers, for example, beginning in the seventeenth century, often and regularly described their spiritual journeys, doubts, questions, and beliefs. John Wesley, the founder of Methodism, kept volumes recording his symbolic relationship with his God. Indeed, many Puritans recorded their trust in God, doubt, uncertainty, miseries in their lives, sins, omissions of goodness, and so on. The voyage of the *Mayflower* is eloquently and curiously described in journal form. For people who were embarking on new adventures, the journal became an outlet for fears and moments of deep despair on the voyage. The use of the journal, ranging from spiritual record to political record, flourished as well. Remember, at these points in time, writing was a key means of communication. There were no telephones, pagers, computers, televisions, or news media as we know them. For example, during the French Revolution, many writers produced "journals in time." These were personal accounts of arguments regarding the Revolution, and they revealed deep and passionate feelings of patriotism, nationalism, and disgust for the corrupt monarchy.

Similarly, in the United States during the westward expansion movement, explorers such as Meriwether Lewis and William Clark chronicled their journey to the West, describing relationships with the Native Americans and encounters with existing communities. Likewise, pioneer women not only cooked around the campfires but also took the time to record personal impressions of the westward movement. Later, these would be chronicled in the play *Quilters*. This play powerfully documented a history of depression, sorrow, joy, misunderstanding, and treachery. There would be no sugarcoating of injustice and bigotry in all these diaries. In addition, an eloquent account of the brutality of slavery in the United States is chronicled in the slave narratives. The clarity, suffering, and degradation described in these works inform our understanding of a history of the black diaspora. Were it not for these detailed accounts, a critical piece of American history would certainly have been lost.

Yet literary and historical figures are not the only journal writers. The field of psychology has long made use of journal writing as a therapeutic aid. The cathartic function of journal writing has been widely recommended by many schools of therapy. Therapists view the journal as an attempt to bring order to one's experience and a sense of coherence to one's life. Most recently, Ira Progoff (1992) has written of an "intensive journal." Progoff developed a set of techniques that provide a structure for keeping a journal and a springboard for development. As a therapist himself, he has conducted workshops and trained a network of individuals to do workshops on keeping an intensive journal for unlocking one's creativity and coming to terms with one's self. The intensive journal method is a reflective, in-depth process of writing, speaking what is written, and in some cases sharing what is written with others. Feedback is an operative principle for the Progoff method. The individual needs to draw upon inner resources to arrive at the understanding of the whole person. The journal is a tool to reopen the possibilities of learning and living. Progoff advocates (1) making regular entries in the journal in the form of a dialogue with one's self; (2) maintaining the journal as an intensive psychological workbook in order to record all encounters of one's existence; and (3) participating in some type of sharing of this growth through journal writing with others.

The method makes use of a special bound notebook divided into definite categories that include dreams, stepping stones, dialogues with persons, events, work, and the body. The writer is asked to reflect, free-associate, meditate, and imagine that which relates to immediate experience. The latest version of his text (1992) is a definite testimonial to and a solid example of techniques for keeping a journal.

Beyond the psychologists, perhaps the two most identifiable writers of journals in our memory are Anne Frank and Anais Nin. In fact, *The Diary of Anne Frank* and the many volumes of *The Diary of Anais Nin* are published in over twenty languages. Anne Frank's lived experience hiding from the Nazis not only details her feelings of growing up under these conditions but also offers a political and moral interpretation of humanity's failures. On the other side of the coin, Anais Nin describes and explains her journey to understand her self, her body, and her mind. The genre of journal writing is alive and well, and teachers and learners should not be afraid of trying to keep a journal specifically to deepen critical thinking about oneself and one's experiences and the meaning therein.

In fact, journal writing is so prevalent now that one only has to surf the Internet to see thousands of journal resources, examples, and personal histories on-line. For example, there is an on-line course on journal writing offered by Via Creativa, a Web site entirely devoted to Ira Progoff's Intensive Journal Workshop, chat rooms on journal writing, exemplars of diaries and journal writing, and literally thousands of resources. You will be somewhat overwhelmed by the multitude of sources. As with anything on the Internet, you will have to sift through to see what is best for your learning style. In general, the common thread that unites all these resources on the Internet is the agreement that journal writing is a way of getting in touch with yourself in terms of reflection, catharsis, remembrance, creation, exploration, problem solving, problem posing, and personal growth.

Why Journal Writing?

Students and colleagues have often asked, Why should one invest the time in journal writing? Journal writing allows us to reflect, to dig deeper if you will into the heart of the words, beliefs, and behaviors we describe in our journals. The clarity of writing down our thoughts will allow for stepping into the inner mind and reaching further into interpretations of the behaviors, beliefs, and words we write about.

Great journal advocates such as Progoff encourage daily writing. In fact, Progoff encourages writing a journal as a dialogue with one's self. He talks about keeping a daily log. Yes, there is no getting around it—you need to write in this journal every day. There is only movement forward. He suggests keeping dialogues with key persons in our lives, with our bodies, with our works, with our roads not taken, with events that were critical in our lives, with society, and with our dreams. In other words, we write our journals in a dialogue form that prompts us to think in new ways, to be more critical and reflective.

Another journal writer is Thomas Mallon. His 1995 text, *A Book of One's Own: People and Their Diaries*, is an overview of diarists and journal writers. He categorizes the writers as follows:

> *Chroniclers:* people who keep their diaries every single day as if recording the news
>
> *Travelers:* people who keep a written record during a special time, such as a vacation or a trip
>
> *Pilgrims:* People who want to discover who they really are
>
> *Creators:* People who write to sketch out ideas and inventions in art or science
>
> *Apologists:* People who write to justify something they have done to plead their case before all who read the journal
>
> *Confessors:* People who direct ritual unburdenings, conducted with the promise of secrecy or anonymity
>
> *Prisoners:* People who must live their lives in prisons or who may be invalids and as a result must live their lives through keeping a journal

Of course, any writer might be a combination of any of these categories, but the categories just listed might be useful as a tool to understand different approaches to keeping a journal. Currently, there are many wonderful resources on journal writing in popular culture and specifically accessible through the Internet. Recently, in a search on the World Wide Web, by entering the words *journal writing* I saw over 4 million entries! In fact, there is even a journal-writing course on the Web. In our culture, our media, and the schools, we have numerous opportunities to find examples of actual journal writers and journal writing itself. Keeping a journal, although there is a long and reliable history attached, is actually a current, state-of-the-art curriculum trend. However, journal writing and WAC are not the only trends that engage critical thinkers. The movement in integrating the arts into the curriculum is a most promising trend.

Arts-Based Curriculum Trends

Arts-based curriculum trends are similar to the writing across the curriculum trend in that arts-based work is holistic and cross-disciplinary and aims to foster critical thinking. The arts, in the form of music and visual art instruction, have been a part of the American public school curriculum for over a century. In fact, some writers call art the fourth *R*, as in "reading, 'riting, 'rithmetic, 'rt." But only recently have the arts begun to take their rightful place as equal in importance and value to reading, science, and mathematics. It was not until the U.S. Office of Education published its Interdisciplinary Model Programs in the Arts for Children and Teachers (IMPACT) report in the late 1970s that the arts gained recognition as having a positive, central role in integrative learning. Arts-based curriculum has since gained support from public and private institutions as a means by which to bring comprehensive reform to both teaching and learning. Organizations such as the John F. Kennedy Center and the Getty Foundation have provided funding for arts-based programs. Likewise, the National Endowment for the Arts (NEA) established programs to honor and award partnerships between arts-based education and business organizations.

Arts-based curriculum may be used to teach and reinforce concepts and skills in other subjects as well as nourish the creative spirit. Since it is relevant across all cultures, arts education is also multicultural and can be used to initiate discussions and understanding of a multicultural nature. Instructional activities utilizing the arts can include music, dance, drama, sculpture, design, storytelling, painting, writing, photography, puppetry, quilting, and more. Arts-based curriculum is being used to teach students how to use computer software applications. Students are encouraged to use their own photographs, videos, poetry, drawings, and personal stories to build personal Web pages and design with digital cameras all kinds of projects. Even mass-media advertising for major computer companies includes the use of graphics and digital camera work for kids.

There are several benefits to utilizing arts in the classroom. Art is a necessary component for human development. Many of the intelligences that will help the child succeed in other areas of school, work, and life can be enhanced through the use of arts-based curriculum. Integrating the arts across all academic disciplines permits educators to draw upon and nurture the child's innate capacity to be creative and to think creatively. Curriculum centered on the value of the arts can enhance the child's originality, imagination, and analytical skills. By using the child's creative instinct and artistic expression as a means by which to enhance creative thinking, the learning experience becomes more satisfying. The classroom learning environment becomes transformed through the use of art in curriculum. Students become stimulated, enthusiastic, motivated, and self-determined. The arts teach students about the discipline required to excel in school and society. The arts also provide students with a concrete reward for diligence and sustained effort. These factors encourage higher attendance, and many would argue that they increase achievement all the way around. The discipline involved in the study of music, dance, performing arts, and painting, for example, often carries over into the academic arena.

A Model for Arts Education:
Discipline-Based Arts Education (DBAE)

Perhaps the most recognized model in arts education is the model created by the J. Paul Getty Education Institute for the Arts, known as discipline-based arts education (DBAE). In this model, a comprehensive, holistic approach to arts education is prominent. Students learn art history so there is context for their own work, whatever medium they select. Further, art criticism is taught and nurtured so that students can compare their own work with others as well as understand key elements of the great artists' works. In addition, aesthetics is taught, and students must apply aesthetic principles to their own work. All this is in addition to painting, sculpting, performance, music, dance, acting, cinema, etc. Thus, the DBAE model works to provide a complete curriculum approach. This trend will certainly continue to inspire young artists and their teachers. It is a strong working model, and the Getty Foundation almost single-handedly has seen to it that supplies, materials, and personnel are available to the thirty-six states so far that have adopted frameworks using this model.

Summary of Postmodern Alternative Curriculum Trends

In this section, a review of three types of alternative curriculum trends were described: home schooling, Montessori Schools, and Waldorf Schools. All three depart from the traditional and have traces of reconceptualist traits and postmodern traits. All three approaches offer a wider perspective in terms of educating the whole child, encouraging communication, and fostering a sense of community, meaning in one's life, and responsibility for actions. In addition, writing across the curriculum and journal writing were described as postmodern trends, and the integration of the arts into the curriculum was described as well. Teachers freely use these techniques to help students and themselves in all fields. Ethics became part of the entire educational process as a result of the questions posed by postmodern educators. All three approaches offer educators something to think about in their own worlds. Each may serve to inspire curriculum workers in current settings to broaden their understanding of what is possible in terms of curriculum trends. In a way, postmodernism in all fields has made curriculum workers more prone to examine their own practices by virtue of seeing alternatives that go beyond the present circumstances. The hot-button issues involving educational reform will always have a component that has to do with evaluation, assessment of practice, and finding and making sense of that practice. Thus, postmodern trends include assessment and standards as key issues in the next logical step for attempting school reform and change.

CURRICULUM TRENDS, SCHOOL REFORM, STANDARDS, AND ASSESSMENT

When we think about the amazing movement forward in terms of curriculum trends in schools today, we cannot overlook the emphasis on standards and assessment. Looking back at the history of the standards movement, we see that it is often linked to the educational reform movement sparked by the report *A Nation at Risk* (1983). Of course, we can easily claim that educational reform has been a pastime for over a century, as many writers have done (see Cuban 1990). More recently, however, individual educators and professional organizations have demanded standards as a remedy to almost every educational problem. Consider these points regarding school reform movements, recently elucidated by Susan Orlich (1998), a leader who questions reformers.

Although school reform might be operationally defined as "anything you can get away with," the bulk of reforms in the United States seem to exhibit eight general characteristics:

1. The reforms are politically inspired and coerced by state governments.
2. The stress on higher student achievement is based on standards-based reports that were prepared by professional associations, not by local school boards.
3. Content standards tend to be collections of outcomes or student behaviors, assembled in a nonsystematic manner and without content hierarchies clearly shown.
4. Cost-benefit analyses are lacking from the reports on state school reforms.
5. Control of education has shifted to the national and state levels and away from localities.
6. The reform agendas, though fragmentary, are broad in scale and encompass most of the fifty states.
7. Politically inspired as the education reform movement has been, it must still be classified as being theoretical, that is, its basic premises are grounded not in empirically sound studies but rather in political enthusiasms and intuitions.
8. Implied within these reforms is the conclusion that, as a consequence of standards and high-stakes state testing and assessment programs, there should be a dramatic increase in student achievement.

The time has come to revisit the premise that massive funding, written standards, and a firm resolve to create reform will cause students to achieve at higher levels, since there are developmental limits to student achievement. Other writers have argued that the notion of setting high standards for all students is hard to resist. For example, it is difficult to argue against high standards. Yet if we go deeply into the complex issues related to standards, this house of cards may easily tumble. In terms of curriculum trends, standards and the follow-up to standards, assessment, cannot be avoided.

SOME ETHICAL PROBLEMS WITH
THE STANDARDS MOVEMENT

Keep in mind these eight characteristics of educational reform movements in general, and now think about the standards movement framed with the following questions:

1. Who benefits from setting standards?
2. Whose voice is taken into account when the standards are formulated?
3. Are we creating new inequalities by advocating standards?

As you can see, the problems created by setting standards are complex. Let's look at the first problem: who benefits from setting standards? As Donald Gratz (2000) correctly argues, reforms—especially the standards reforms—present us with the problem of overpromising and underdelivering. Likewise, he points out that even if a new idea is tested in one setting, it may never be suitable for widespread implementation. So when we ask, as he puts it, "High standards for whom?" we uncover a host of questions. He reminds us that educational accountability is in its infancy and most often relies on the single measure of test scores. The extremely high monetary cost of the tests themselves, the upkeep of all the prep materials, and the like illustrate the very high cost of testing. Clearly, the testing industry benefits from encouraging testing. In addition, those of us with a life in education realize testing is often handled questionably. Some educational leaders suggest that the teacher should actually teach for the test alone, thereby casting teaching as test preparation. In fact, the standards movement was initiated with grandiose aims such as world-class high standards. Yet in actual cases—in the State of Texas, for example—the standards movement has become distorted by politics and expediency. Let's look at this more closely as we examine the case study of Texas, for it illustrates the political and economic consequences of the push for standards.

Learning from the Texas School Reform Case

The well-known researcher Linda McNeil (2000) has done a thorough analysis of the contradictions of school reform in a book by that title, and she particularly examines this reform movement in Texas from the mid-1980s to the present time. She completed the first study to document and track standardized reforms from their beginnings in the state legislature to their effects on the curriculum in schools, teacher reactions, and, subsequently, student achievement. The "reform" in Texas, begun by Ross Perot, basically took local control of schools away from the public and professional teachers, putting it into the arms of business-controlled external management and accountability systems. This major shift from public to private is a key underlying and barely examined reality. The accountability system in Texas is called the Texas Assessment of Academic Skills (TAAS). TAAS is basically promoted for the following reasons:

1. It has shaped up the schools.
2. Teachers and principals are held accountable for test scores.
3. "Performance contracts" are used for evaluating principals based on test scores.
4. Test results are used for decisions about school practice.

Perot was very articulate about how to improve schools through testing and basically argued that if testing is good enough for business, it's good enough for schools. Thus, the injection of a business orientation as well as a political one complicates matters even further. But McNeil looks closely at this situation and points out the flaws in this simplistic approach to education.

For one thing, she raises the issues of historical inequities in school funding, staff allocation, investment in materials, and support from the broader community. In fact, many writers point out that what drives the standards movement in general can be distilled into two assumptions, both based on fear:

1. Our nation is losing its competitive edge, so we must demand more from all students. We are falling behind other countries, and in order to compete in the global marketplace, we must push students to learn more and learn faster. We can do this by raising standards.
2. If we raise standards for all students, we automatically address the disparity between high and low achievers. Thus, the argument goes, minority students will benefit, since they are generally found in urban schools with low achievement records.

Oddly enough, earlier in our history, John Dewey argued for a child-centered, rather than test-centered, curriculum in the attempt to address some of the key points on inequality. In our present day, we are listening to test makers who obviously argue for more tests as the way to resolve the serious complexities of standards. They contend that by raising standards and using an appropriate test to measure achievement, we automatically improve education and our place in a competitive global economy. If only it were that simple. Let's look again at the Texas case. McNeil reports on various teachers' reactions and changed behavior when a mandated curriculum driven by testing was in place. Basically, teachers explained that the TAAS prep component of curriculum totally recast the teachers' and principals' roles. Teachers were silenced and marginalized. They had little voice in the matter. Likewise, principals also lost their voice. But what is the cost of standardization and compliance? Where is the space for the "public" in "public schools"? As we increase standardization, will we eliminate the voice of parents, teachers, and other community members? And who benefits most from the noise about raising standards? In the highly politicized milieu of an election year, politicians especially love the opportunity to get tough with standards.

Basically, mandatory typical tests will be used as the means for implementing state standards. Gratz (2000) argues that those accountability systems designed to help students and schools almost always downplay cross-school comparisons. Thus, another problem emerges. By aggregating test scores, the reality of disparities within and between schools is masked. For example, a suburban school, he states, may do well in preparing college-bound students. At the same time, they may not do well at all in preparing non-college-bound students. Yet by aggregating all the scores, someone looking at the test data may see the school as excellent. Thus, the way data are reported is a problem and has political, racial, and economic overtones.

To add to the latest information on the Texas case, Raymond A. Horn Jr. and Joe L. Kincheloe have compiled a text entitled *American Standards: Quality Education in a Complex World—The Texas Case*. This text touches on not only the ethics but also the legal issues involved in Texas. For an example, in 1979 and 1980, the Texas Assessment of Basic Skills (TABS) was given to students. The results of the tests were used in district planning and specific curriculum content. There was a focus on teaching the state curriculum according to legislative requirements. The teachers also had to pass a basic skills test in reading and writing and another test on specific disciplines. A list of standards was created for teachers and administrators to know and be able to demonstrate to students. Many saw these changes as too rigid and without enough input from educators, parents, and community members.

From 1995, there was a move toward site-based management with input from community members and school personnel in Texas.

Some believed that this kind of management would create greater accountability. This plan called for educators, parents, and community members to implement chosen strategies, determine goals, and assess outcomes. Teacher development also became more site-based. Campus-level teams were charged with identifying areas in which teachers needed improvement and implementing the programs. But not everyone agreed with the high-stakes TAAS testing. Parents, school personnel, and students objected to the testing, since they initially had no input into a process that required input. In fact, some students went to court over this matter. In *GI Forum v. TEA*, seven minority students who did not receive their high school diplomas because of not passing the TAAS sued their district. Of course, this led the way for other suits, which remain unresolved.

In the case mentioned here, the evidence provided by both sides indicates that the TAAS is deeply entrenched in the factory-system paradigm of education. It is important for us to remember that the factory system of the nineteenth and twentieth centuries had a strong racially biased component that was not challenged until the 1960s. In terms of curriculum trends, it was most like the traditionalist model. The biggest controversy in the popular press arose over the issue of teaching for the test alone.

Teaching for the Test

McNeil (2000) reported that in Texas, many of the schools she studied used large amounts of time practicing for tests. Students practiced "bubbling" in answers and learned to recognize that test makers never have the same letter choice for a correct answer three times in a row. In fact, to help students remember this, a catchy phrase was repeated. They said, "Three in a row, no, no, no." What are we to make of this? Still further, principals who participated in the study reported using the lion's share of the budget to purchase expensive study materials. I highly recommend reading McNeil's book for more particular and extensive examples of what can be problematic in terms of standards and testing. For a more detailed account of all this, see my own work (Janesick 2000) on the complexities of assessment.

The case of Texas teaches us that some schools can improve, but most do not have financial support to do so. Texas school partnerships offer networking and partnerships as a solution to offset the heavy cost of school improvement and reform. At the same time, they stress the enormous cost for what needs to be done in schools if we are to authentically improve achievement for all students. Schools must have a structure to accommodate and support the host of reforms, requirements, and ongoing demands of the curriculum. Without this, what chance can any reform have in a climate with few or shrinking resources?

A Major Contradiction: The New Discrimination

What is most distressing about centralized, standardized testing is how it masks ongoing inequality. As McNeil (2000) and others point out, minority students who may be disadvantaged to begin with are now thrown into the pool of the entire school. As the curriculum narrows to a focus on test preparation, a new kind of discrimination emerges. Instead of outright tracking and stratification, the new discrimination uses the *appearance of sameness* to cover up inequalities. Most of the "basics" or "back to basics" mantra is historically rooted in the mistaken notion that sameness produces equity. Nothing could be further from the truth. Is there any evidence that standardization brings up the bottom-scoring students? One would have to look very far and wide to find evidence for this, given McNeil's text. In fact, she argues persuasively, based on the Texas case, that the TAAS system is actually harming students, teaching, curriculum development, and the faith and trust in public schooling. This makes sense given the almost unquestioned faith in the business model so prominent in states such as Texas. McNeil argues that substituting a rich curriculum in poor and minority population schools with drill and repetition exercises is the new discrimination. Even if standardization and drill and repetition exercises raise scores in the present moment, children's learning is not often enhanced or enriched. Because of the controversy aroused by the TAAS, research is in progress that is designed to examine the issues in Texas, and we shall have to wait and see what is found. In an unpublished paper, the researcher W. Haney (1999) did a study of data from Texas on dropout rates before and after the TAAS system was implemented. His preliminary results are disturbing. McNeil summarizes his data. Haney looked at statistics from 1978 (pre-TAAS) to the present. The data were collected by the Texas Education Agency. In 1978, more than 60 percent of black students and nearly 60 percent of Latino students graduated from high school, 15 percent below the average for white students. Yet by 1990, four years after the Texas reforms, graduation rates for all three groups dropped. By 1990, fewer than 50 percent of all black and Latino ninth-graders made it to graduation. The graduation rate for whites was 70 percent. Thus, the gap between minorities and whites actually grew! Even more problematic, Haney found that by 1999, the white student graduation rate had risen to about 75 percent, yet the rate for minority students remained at below 50 percent.

Has the TAAS system enhanced or enriched the curriculum or student learning? These data give us a great deal to examine more closely. McNeil concludes that we are actually creating new inequalities, and we cannot avoid a serious examination of this problem. Again, I return to the three questions mentioned earlier:

1. Who benefits from standards?
2. Whose voice is taken into account when standards are formulated?
3. Are we creating new inequalities by advocating standards?

Let the reader decide the response here. There will always be a debate on these issues. For example, in Texas, for every person you find to expose the problems with the TAAS system, you will find someone who thinks it works. In any event, check the data themselves.

Continuing Ethical Questions Regarding Norm-Referenced Tests (NRTs)

Related to the ethical concern about standards is the ethical concern about the tests themselves. For example, let's think about the ethics of the use of norm-referenced tests (NRTs). You may know that a norm-referenced test compares a student's score with the scores of a group of people who already took the exam. All of us involved in education are now accustomed to seeing scores in the newspaper that disclose a school's percentile rating. This is based most often on a norm-referenced test. NRTs are designed to rank order the test taker in order to accommodate the bell curve. In other words, test makers want to see that the results of students' scores can be represented by the bell-shaped curve. Test makers, often bureaucrats outside of education, actually construct the tests so that most students will fall in the middle. Only a few are expected to score very high and very low. In addition, most of these tests are multiple-choice tests. Given what we know about the complexity of the mind and how learning and cognition take place, it seems questionable to rely on multiple-choice tests in general. Not only that, the political climate of our times is such that governors and other politicians call for *all* students to score above the national average. However, this is impossible with the NRT. NRTs are constructed so that half the population is below the midpoint or average. Thus, we contribute to the "dumbing down" of the educational process. Is it surprising that students feel put upon when they see their scores or their school scores below the midpoint? In addition, to compound the problem, NRTs are designed to rank order and compare *only some* of the students' scores. A commercial NRT, such as the California Achievement Test (CAT), does not compare *all* the students who take the test in a given year. The test is "normal" on a "sample," which is advertised as representing all in a given group. Why is this done? One reason is that it is easier to do it this way. The problem with doing it this way is that one question right or wrong can cause a student score to jump up or go down more than ten points. Likewise, if a particularly intelligent student is absent on test day, the school's score might plummet. If a particularly nonintelligent student is absent, the score may skyrocket. In any of the cases, the score is hardly reflective of a given student, class of students, or school.

Is the NRT Test Score Accurate?

Obviously, the test score cannot be accurate. Since the questions are posed as multiple-choice tests, the items on the test only reflect a sample of possible questions. At best, the test score is more like an estimate. Anyone who studies testing and measurement knows that no test is completely reliable. To add more confusion, because a school's score goes up or down does not ensure that a given school is better or worse than others. Remember, when new tests are used, scores usually go down, for example. Presumably, if teachers teach to a particular test but another test is, in fact, administered, of course the scores go down. In addition, the claims of politicians that all students will achieve a particular score don't make sense. This is impossible, since NRTs are designed so that one-half of the test takers score *below* the average. One can only conclude that these test scores are not truly accurate. In fact, test makers actually have gone on record to state "in elementary or secondary education, a decision or characterization that will have major impact on a test taker should *not* be made on the basis of a *single score*" (emphasis added). This statement was issued by the testing profession in its "Standards for Educational and Psychological Measurement." Furthermore, since NRTs are focused on routine, drill, and memorization and since many teachers teach only to the test, one can conclude that even more damage is being done here. By lowering expectations and by de-emphasizing problem solving, critical thinking, and content knowledge, it appears we are not helping children to learn. We are teaching them to conform.

Race, Class, and Gender Bias in Testing

One of the major criticisms of standardized testing is the criticism of bias. Since the 1980s, standardized tests have been criticized for score gaps that indicate racial, socioeconomic class, and gender bias. Just to take one example, the American College Testing Group (ACT) admits that ample evidence exists to support the claims of test bias. For some background, the ACT is a standardized multiple-choice test. It is intended to predict student grades and success in the first year of college. In 1989, the ACT program personnel actually attempted to respond to their critics and vowed to change the test accordingly. However, there is little evidence today to support their promise. Many organizations listed in later chapters in this text have indicated the glaring biases of the ACT. For example, the data clearly show that whites outscore all other groups. As Fairtest, the watchdog organization of the testing industry points out, if the test was not biased in this category, one would expect Asian Americans to score higher, since they take more academic courses than any other group. Likewise, Asian Americans would rank first when scores are not adjusted for family income, course work, and grades. Thus, we see an example of the bias of this test.

Furthermore, there are many other biases of the ACT, as disclosed by the Fairtest organization. Here are just the three main categories of bias:

1. *Biased format:* Research shows that a multiple-choice format favors males over females. Guessing, a risk males are more likely to take, is rewarded. Since multiple-choice items do not allow for shades of meaning, they work against females' more complex thinking styles.

2. *Biased language:* Idiomatic expressions such as "thumb its big nose at" and "straight from the horse's mouth" may not be familiar to many test takers, particularly those whose first language isn't English, causing them to choose wrong answers.

3. *Biased question context:* Studies show test takers do better on questions they find interesting or that are set in familiar situations. Many more English and reading ACT passages cover topics that are likely to be more familiar to whites and males than to minorities and females. One reason for this is that people of color and women are seldom featured on the ACT. Of four publicly disclosed tests, one did not include a single reference to a person of color, and two mentioned only one. Similarly, men appeared in items five times more often than women. When people of color and females are mentioned, they rarely have the status of whites and males. For example, one test featured twenty-one white males, including famous scientists, politicians, and artists. The single minority group

member was a nameless Japanese tea master. The five females included a "she" and four characters in a fiction passage.

Thus, one can only conclude this test is problematic. For a more detailed analysis of this issue, see my earlier work (Janesick 2000). Again, the use of this example of the ACT points out problems and emphasizes that each of these flaws raises serious ethical questions. We have not even begun to address these ethical questions. Educators raise some of these questions in their respective local settings. On a hopeful note, there is one group already challenging gender bias in testing, and that is the group of female athletes in those universities that are members of the National Collegiate Athletic Association (NCAA). In addition, ongoing research by Howard Gardner, the medical doctor with a lifetime of research on multiple intelligences, is complicating matters even further.

Ethical Questions Raised as a Result of the Work on Multiple Intelligences: Searching for New Ways to Explain Learning

The theory of multiple intelligences was developed by Gardner and his colleagues at Harvard University and became known through the text *Frames of Mind.* Also, the text *Multiple Intelligences: The Theory and Practice—A Reader* helped to fully explain this work. Gardner had worked for over twenty-five years on this research and was guided by the questions of how we learn what we learn and how the mind works. Basically, Gardner found that we have at least eight intelligences. These include bodily kinesthetic intelligence, visual-spatial intelligence, mathematical-logical intelligence, musical intelligence, linguistic intelligence, interpersonal intelligence, and intrapersonal intelligence; the eighth category, naturalist intelligence, was added after 1996. Unfortunately, our school system functions with attention to only two of these intelligence categories: mathematical-logical and linguistic. Thus, so much of what could be possible in schools is left out. First, let us examine the basic categories and the definitions of each intelligence.

- Bodily kinesthetic intelligence refers to knowledge gained through bodily movement, which is seen as a type of problem solving. For example, to express emotion through the body as in dance or to invent something physically or to play a game such as football involves bodily kinesthetic intelligence.
- Visual-spatial intelligence refers to problem solving through visualizing an object, as in map reading, navigation, drawing, etc.

- Mathematical-logical intelligence refers to the ability of individuals to solve problems rapidly and mathematically and nonverbally. Many scientists show evidence of this, especially in solving a problem nonverbally before putting the solution down on paper, for example. Thus, a solution is found before it is articulated.
- Musical intelligence refers to the ability to compose music and/or play a musical instrument by virtue of the problem solving involved and the creation of a product, in this case music.
- Interpersonal intelligence refers to the ability to get along with others and all that entails.
- Intrapersonal intelligence refers to an individual's ability to understand and work with him- or herself, as well as be intuitive and creative.
- Linguistic intelligence refers to the production of words, language, etc.
- Naturalist intelligence refers to observing, collecting, categorizing, and understanding patterns in the natural environment, much like a researcher or naturalist would do.

Thus, the work of Gardner expands our understanding of how the mind works, and although schools pay attention to only two of these categories by and large, that does not mean we should forget about the others. Furthermore, our standardized tests cater to only two of these intelligences. Does that make any sense, given what we know about the complexity of the brain?

In addition, what Gardner is striving for is a clear vision of what education ought to be. Rather than merely using testing to illustrate what a student knows, Gardner and his colleagues remind us, fostering a deep understanding of content should be our goal. Furthermore, students should work toward understanding whether something is considered true or false and why it is thus, and they should be able to recognize what is beautiful and even unexplainable. We need to expand our understanding of human knowledge and human differences in respect to culture, context, and the social world. The theory of multiple intelligences can help teachers and students to enhance understanding in at least three ways:

1. By providing powerful points of entry—knowing when to introduce subject matter and how to introduce it and which

students learn in which primary mode of the multiple intelligences can be beneficial
2. By offering apt analogies—teachers may use analogy to convey the complexity of a subject, for example
3. By providing multiple representations of an idea or topic

In other words, rather than relying on only one or two of the multiple intelligences, try to use as many ways as you can to introduce content. In the text *The Disciplined Mind,* Gardner uses examples to illustrate these major ideas of his, especially in respect to his vision for schooling and learning. All rest on the notion that students are best served when we strive for deep understanding of any given content. But this goes along with the notion that students must have ways to grapple with what is true and false, what is beautiful and what is not so, and what is good and what is reprehensible. It seems to me that this alone calls into question many of our practices regarding the testing of children.

Thus, Gardner, whose curriculum trend tradition is part reconceptualist and part postmodern, has done a great deal to raise questions concerning the problems with testing in terms of one type of intelligence.

NO EASY QUESTIONS:
THE MANUFACTURED CRISIS

When faced with criticism of the public schools, many look for easy answers, quick fixes, and a way to make the situation better. Often, their arguments are weak, such as "American students don't work hard enough." Individual cases aside, there is very little compelling evidence to support such a claim. Will students work harder for drill and repetition type work or on cognitively developmentally appropriate work? You be the judge. David Berliner and Bruce Biddle (1995) have warned against the rush to easy answers given compelling evidence. In fact, they conducted research over time to get at the public distrust in education and the myths, fraud, and outright attack on education. Their text is the most powerful repository of evidence that argues against the politicization of issues such as standards, testing, and school reform in general. They debunk the phony claims and false statistics used by newspapers, politicians, and others, which are simply wrong. With mounds of proof, Berliner and Biddle show the reader that, in fact, schools are performing amazingly well given that in just a short span of thirty years or so, schools have widened the pool of students by including the disenfranchised in every single so-called measure of accountability. For example, the authors counter with evidence the politicians' claims that Scholastic Achievement Test (SAT) scores are lower, that private schools are better than public, and that privatization of schools somehow will fix all problems. The data show that these kinds of claims are almost impossible to support. The authors refer to the myths as "the manufactured crisis," the title of their book, and their exploration of one myth after another uncovers some of the threads that relate directly to the standards movement and its endless problems. Let's look at some of the myths the authors have pulverized:

- Student achievement in American primary schools has declined.
- The performance of American college students has declined.
- The intellectual abilities and abstract problem-solving skills have declined.
- America's schools always come up short when compared with those of other nations.
- America spends more money on schools than other nations.
- Investing in schools has not brought success, or money is not related to school performance.
- The productivity of the American worker is down.
- American teachers are not prepared to teach.
- Private schools are better than public.

These are just a part of what Berliner and Biddle address in their text, and they show that these claims are utterly phony. They are manufactured not to help students or teachers succeed but to deter us from the facts. The authors carefully follow the deliberate attack on schools that began in the 1980s and analyze why the change in the political milieu occurred at that time. The business and industry model took the place of the social services and learning model, and the attack goes on into this the new millennium. But the even sharper analysis of the authors shows that the myths not only are foolish but also can be harmful. The harm comes in preventing students of all groups from learning, and additional harm is found in the simplistic notion that everything can be fixed with simple solutions. I invite the reader to carefully read Berliner and Biddle's text, as it provides a context for understanding how the standards movement and testing as the easy answer can be framed. In addition, I agree with the authors that if we are to have effective school reforms of any type, adequate funding and the structure for reform should be the first goals. Thus, the notion of simple answers can never address the complexity of the issues before us. In particular, the idea that setting standards for students and testing them will in some way automatically ensure high achievement simple does not make sense. There are many writers who echo these same thoughts, and in particular, the work of Grant Wiggins (1993, 1998) stands out.

UNDERSTANDING CURRICULUM THROUGH STANDARDS AND ASSESSMENT

Standards make sense when the assessment system in place makes sense. Wiggins (1993) argues that there are equitable, fair, and authentic means of assessment.

Here are some of his major guidelines:

1. Assess the student's accomplishments and progress, not merely the total score that results from points subtracted from a collection of items. In other words, score longitudinally toward exemplary performance at exemplary tasks, not by subtraction from "perfection" on simplistic and isolated tests.
2. Devise a scheme that assigns degree-of-difficulty points to assignments and test questions, thus distinguishing the quality of the performance from the degree of difficulty of the task.
3. Give all students the "same" demanding work but differently scaffolded assessments based on equitable expectations.
4. Devise a sliding grading system wherein the proportion of what is counted over time varies. Move toward increased emphasis on achievement, with a weight for effort and progress.

In other words, Wiggins has suggested that there are ways to test students, still maintain standards, and be fair and equitable in the process. His system of authentic assessment (1998) is based on the following premises:

1. Authentic tasks must be realistic. The task must match the real knowledge and abilities based in the real world of experience with that task.
2. Authentic assessment requires students to use their judgment and their imagination. The learner has to use knowledge,

theory, and skills wisely in order to solve problems or pose problems.

3. Ask students to "do" rather than recite, memorize, replicate, or restate information. In other words, let students demonstrate what they have learned.

4. Authentic assessments are related to the real-world context in which adults are tested in the workplace. Typical tests are contextless (Wiggins 1998, 24). He argues that students need to experience what it is like to do tasks in real-life situations.

5. Assess the learners ability to efficiently and effectively use a repertoire of skills and knowledge to negotiate complex tasks.

6. Allow appropriate opportunities to rehearse, practice, consult resources, and get feedback on and refine performance and products.

Thus, Wiggins asks us to imagine a new way to look at testing and assessment and a new way to help students learn and grow. If we follow his tenets, there is room to use information from authentic assessments in a way that is healthy, respectful, fair, and demanding for students, without reducing their work to one and only one indicator.

Reviewing Some Problems with High-Stakes Testing

In order to fully understand the importance of the assessment movement, one needs to put into perspective the problem with high-stakes testing. *High-stakes testing* is the term used to label the testing of children where the stakes are extremely high. Most recently, the high stakes have involved tying school funds to tests scores. Historically, this kind of testing went on in the South. Southern states have never funded their schools to the extent that other states have. Many writers and critics believe that this lack of commitment to education has its roots in racism. Monty Neill, executive director of the National Center for Fair and Open Testing (also known as Fairtest), has called this "an unnecessary and harmful intrusion in the process of school reform" (on the Fairtest Web site, www.fairtest.org), and the group urges all citizens to get active about this serious problem. Neill and others listed in the resources section of this book have long argued that there is no need to require all states and all children to fit into a "one size fits all" model. The belief that we can test our way to better schools makes no sense. If you look at the results of states that employ high-stakes testing—again, typically and historically the southern states—you'll see the approach has not succeeded. Why would the entire country want to adopt a model that has failed?

What the Activist Organization Fairtest Is Teaching Us

Fairtest has numerous publications and calls to action on its Web site. In addition, it keeps track of what is happening in terms of testing in each state. The organization has also rated the states as to the extent to which assessment is used to help our children. Fairtest has produced "A Report Card on Assessment," choosing to focus on the positive aspects of assessment rather that the negative aspects of testing.

A brief history of standardized testing is in order here to frame the assessment debate. Basically, since the 1920s, we have used standardized tests. At that time, only a few students went to school. In our society then, the factory model of education was in full swing. Students were sorted hierarchically by virtue of their test scores. Indeed, the hope and promise of the school reform movement of the 1990s and into the early years of the new century are tied to breaking with the factory model. Assessment of students offers a strong alternative to support high standards without standardization. In the study conducted by Fairtest on how well states are seriously using assessment practices, standards were used to judge the merits of each state's progress. In 1995, a publication called *Principles and Indicators for Student Assessment Systems* was disseminated. This statement was written by a coalition of education and civil rights groups from the National Forum on Assessment. The "principles" document calls for assessments that are:

1. Grounded in solid knowledge of how students learn
2. Connected to clear statements of what is important for students to learn
3. Flexible enough to meet the needs of a diverse student body
4. Able to provide students with the opportunity to actively *do* work, to produce work and *demonstrate* learning

Surprisingly, what investigators found was that two-thirds of the states fundamentally have not used assessment but rather continue using standardized tests. Even worse, some states have relabeled testing as assessment! Most programs rely on traditional, multiple-choice tests, and they often use them inappropriately as high-stakes indicators. Overall, the detailed survey and data sources revealed that one-third of the state systems need a *complete* overhaul, another third need major improvements, and the remaining third have positive components but still need improvement.

Thus, we have a long way to go. Fairtest reminds us that two-thirds of the states need serious work. In those states, testing systems *impede* rather than help students. Here is a summary of the organization's findings on how this two-thirds uses testing systems. They are not advancing reform because:

⇢ Rather than holding schools accountable for providing a rich, deep education and reporting on such achievement to the public, most state testing programs provide information on a too limited range of student learning in each important subject area.

⇢ Rather than supporting and assessing complex and critical thinking and the ability to use knowledge in real-world situations, most state tests continue to focus too much on measuring rote learning.

⇢ Rather than making decisions about students based on multiple sources of evidence, too many states use a single test as a mandatory hurdle.

The Major Problems

As we review the major problems with standardized high-stakes testing, it is a good idea to categorize the problems into the following areas:

1. Problems with the construction of the tests
2. Problems with scoring and interpretation of tests
3. Problems with penalties of the tests if test takers are below par
4. Problems with issues of fairness
5. Problems with teachers teaching to the test

Throughout this chapter, the issues involved raise many serious questions and point to the complexity of curriculum trends, assessment, and standards. For schools to succeed, they must have a sensible way to assess what they are doing. In this current age of evolving postmodernism in curriculum, educators must keep up with the unfolding development of assessment techniques, be aware of the pitfalls of embracing standards without critique, and see the complexities of school reform.

HOPEFUL SIGNS

Educative assessment offers hope to teachers, students, parents, administrators, and all community members. Assessment allows for developing a sense of community. For example, since parents are involved in portfolio development, they obviously have more contact with the teacher and feel welcome in the school. Thus, by virtue of coming in to the school building, the first steps toward a stronger community spirit are taken. When interested parents, teachers, students, and administrators get together and work on assessment in its many forms, good things happen for all. But this is only one sign of the hope offered by educative assessment. As the chapters in this text reveal, other characteristics of assessment offer hope for the future. For example, look at this list to see the possibility of stronger schools and communities.

Educative assessments do the following:

- Ask and demand that students be actively involved in learning by having them create, perform, produce a product, or *do* something
- Ask and demand of students that they use problem-solving skills on a regular basis
- Require actual people to score, grade, and evaluate a student's work, rather than have a machine do so
- Demand new roles for teachers and administrators

Based on this, there is hope for the future in our schools. For those who are dissatisfied with the standardized testing movement, authentic, educative assessment is a good and powerful alternative. Assessment must be part of a learning environment. The student's ability to perform learning tasks and the ability to think, to solve problems, and to articulate what and why he or she is doing something are all parts of a learning environment. Assessment must go hand in hand with the curriculum. Current curriculum trends demand a watchfulness and return to the basic questions in the field of curriculum: What do we teach? And how best can we teach it?

SUMMARY

In this overview chapter, I have described some of the key organizing ideas for the remainder of this reference handbook. The three major categories of traditional, reconceptual, and postmodern trends in curriculum were outlined. Examples were given of each orientation. Examples of postmodern writing were used to show the critical elements of the postmodern trend in terms of autobiography, ethics and aesthetics, and alternative schooling models. To complicate matters, let me add three other critical points at this time. In order to understand all the trends and orientations described earlier, one needs to be aware of three curricula that all schools teach, as described by Eisner (1985):

1. The *stated* actual content of the subject taught, such as math, history, etc.
2. The *hidden,* or implicit, curriculum, such as what is not explicitly taught but what a student may learn. For example, as early as preschool, children are learning some reading skills in reading class. Yet at the same time, they are learning some hidden messages. They learn they have to stand in line. They learn they have to raise their hands to even get noticed. They learn who is the smartest person in class, etc. So all these unintended messages are indeed part of the curriculum yet are hidden from the plan or syllabus.
3. The *null* curriculum, or that which is not taught. Think about all that we do not teach, such as how to resolve conflict, how to express emotions, how to deal with money, how to deal with death, and so on. In fact, schools have been so preoccupied with cognitive process and the great books, they have forgotten about the people who are experiencing those books.

All this should be kept in mind as an advance organizer for understanding curriculum trends. In addition, five legal cases that are crucial to current curriculum trends were described. Furthermore, the connections between curriculum trends, school reform, standards, and assessment were described and explained. Within that context, the work on multiple intelligences by Howard Gardner was briefly described to help understand the complexity of any school reform activity, particularly those reforms related to testing and assessment. The applications of postmodernism in the classroom were evidenced with two examples of integrated thematic units at two different grade levels.

In the next chapters, you will find a chronology of curriculum trends and numerous resources in print and nonprint media. You will find descriptions of organizations devoted to curriculum trends and to understanding those trends on a professional level. You will also find a chapter on the future trends. Near the end of the text, useful examples of each trend and a glossary of terms will help you to navigate the wide ocean of curriculum trends.

REFERENCES

Adler, M. J., and the Paideia Group. (1982). *The Paideia Proposal: An Educational Manifesto.* New York: Collier Books.

Berliner, David C., and Bruce Biddle. (1995). *The Manufactured Crisis: Myths, Fraud and the Attack on America's Public Schools.* Reading, MA: Addison-Wesley.

Bobbitt, J. F. (1918). *The Curriculum.* Boston: Houghton Mifflin.

Charters, C. W. (1923). *Curriculum Construction.* New York: Macmillan.

Cuban, L. (1990). "Reforming Again, Again and Again." *Educational Researcher* 19, no 1: 313.

Dewey, J. (1897). "My Pedagogic Creed." *School Journal* 54, no. 3: 77–80.

———. (1899). *The School and Society.* Chicago: University of Chicago Press.

———. (1902). *The Child and the Curriculum.* Chicago: University of Chicago Press.

———. (1910). *How We Think.* New York: D. C. Heath.

———. (1916). *Democracy and Education.* New York: Macmillan. Reprint, New York: Free Press, 1966.

———. (1934). *Art as Experience.* New York: Minton Balch.

———. (1938). *Experience and Education.* New York: Macmillan.

Doll, R. (1989). *Curriculum Improvement: Decision Making and Process.* Boston: Allyn & Bacon. Previous editions in 1986, 1982, 1978, 1974, 1970, and 1964.

Doll, W., Jr. (1990). "Teaching a Post-modern Curriculum." In J. Sears and D. Marshall, eds., *Teaching and Thinking about Curriculum,* 39–47. New York: Teachers College Press.

Doll, W. E. (1993). *A Post-modern Perspective on Curriculum.* New York: Teachers College Press.

Donmoyer, R. (1985). "The Rescue from Relativism: Two Failed Attempts and an Alternative Strategy." *Educational Researcher* 13, no. 20 (December).

Eisner, E. (1985). *The Educational Imagination: On the Design and Evaluation of School Programs.* New York: Macmillan.

———. (1991). *The Enlightened Eye: Qualitative Inquiry and the Enhancement of Educational Practice.* New York: Macmillan.

Eisner, E., and Elizabeth Vallance, eds. (1974). *Conflicting Conceptions of Curriculum.* Berkeley, CA: McCutcheon Press.

Farenga, P. (1999). "John Holt and the Origins of Contemporary Homeschooling." In P. Farenga, ed., *Paths of Learning,* 34–37. Brandon, VT: Foundation for Educational Renewal.

Freire, Paulo. (1973). *Pedagogy of the Oppressed.* New York: Seabury.

Gardner, Howard. (1993). *Multiple Intelligences: The Theory and Practice.* New York: Basic Books.

———. (1999). *The Disciplined Mind: What All Students Should Understand.* New York: Simon and Schuster.

Giroux, H. (1988). *Teachers as Intellectuals: Toward a Critical Pedagogy of Learning and Educating.* South Hadley, MA: Bergin & Garvey.

———. (2000). *The Mouse That Roared: Disney and the End of Innocence.* New York: Rowman & Littlefield.

Gratz, Donald B. (2000). "High Standards for Whom?" *Phi Delta Kappan* 81, 9: 681–687. EA 537 202.

Greene, M. (1971). "Curriculum and Consciousness." *Teachers College Record* 73, no. 2: 253–269.

———. (1978). *Landscapes of Learning.* New York: Teachers College Press.

Haney, W. (1999). *Supplementary Report on Texas Assessment of Academic Skills Exit Test (TAAS-X).* Chestnut Hill, MA: Boston College Center for the Study of Testing Evaluation and Educational Policy.

Home School Legal Defense Association (HSLDA). (2002). "Homeschooling." Retrieved from HSLDA Web site at http://www.hslda.org.

Horn, Raymond, and Joe L. Kincheloe. (2001). *American Standards: Quality Education in a Complex World—The Texas Case.* New York: Peter Lang.

Jackson, P. (1968). *Life in Classrooms.* New York: Holt, Rinehart and Winston.

Jackson, P. W., ed. (1996). *Handbook of Research on Curriculum,* 3–40. New York: Macmillan Library Reference.

Janesick, Valerie J. (2000). *The Assessment Debate: A Reference Handbook.* Santa Barbara, CA: ABC-CLIO.

Mallon, Thomas. (1995). *A Book of One's Own.* Saint Paul, MN: Hungry Mind Press.

McLaren, P. (1989). *Life in Schools: An Introduction to Critical Pedagogy in the Foundations of Education.* New York: Longman.

McNeil, Linda M. (2000). *Contradictions of School Reform: Educational Costs of Standardized Testing.* New York: Routledge.

Nin, Anais. (1976). *The Diary of Anais Nin, 1955–1966.* Edited by Gunther Shulman. New York: Harcourt Brace Jovanovich.

Noddings, Nel, and P. Shore. (1984). *Awakening the Inner Eye: Intuition in Education.* New York: Teachers College Press.

Orlich, D. C., R. J. Harder, R. C. Callahan, and H. W. Gibson. (1998). *Teaching Strategies.* Boston: Houghton Mifflin.

Pinar, W. F., W. M. Reynolds, P. Slattery, and P. M. Taubman. (1995). "Understanding Curriculum as Political Text." In their *Understanding Curriculum.* New York: Peter Lang.

Progoff, Ira. (1992). *At a Journal Workshop.* Los Angeles, CA: J. P. Tarcher.

Ruenzel, D. (1997). "The Montessori Method." *Teacher Magazine* (on-line) 8, no. 7. Retrieved from http://www.teachermagazine.org/vol-08/07mont.h08.

"Standards for Educational and Psychological Measurement." Educational Testing Service. www.ets.org.

Tyler, R. W. (1969). *Basic Principles of Curriculum and Instruction.* Chicago: University of Chicago Press.

Wiggins, Grant. (1993). "Assessment Authenticity, Context, and Validity." *Phi Delta Kappan* 75, no. 3: 200–214.

———. (1998). *Educative Assessment: Designing Assessments to Inform and Improve Student Performance.* San Francisco, CA: Jossey-Bass.

Chapter Two

•◆ Chronology

Curriculum trends may be as old as education itself. For the purposes of this text, however, it makes sense to revisit the 1890s where one writer, W. W. Charters, wrote a text that began a fascinating journey into understanding what teachers need to teach and how teachers might teach their subject matter. That is the heart and soul of the field of curriculum. It is the field that is formed around two questions: What do we teach? And how best do we teach it?

Yet it took from the 1890s to the 1940s before curriculum became a legitimate field of study. As a result of the need to emphasize those two basic questions of curriculum, educator Ralph Tyler stepped forward. When Tyler wrote his famous *Basic Principles* text, the field began to percolate with ideas, with controversy, and with competing conceptions of curriculum. Understanding that all texts are bound by time, history, and cultural context, this chronology will focus on schools in the United States. As I define, describe, and explain the chronology, all efforts will be made to trace those time periods to international influences from England, other parts of Europe, and Asia. Before I begin, the reader should understand that the American system clearly followed from the British system. The United States evolved from Great Britain and what we now call the United Kingdom (UK). Thus, the chronology begins in the 1890s, though that period is only briefly described, to set the historical context of where we came from and where we are today.

FROM THE 1890S TO THE 1920S: THE PRETRADITIONALIST ERA

Schooling in the United States, as in Great Britain, began in the context of religious schools. Typically, the students, usually male, studied the Bible, and good character traits, as defined by the local Puritan culture, were stressed. Teachers were typically male clergy. Historically church-based parish schools continue to exist today, although in the United Kingdom and United States they are subject to state, local, and national requirements. It was not until major wars and turbulence occurred that women entered the labor market as teachers. Thus, gender began to be an issue in curriculum trends as early as World War I.

In the 1890s, thirty years after the first education reform bills in England, the United States experienced a decade of making curriculum a serious issue legally and socially. A classical view of curriculum was put forth by Charles W. Eliot (1834–1926), president of Harvard University. He was the chairperson of three committees appointed by the National Education Association. The committees were:

The Committee of Ten on Secondary School Studies
The Committee of Fifteen on Elementary School Studies
The Committee on College Entrance Requirements

Note that beginning in the 1890s, these committees focused on subject matter with firm beliefs in discipline, a focus on study, and a heavy emphasis on grammar and arithmetic. This is important, for as the old saying goes, "History repeats itself." Today, we are still grappling with these same issues regarding subject matter emphasis.

Another important influence appeared for U.S. curriculum specialists in the 1890s. Many traveled to Germany to study the work of the German philosopher Johann Friedrich Herbart (1776–1841). Herbart believed the entire reason for education was the development of character. He stressed that education was indeed a moral activity. He believed students were basically good and that the job of the teacher was to elicit and develop the goodness of the student through study, concentration, and application of what was taught. The many Americans who traveled to Germany to study Herbart's thoughts formed the Herbart Club in 1892, which then became the National Herbart Society somewhere in the late 1890s. Each year beginning in 1894, the group published a yearbook related to curriculum issues and trends. It still continues to this day.

FROM THE 1920S TO THE 1950S:
THE TRADITIONALIST ERA

During this period, written texts were preoccupied with subject matter, curriculum development, and improving education. As usual, the focus was indeed on grammar and arithmetic—what we now call reading and language arts and mathematics. This period can be called the traditionalist period. It evolved from the 1890s and has stayed in many forms through to the present day. It is usually spelled out with clear goals and objectives, with the assumption that all children can learn all data at the same time. Traditionalist writers influenced many current writers and so-called reform movements. They laid the groundwork for the work of Ralph Tyler, the grandparent of curriculum in the traditional form. The traditionalist period, described earlier, evolved into an even more basic, technocratic period in the 1940s and 1950s. World War II disrupted all aspects of life across the globe. It made sense that schools and curriculum would remain traditional. This was not a period of great change for curriculum. In fact, Tyler's 1949 *Basic Principles of Curriculum and Instruction* is almost a cookbook approach to curriculum. I mention this text for it may have been a wake-up call to educators to go more deeply and artistically into the field of curriculum and instruction—what we now call curriculum studies. In fact, one might argue that Tyler's work caused so many writers to be upset that they began the counternarratives and branched out into all the complexities of the curriculum questions and practices of the time. Subsequently, new ideas were percolating and directly questioning all that Tyler had left out of his format.

FROM THE 1960S TO THE 1980S: THE RECONCEPTUALIST ERA

Society was changing in the 1960s and 1970s. Experimentation was evident in nearly every facet of living. The civil rights movement, feminist movement, and gay rights movement began the journey into reconceptualizing how we think about our world. Of course, this would be reflected in schools. Remember that the schools are the slowest institutions to change overall. Yet the first seedling of major change emerged at this time. For example, tests that focused on curriculum development began to appear and include more than discussion of subject matter. In 1957, B. Smith, W. Stanley, and H. Shores's text *Fundamentals of Curriculum Development* began to use examples of implications and lessons learned from actual cases. In 1962, Hilda Taba's text *Curriculum Development: Theory and Practice* offered models for educators to follow. In 1975, Daniel and Laurel Tanner's *Curriculum Development: Theory into Practice* went even further to illustrate how to create, develop, and evaluate curriculum. These writers had the classroom teacher in mind in order to deal with real-world issues and problems. Still, it was not until the 1980s that the field of curriculum studies began to blossom. Beginning in the late 1970s, writers such as Henry Giroux and

Michael Apple set off an earthquake in the field by asking questions about economics, politics, and teachers as intellectuals rather than teachers as technocrats.

Here began a major paradigm shift from the technocratic, nuts-and-bolts approach to curriculum to *understanding* curriculum. The major wake-up call came from the brilliantly written 1986 text by William H. Schubert, *Curriculum: Perspective, Paradigm, and Possibility.* Here, the author seriously grappled with the state of the field, viewing it through three lenses: those of the traditionalists, the social behaviorists, and the experientialists. Schubert's orientations can be described as follows.

The Traditionalists

The name says it all. Basically, this group of educators believes the curriculum should consist of all courses in the liberal arts tradition. They value the great books, *The Encyclopedia Britannica,* and the classics of the Western world. This group is sometimes reluctant to include writings of minority groups, Eastern philosophy or thought, and alternative literature.

Traditionalists believe the mind is to be developed fully through serious study of Western culture. Mortimer Adler speaks of six great ideas: truth, beauty, goodness, liberty, equality, and justice. Any questions can be related to these ideas for the traditionalists. Traditionalists also believe that education proceeds through life, beyond the K–12 grades. In our present day, those educators who argue for the three Rs and the reduction of music, arts, and sports are the best examples of traditionalist thought.

The Social Behaviorists

Now we come to a group of efficiency experts that like to catalog all of learning into specific sets of skills for every content area. This is related to the traditionalist approach in that the basic content area still remains classical Western literature. However, the social behaviorists are taken with science, scientific thinking, and great scientific discoveries. In general, they believe we need more and better research on learning and teaching. Curriculum is viewed as a set of skills to be mastered. Of course, the emphasis should be on science and math, the "hard" subjects. That emphasis should include technology and workplace preparation, not just lofty discussion. Social behaviorists like to function on basic skills of reading, math, and writing. An example in today's world of this type of thinking would be educators who want charter schools, specific schools of science, etc.

The Experientialists

John Dewey is most often recognized as the father of the experientialists. He described learning as beginning with the learner's experience and interests. Experientialists believe interests are deeply ingrained in the individual learner and should be developed. Students need to take an active role in the learning process rather than a passive role. Thus, we are the agents of our own learning agenda. Learning is also for the good of the community. For the experientialist, students, teachers, leaders, and parents in a given community teach and learn from one another for a better world. The key questions of what and how to teach have to be socially constructed so as to allow for freedom from oppression. For the experientialist, what is good is a democratic learning community. Thus, all in the community benefit from a pedagogy that allows for maximum growth and development.

In addition, the 1980s brought about an aesthetic look at curriculum. Maxine Greene wrote of curriculum consciousness. She used autobiography as a technique to explore the meaning of curriculum. Likewise, William Pinar wrote of sanity, madness, and schooling. Essentially, he asked educators to consider the harm caused by education that mesmerizes, anesthetizes, and prevents critical thinking. Still further, Elliot Eisner wrote of the freeing aspect of art and aesthetics for curriculum in all fields of study. Thus, in the 1980s, serious questions that challenged the traditionalists and social behaviorists began to be posed.

FROM THE 1980S ONWARD: THE POSTMODERN CRITICAL ERA

The 1980s began an exciting time in the field of curriculum. Key writers since the 1970s had begun to make a difference in curriculum. The idea of critical pedagogy most often associated with Henry Giroux had great influence in terms of making educators aware of critique and the impact of culture in schools. His many writings in the area of cultural studies and education made many people stop and assess some key icons in our culture. For example, Giroux's 1999 text critiquing the Disney Corporation and its influence on children made parents ask more questions about the mouse that roared, so to speak. Giroux wanted parents, teachers, students, administrators, and everyone else to question the time and money spent on Disney products and how that affected children's thoughts and behaviors. His work remains a classic in the field.

Giroux, Michael Apple, and Peter McClaren all wrote that basically schools are functioning to reproduce the structure of the workplace. As a result, there is an attempt to deskill teachers and to dumb down their education. Thus, the teacher becomes a minimal force in curriculum practice. In order to have hope, teachers needed to resist the deskilling of teaching and the dumbing down of curriculum. So resistance became a theme in the literature. These writers argued that by looking at the contradictions in schools and through the cracks of what is not working, we arrive at a critique of the status quo. Next, action is needed to ensure that teachers are critical, reflective agents in the process of educating students. In order to get there, educators need to examine issues of race, class, gender, and multiculturalism. These writers and many others argued for including the voices of groups traditionally left out of the conversation on curriculum. Those were the voices of women, ethnic and linguistic minorities, and nonmainstream groups.

Since 2000, one might say that more than ever, writers who raise questions regarding race, class, and gender have been very active. They have to raise these serious questions in the never ending fear of falling backward to a drill-and-memorize, fact-based model of curriculum. One of the reasons the traditional, fact-based model has gained attention is the practical use of the "testing" movement as fodder for politicians. Especially during election years, many a candidate names him- or herself "the education candidate." Thus, writers who are reconceptualists and postmodernists are constantly on their toes responding to manufactured and false claims about curriculum issues. This trend should continue in the future as we see, particularly in the arena of testing, increasing challenges to the high-stakes testing movement. Not only are curriculum writers exposing the flaws in overtesting and high-stakes testing movements, we now also have parents and citizens' groups raising questions. In fact, parents have begun a grassroots movement called the Coalition for Authentic Reform of Education (CARE). In Cambridge, Massachusetts, Jonathan King was a key actor in funding this movement.

King is a father of two and a professor at the Massachusetts Institute of Technology (MIT), and he and many others nationwide have voluntarily pulled their children out of the testing process. This movement will only continue, as King and others claim the tests are turning schools into a "police state." Oddly enough, we come into an era of contradiction. On the one hand, we have the high-stakes testing going on. On the other hand, we have a grassroots, antitesting movement. The organization Fairtest (www.fairtest.org) is in full swing, and other similar groups have also developed, such as CARE. The trend can only continue due to the continuing failure of predominantly minority schools in high-poverty areas to meet minimum achievement levels set by the test makers. It is easy to see why curriculum writers and education in general will continue to raise the postmodern issues of race, class, and gender. These topics took hold earlier, during the 1970s, when the reconceptualists basically asked: Are we doing enough for minority students? Under what conditions can poverty-level children learn to read, write, think, and do math? *What* should we be teaching in a multicultural, multilingual nation?

SUMMARY

As we've reviewed curriculum trends in the United States, three major categories have been selected to describe the time line of development.

1. Traditionalists: those favoring the Western canon and the three Rs—reading, writing, and arithmetic.
2. Reconceptualists: those who include traditionalist beliefs and add an overwhelming reverence for scientific progress. For them, the need to offer alternatives to the traditional approaches is critical.
3. Postmodernists: those who ask questions beyond the obvious, which include questions on race, class, gender, multiculturalism, and cultural issues.

In addition and following from the postmodernist period, future trends are focused on the critical turn of events. Trends in curriculum and autobiography, ethics, aesthetics, critical thinking, and critical pedagogy prevail. These will be discussed more thoroughly in a subsequent chapter in this text.

Figure 2.1 Time Line of Curriculum Trends

Pre-1890s–1920s	1920s–1950s
Pretraditionalist Era · Church-based · Mostly male students and teachers · Few in school · Subject matter focus, drill, repetition, testing	*Traditionalist Era* · Committees formed to study curriculum trends by well-known educators · Emphasis on objectives and outcomes · More students in school · Development of character · Subject matter focus, drill, repetition, testing

1960s–1980s	1980s–Present
Reconceptualist Era · Examines student cognition, goals · Values the person as learner · Questions rote and repetition · Calls for school as community center · Inserts the child into the curriculum · Examines the importance of the arts · Begins the questioning of race, class, gender equity in curriculum trends	*Postmodern Critical Era* · Critical social issues raised as curriculum issues · Race, class, and gender are inserted into the curriculum discourse · Equity, equality, ethics, and empowerment are critical themes · Social justice is key · Raises ethical concerns about high-stakes testing · Alternative schooling

Chapter Three

●◆ Organizations That Support or Relate to Curriculum Trends

This chapter offers the reader a menu of key organizations and educational groups that are connected to curriculum trends and development. Are there more such organizations? Yes of course, but in the interest of space, I have selected the top groups and most active organizations, which is a very good start. As I was researching this chapter, I was struck—and I hope the reader will be struck—by the many organizations out there in this field. In fact, some people would question why so many overlap and why so many goals of these organizations are nearly identical. Part of the reason was the push for specialization by the traditionalists early on in the last century. However, this may also point to the need to find common ground and build coalitions, a postmodern idea. In any event, know that these organizations are in one way or another related to curriculum in a solid and authentic manner.

RELATED KEY ORGANIZATIONS

American Association of Colleges for Teacher Education (AACTE)
1307 New York Avenue, NW
Suite 300
Washington, DC 20005-4701
202-293-2450
Fax: 202-457-8095
http://www.aacte.org
E-mail: see Web site (contact link)

The American Association of Colleges for Teacher Education provides leadership for the continuing transformation of professional preparation programs to ensure competent and caring educators for all of America's children and youth. It is the principal professional organization for college and university leaders with responsibility for educator preparation.

American Association of School Administrators (AASA)
1801 North Moore Street
Arlington, VA 22209-1813
703-528-0700
Fax: 703-841-1543
http://www.aasa.org
E-mail: webmaster@aasa.org

The American Association of School Administrators, founded in 1865, is the professional organization for over 14,000 educational leaders across America and in many other countries. AASA's mission is to support and develop effective school system leaders who are dedicated to the highest quality of public education for all children. The four major focus areas for AASA are: (1) improving the condition of children and youth, (2) preparing schools and school systems for the twenty-first century, (3) connecting schools and communities, and (4) enhancing the quality and effectiveness of school leaders.

American Educational Research Association (AERA)
1230 Seventieth Street, NW
Washington, DC 20036-3078
202-223-9485
Fax: 202-775-1824
http://www.aera.net
E-mail: wrussell@aera.net

The American Educational Research Association is concerned with improving the educational process by encouraging scholarly inquiry related to education and by promoting the dissemination and practical application of research results. AERA is the most prominent international and professional organization with the primary goal of advancing educational research and its practical application. Its more than 22,000 members are educators; administrators; directors of research, testing, or evaluation in federal, state, and local agencies; counselors; evaluators; graduate students; and behavioral scientists.

American Federation of Teachers (AFT)
555 New Jersey Avenue, NW
Washington, DC 20001
202-879-4400
http://www.aft.org

The AFT represents 900,000 teachers, paraprofessionals, school-related personnel, public and municipal employees, higher education faculty and staff, and nurses and other health professionals. It advocates national standards for education, the professionalization of teaching, and disciplined and safe environments for learning.

The AFT has actively promoted safe-schools practices over the years. One recent initiative is its "zero tolerance" policy for drugs, weapons, violence, and disruptive behavior in and around schools. The AFT is currently waging a national campaign called "Responsibility, Respect, Results: Lessons for Life." It has a strong antiviolence component and promotes higher academic and discipline standards.

ArtsEdge

The John F. Kennedy Center for the Performing Arts
2700 F Street, NW
Washington, DC 20566
Fax: 202-416-8876
http://artsedge.kennedy-center.org/

ArtsEdge was established under a cooperative agreement between the John F. Kennedy Center for the Performing Arts and the National Endowment for the Arts to support an arts-based curriculum through the use of appropriate and creative technology. ArtsEdge provides teaching materials and professional resources to help educators teach about, through, and in the arts.

Arts Education Partnership (AEP)

One Massachusetts Avenue, NW
Suite 700
Washington, DC 20001-1431
202-326-8693
Fax: 202-408-8081
http://aep-arts.org/
E-mail: aep@ccsso.org

The Arts Education Partnership (formerly the Goals 2000 Arts Education Partnership) is a national coalition of education, business, art, government, and philanthropic organizations that promotes the role of the arts as an essential component in the learning and development of every child. AEP also includes state and local partnerships to improve schools and influence education policies to promote quality arts education.

Getty Center
1200 Getty Center Drive
Los Angeles, CA 90049-1679
310-440-7300
http://www.getty.edu

The J. Paul Getty Center offers grants to individuals and institutions for projects that promote the understanding and conservation of cultural heritage and art. The Web site provides visual highlights of exhibitions on view at the Getty Museum, along with information about the collections in the Getty Research Library and an on-line bookstore with a wide array of resources on art, architecture, and the humanities.

National Endowment for the Arts (NEA)
1100 Pennsylvania Avenue, NW
Washington, DC 20506
202-682-5400
http://arts.endow.gov/
E-mail: webmgr@arts.endow.gov

The mission of the NEA is to enrich the nation and its diverse cultural heritage by supporting artistic works, advancing knowledge in the arts, preserving the country's diverse cultural heritage, and strengthening the arts in communities around the United States. The NEA provides federal funding and national recognition to significant artistic projects and has resulted in both classic and new works of art reaching into every corner of the nation.

INFORMATION PROVIDERS

Association for Supervision and Curriculum Development (ASCD)
1703 North Beauregard Street
Alexandria, VA 22311-1714
703-578-9600 or 800-933-ASCD
Fax: 703-575-5400
http://www.ascd.org

The Association for Supervision and Curriculum Development is a unique international, nonprofit, nonpartisan association of professional educators whose jobs cross all grade levels and subject areas. In their diversity, members share a profound commitment to excellence in education. Founded in 1943, ASCD's mission is to forge covenants in teaching and learning for the success of all learners. ASCD sponsors workshops, conferences, and professional development sessions. In addition, books, journals, and videos on topics of interest to educators are available.

Bilingual Education Clearinghouse
George Washington University
Center for the Study of Language and Education
2011 I Street, NW
Suite 2001
Washington, DC 20006
202-467-0867
Fax: 202-467-0867
http://www.ncbe.gwu.edu
E-mail: askncbe@ncbe.gwu.edu

The Bilingual Education Clearinghouse provides information to practitioners in the field on curriculum materials, program models, methodologies, and research findings on the education of limited English proficient (LEP) individuals. It also offers an electronic information system, free to users, where access is available to databases of curriculum materials and literature related to the education of LEP persons. An electronic bulletin board is also available, which contains news from federal, state, and local education agencies, conference announcements, and other current information. The organization's newsletter and other publications are available, many free of charge. They can answer such questions as: (1) How do you mainstream language minority students? (2) What computer programs exist to assist in teaching limited English proficient students? (3) What are some of the issues and practices involved in meeting the needs of gifted and talented minority language students? (4) How can parents become involved in the education of limited English students? and (5) How can teachers integrate multicultural materials in instructional programs?

Center on Reinventing Public Education
Daniel J. Evans Schools of Public Affairs
University of Washington
PO Box 363060
Seattle, WA 98195-3060
206-6850-2214
Fax: 206-221-7402
http://www.crpe.org

E-mail: crpe@u.washington.edu

The Center on Reinventing Public Education seeks to develop and evaluate methods of public oversight that can allow individual schools to be focused, effective, and accountable. The research program, which was established in 1993, is based on research into the current governance and arrangement in public education, which found that the most productive schools follow coherent instructional strategies in an environment free of regulation and compliance imperatives.

Council of Chief State School Officers (CCSSO)
One Massachusetts Avenue, NW
Suite 700
Washington, DC 20001-1431
202-408-5505
Fax: 202-408-8072
http://www.cgcs.org
E-mail: info@ccsso.org

The Council of Chief State School Officers is a nationwide, nonprofit organization composed of public officials who lead the departments responsible for elementary and secondary education in the States, the U.S. extrastate jurisdictions, the District of Columbia, and the Department of Defense Education Activity. In representing the chief education officers, CCSSO works on behalf of the state agencies that serve pre-K–12 students throughout the nation.

Council of the Great City Schools
1301 Pennsylvania Avenue, NW
Suite 702
Washington, DC 20004
202-393-2427
Fax: 202-393-2400
http://www.cgcs.org

The Council of the Great City Schools is a coalition of nearly sixty of the nation's largest urban public school systems. Founded in 1956 and incorporated in 1961, the council works to promote urban education through legislation, research, media relations, instruction, management, technology, and other special projects designed to improve the quality of urban education.

Education Commission of the States (ECS)
700 Broadway, #1200
Denver, CO 80203-3460
303-299-3600
Fax: 303-296-8332
http://www.ecs.org
E-mail: ecs@ecs.org

The Education Commission of the States is an organization created in 1965 to improve public education by facilitating the exchange of information, ideas, and experiences among state policymakers and education leaders. As a nonprofit, nonpartisan organization involving key leaders from all levels of the education system, ECS creates unique opportunities to build partnerships, share information, and promote the development of policy based on available research and strategies.

Geraldine R. Dodge Foundation
163 Madison Avenue
PO Box 1239
Morristown, NJ 07962-1239
973-540-8442
Fax: 973-540-1211
http://www.grdodge.org
E-mail: info@grdodge.org

The mission of the Geraldine R. Dodge Foundation is to support and encourage those educational, social, and environmental values that contribute to making our society more humane and our world more livable. The foundation works in two ways: (1) by responding to imaginative proposals that fall within the declared areas and promise to have impact, to be replicated, and to effect systemic change, and (2) by developing initiatives shaped by close listening to practitioners and resource people in areas where the concentration of funds is likely to improve the quality of life.

RELATED EDUCATIONAL GROUPS

Education Publications Center
U.S. Department of Education
PO Box 1398

Jersup, MD 20794-1398
Fax: 301-470-1244
http://www.ed.gov

The nation's report card, the National Assessment of Educational Progress (NAEP), is the only nationally representative and continuing assessment of what America's students know and can do in various subject areas. Since 1969, assessments have been conducted periodically in reading, mathematics, science, writing, history, geography, the arts, and other fields. By making information on student performance—and instructional factors related to that performance—available to policymakers at the national, state, and local levels, NAEP is an integral part of the nation's evaluation of the condition and progress of education.

Educational Research
Office of Educational Research and Improvement's
Information Service
U.S. Department of Education
Education Information Branch
Capitol Plaza Building
Suite 300
555 New Jersey Avenue, NW
Washington, DC 20208-5641
800-424-1616
http://www.ed.gov/offices/OERI

The Education Information Branch staff specialists can provide information on topics such as early childhood education, elementary and secondary education, higher education, adult and vocational education, education finance, longitudinal statistical studies, and special education. They have publications and reports, many of which are free. They can answer such questions as:

- ➤ What statistics are there on the number of students who receive loans, grants, and work-study assistance from state sources?
- ➤ What are the statistics on private postsecondary education, such as enrollment, earned degrees conferred, full- and part-time faculty members and their salaries, and more?
- ➤ What information is available on how to choose a school for a child, and what makes a school good?
- ➤ How can parents help their children become better readers?

•• What are the enrollment outcomes for recent master's and bachelor's degree recipients?

Educational Resources Information Center (ERIC)
Aspen Systems Corporation
2277 Research Boulevard
Rockville, MD 20850
800-LET-ERIC
Fax: 301-309-2084
http://www.accesseric.org
E-mail: accesseric@access.ericorg

Educational Resources Information Center is a nationwide information service set up to collect materials about current developments in education and make them available to the public. The system includes sixteen clearinghouses, each of which is responsible for acquiring, processing, and disseminating information about a particular aspect of education. The ERIC database contains bibliographic information, including key descriptors and abstracts, on over 950,000 research documents, journal articles, curricular materials, and resource guides. The clearinghouses offer a wide variety of services and products, and staffers can answer questions about subject fields; run computer searches; develop short bibliographies, newsletters, and other free or inexpensive materials; publish monographs; publish handbooks; and develop materials to help you use ERIC.

ACCESS ERIC is the main center for the ERIC clearinghouses. Staff members answer all questions on how to use ERIC and help people stay up-to-date on the latest developments in the education field. They can answer such questions as:

•• How can I use ERIC to answer my education question?
•• What is required to have a database search run on a topic?
•• How can I have something that I have written entered into the ERIC system?
•• Where can I find the latest statistics on an education topic?
•• How can school administrators develop new management tools and practices?

Educators for Social Responsibility (ESR)
23 Garden Street
Cambridge, MA 02138
800-370-2515 or 617-492-1764

Fax: 617-864-5164

http://www.benjerry.com

The ESR provides resources and services for educators and parents, including books; curricula; and workshops and training on violence prevention, conflict resolution, intergroup relations, and character education. Query the Web site for information on the highly regarded Resolving Conflict Creatively Program and other materials.

ERIC Clearinghouse on Information and Technology
Syracuse University School of Education
621 Skytop Road
Suite 160
Syracuse, NY 13244-5290
800-464-9107 or 315-443-3640
Fax: 315-443-5448
http://www.ericir.syr.edu/home
E-mail: eric@ericir.syr.edu

The Clearinghouse on Information and Technology provides information covering educational technology and library and information science at all levels. Topics covered include: instructional design, development, and evaluation with emphasis on educational technology; computers; audio and video recordings; and more. The staff can answer such questions as:

1. What is the latest research on the value of using computers and applying video technology to enhance learning?
2. What are the various studies comparing the different types of computer-based media?
3. Is there an overview of instructional television and its effectiveness for teaching children?
4. At what grade level are computers introduced in the classroom, on average?
5. Are audio recordings an effective tool for teaching foreign languages?

ERIC Clearinghouse on Teaching and Teacher Education
American Association of Colleges for Teacher Education
1307 New York Avenue, NW
Suite 300
Washington, DC 20005
800-822-9229 or 202-293-2450

Fax: 202-457-8095
http://www.ericsp.org
E-mail: query@aacte.edu

The ERIC Clearinghouse on Teaching and Teacher Education acquires, publishes, and disseminates documents conveying research, theory, and practice in teacher education and in all aspects of health education, physical education, recreation education, nutrition education, and more. Staff members can answer such questions as:

1. What are the teacher certification requirements?
2. How effective are student teachers in the classroom?
3. What computer games are there to help kids learn math?
4. What techniques can a teacher use to improve classroom productivity?
5. What are "at-risk" students, and how can they best be served?

ERIC Clearinghouse on Urban Education
Teachers College
Columbia University Institute for Urban and Minority Education
Main Hall
Room 303
Box 40
New York, NY 10027
800-601-4848 or 212-678-3433
Fax: 212-678-4012
http://eric-web:tc.columbia.edu
E-mail: eric-cue@columbia.edu

The Clearinghouse on Urban Education provides information on the programs and practices in schools in urban areas. In addition, the education of racial/ethnic minority children and youth in various settings is studied in terms of: local, national, and international levels; theory and practice of education equity; and urban and minority experiences. A publications list and price sheet are available. Clearinghouse personnel can answer such questions as:

1. What is the current research on effective programs for reducing the dropout rates among inner-city high school students?
2. What research is available on the number of pregnant, minority teenagers who obtain their high school diplomas in inner-city schools?
3. What information is there on mentoring programs?

4. What issues are involved in linking schools with human service agencies?
5. Are urban schools financed equitably?

Home School Legal Defense Association (HSLDA)
PO Box 3000
Purcellville, VA 20134-9000
540-338-5600
Fax: 540-338-2733
http://www.hslda.org
E-mail: info@hslda.org

HSLDA is a nonprofit advocacy organization for families that home school. HSLDA provides legal consultation and representation to its members, for the purpose of defending and advancing parents' right to home school their children. HSLDA advocates in the media—on TV, on radio, and in newspapers. It also publishes a bimonthly magazine, *The Home School Court Report.* In addition, HSLDA works to defeat harmful federal legislation, and it assists individual state legislatures in drafting language to improve their home-school laws.

International Reading Association
Public Information Office
800 Barksdale Road
PO Box 8139
Newark, DE 19714-8139
302-731-1600
Fax: 302-731-1057
E-mail: pubinfo@reading.org

The International Reading Association is a dynamic and diverse organization that includes classroom teachers, reading specialists, consultants, administrators, supervisors, college teachers, researchers, psychologists, librarians, media specialists, students, and parents. The association has more than 90,000 members in ninety-nine countries and represents over 350,000 individuals and institutions through its affiliated councils worldwide.

The International Reading Association seeks to promote high levels of literacy for all by improving the quality of reading instruction through studying the reading process and teaching techniques; serving as a clearinghouse for the dissemination of reading research through conferences, journals, and other publications; and actively encouraging the lifetime reading habit.

Learning Research and Development Center,
University of Pittsburgh
3939 O'Hara Street
Pittsburgh, PA 15260
412-624-7020
Fax: 412-624-9149
http://www.lrdc.pitt.edu
E-mail: webmaster@lrdc.pitt.edu

The Learning Research and Development Center at the University of Pittsburgh is a multidisciplinary research center whose mission is to understand and improve learning by children and adults in the organizational settings in which they live and work: schools, museums, and other informal learning environments as well as workplaces. Fields of research include: processes of learning, learning in schools and museums, policy research, outreach and implementation, learning and technology, and learning and work.

National Alliance of Black School Educators (NABSE)
2816 Georgia Avenue, NW
Washington, DC 20001
202-483-1549
Fax: 202-483-8323
http://www.nabse.org

The alliance consists of black educators and community leaders whose focus is the equitable education of black youth. NABSE advocates through legislative practice, public awareness, network building, and professional preparation of educators.

National Association of Secondary School Principals (NASSP)
1904 Association Drive
Reston, VA 22091-1537
703-860-0200
Fax: 703-476-5432
http://www.nassp.org

Established in 1916, the NASSP has more than 41,000 members and is the nation's largest school leadership organization for middle and high school administrators. It provides a wide range of programs, services, publications; promotes the interests of school administrators in Congress; provides consulting services on such topics as instructional improvement, student government, and urban education; and sponsors student-oriented programs such as the National Association of Student Councils, the National Honor Society, and Partnerships International.

National Association of State Boards of Education
277 South Washington Street
Suite 100
Alexandria, VA 22314
703-684-4000
Fax: 703-836-2313
http://www.nasbe.org
E-mail: boards@nasbe.org

The National Association of State Boards of Education is a nonprofit organization that represents state and territory education. The principal objectives of the association include: strengthening leadership in educational policymaking, promoting excellence in the education of all students, advocating equality of access to educational opportunity, and assuring continued citizen involvement in public education.

National Board for Professional Teaching Standards
26555 Evergreen Road
Suite 400
Southfield, MI 48076
810-351-4444
Fax: 810-351-4170
http://www.nbpts.org/nbpts/

The National Board for Professional Teaching Standards is an independent, nonprofit, nonpartisan organization governed by a sixty-three-member board of directors. Most of the directors are classroom teachers. The others are school administrators, school board leaders, governors and state legislators, higher education officials, teacher union leaders, and business and community leaders. Their mission is to establish high and rigorous standards for what accomplished teachers should know and be able to do; to develop and operate a national, voluntary system to assess and certify teachers who meet these standards; and to advance related education reforms for the purpose of improving student learning in American schools.

National Conference of State Legislatures
Denver office:
1560 Broadway
Suite 700

Denver, CO 80202
303-830-2200
Fax: 303-863-8003
http://www.ncsl.org

Washington office:
444 North Capital Street, NW
Suite 515
Washington, DC 20001
202-624-5400
Fax: 202-737-1069
http://www.ncsl.org
E-mail: INFO@ncsl.orgE-mail or INFO@ncsl.org

The National Conference of State Legislatures is a bipartisan organization dedicated to serving the lawmakers and staffs of the nation's fifty states and its commonwealths and territories. The conference is a source for research, publications, consulting services, meetings, and seminars.

National Council for Accreditation of Teacher Education (NCATE)
2010 Massachusetts Avenue, NW
Washington, DC 20036-1023
202-466-7496
Fax: 202-296-6620
http://www.ncate.org

NCATE is the profession's mechanism to help establish high-quality teacher preparation. Through the process of professional accreditation of schools, colleges, and departments of education, NCATE works to make a difference in the quality of teaching and teacher preparation today, tomorrow, and for the next century. NCATE is a coalition of thirty-three specialty professional associations of teachers, teacher educators, content specialists, and local and state policymakers. All are committed to quality teaching, and together, the coalition represents over 3 million individuals. It is the performance-based accrediting body for teacher education programs in higher education. NCATE offers on-line publications, policy briefs, and research studies.

National Council for the Social Studies (NCSS)
8555 Sixteenth Street
Suite 500
Silver Spring, MD 20910

301-588-1800
Fax: 301-588-2049
Publications orders: 800-683-0812
http://www.ncss.org/

Founded in 1921, the National Council for the Social Studies has grown to be the largest association in the country devoted solely to social studies education. NCSS engages and supports educators in strengthening and advocating social studies. With members in all fifty states, the District of Columbia, and sixty-nine foreign countries, NCSS serves as a data bank for social studies educators. This data bank includes curriculum materials.

National Council of Teachers of English
1111 West Kenyon Road
Urbana, IL 61801-1096
800-369-6283
Fax: 217-328-9645
http://www.ncte.org
E-mail: Epublic_info@ncte.org

The National Council of Teachers of English, with 77,000 individual and institutional members worldwide, is dedicated to improving the teaching and learning of English and the language arts at all levels of education. Its membership is composed of elementary, middle, and high school teachers, supervisors of English programs, college and university faculty, teacher educators, local and state agency English specialists, and professionals in related fields.

National Governors Association (NGA)
Hall of States
444 North Capitol Street
Washington, DC 20001-1512
202-624-5300
http://www.nga.org
E-mail: webmaster@nga.org

The National Governors Association is the collective voice of the nation's governors and one of the most represented public policy organizations in Washington, D.C. NGA provides governors and their senior staff members with services that range from representing states on Capitol Hill and before the administration on key federal issues to developing policy reports on innovative state programs and hosting networking seminars for state government executive branch officials.

National Middle School Association (NMSA)
4151 Executive Parkway
Suite 300
Westerville, OH 43081
800-528-6672
http://www.nmsa.org

NMSA is a 20,000-member professional organization of teachers, administrators, parents, educational consultants, and community leaders expressly focused on the needs of the young adolescent. In addition to an annual national conference, state conferences and workshops, and several networks such as the National Forum for Middle Grades Reform, NMSA provides professional development, consultant services, and a wealth of resources from books and periodicals to Web links and newsletters. The association sets national standards for higher education teacher preparation programs and is the leading international voice for middle grades education.

National Science Teachers Association (NSTA)
1840 Wilson Boulevard
Arlington, VA 22201-3000
703-243-7100
http://www.nsta.org

The National Science Teachers Association, founded in 1944 and headquartered in Arlington, Virginia, is the largest organization in the world committed to promoting excellence and innovation in science teaching and learning for all. NSTA's current membership of more than 53,000 includes science teachers, science supervisors, administrators, scientists, business and industry representatives, and others involved in science education. To address subjects of critical interest to science educators, the association publishes five journals, a newspaper, many books, and many other publications. NSTA conducts national and regional conventions that attract more than 30,000 attendees annually. NSTA provides many programs and services for science educators, including awards, professional development workshops, and educational tours. NSTA offers professional certification for science teachers in eight teaching level and discipline area categories. In addition, NSTA has a World Wide Web site with links to state, national, and international science education organizations, an on-line catalog of publications, and two "discussion rooms" to foster interaction and ongoing conversations about science education.

National Staff Development Council (NSDC)
PO Box 240
Oxford, OH 45056
513-523-6029
http://www.nsdc.org

This is the major professional organization to focus exclusively on the professional development of educators and the organizational development of educational institutions. The NSDC holds a terrific conference early each December and publishes the quarterly *Journal of Staff Development* and the monthly *Results* and the *School Improvement Team Innovator*. The NSDC maintains an active connection with educational research and theory but keeps its approach very practical and practitioner-oriented. The NSDC specialty is bridging the gap between research, theory, and practice. Members are balanced between school personnel, private consultants, regional educational service center and laboratory staff, and university faculty. NSDC has thirty-six state and provincial affiliates that provide local support to staff developers. (See the section titled "Events" on this site for more information.)

Phi Delta Kappa International (PDK)
408 North Union
PO Box 789
Bloomington, IN 47402
800-766-1156
Fax: 812-339-0018
http://www.pdkintl.org

PDK is an international association of educators. The mission of PDK is to promote high-quality education. Its emphasis is on publicly supported education as essential to a democracy. It sponsors professional development workshops regularly on all areas of interest to educators, including assessment. A newsletter, a journal (*The Phi Delta Kappan*), a series of books, and travel seminars are also offered.

Public Agenda Online
6 East 39th Street
New York, NY 10016
212-686-6610

Fax: 212-889-3461
http://www.publicagenda.org
E-mail: support@publicagenda.org

Public Agenda is a nonpartisan, nonprofit public opinion research and citizen education organization based in New York City. The twofold mission of Public Agenda is to help leaders better understand the public's point of view on major policy issues and to help citizens better understand critical policy issues so they can make their own more informed and thoughtful decisions.

RAND Corporation
Corporate Headquarters
1700 Main Street
PO Box 2138
Santa Monica, CA 90407-2138
310-393-0411
Fax: 310-393-4818
http://www.rand.org
E-mail: godges@rand.org

Washington office:
1200 South Hayes Street
Arlington, VA 22202-5050
703-413-1100
Fax: 703-413-8111
http://www.rand.org
E-mail: godges@rand.org

RAND (a contraction of the term *research and development*) is the first organization to be called a "think tank." The organization's work is exceptionally diverse. The overall purpose of the organization is to help improve policy- and decisionmaking through research and analysis.

Relearning by Design
65 South Main Street
Building B
Box 210
Pennington, NJ 08534
609-730-1199
Fax: 609-730-1488
http://www.relearning.org
E-mail: info@relearning.org

Relearning by Design helps educators build schools around the student's needs as a learner. It provides consultations, in-service workshops, professional development seminars, and national conferences to improve the ways that educational goals and means are organized and assessed. It also provides a variety of printed materials, publications, videotapes, audiotapes, and software on student assessment and curriculum design. Relearning by Design is headed by Grant Wiggins. Most important, it helps educators keep alive the difficult questions at the heart of education:

1. How do we set high standards while also setting fair and reasonable expectations?
2. How do we know that what gets an A in our schools is judged to be quality work in the best schools?
3. If "you are what you assess," why do we so often test only what is easy to test, not what goes to the heart of our aims?
4. Is student boredom inevitable, or is it a sign that our curriculum is inauthentic and ineffective?
5. If feedback is central to learning, why do schools so rarely survey students, parents, alumni, and institutional clients as to what does and does not work?

A vision statement is one thing; policies that make it real and lead to changes in bureaucratic traditions are quite another. At Relearning by Design, educators are asked to judge the gap between their intent and their effect, and they are given help in designing systems that make it likely that the gap is examined and closed.

U.S. Department of Education
400 Maryland Avenue, SW
Washington, DC 20202-0498
1-800-872-5327
http://www.ed.gov/offices/OESE/saa/index.html.
E-mail: customerservice@inet.ed.gov

The Department of Education houses and supports a number of organizations that provide research, evaluation, and statistical information. Included in the list of organizations are groups that deal with standards, assessment, and accountability. Listed under the organization's Web links are issues related to legislation, guidance, communications with the states, and state decision letters regarding Title I standards and assessment issues.

Chapter Four

● Print and Nonprint Resources

In this chapter, the reader has the benefit of viewing a portion of the extensive resources available in print and nonprint forms and on the World Wide Web. This is meant as an introductory guide, as the amount and types of literature and media available are too numerous to catalog. In short, curriculum trends are a key to every aspect of education. The number of texts on curriculum trends and issues is in the millions. Consequently, those summarized here were selected for their contribution to the field, their use on a regular basis, and their grounding in historical movements listed in the chronology chapter. The writers of these texts are some of the most active in the field. The works are listed in alphabetical order.

MAJOR TEXTS ABOUT CURRICULUM TRENDS

Apple, Michael W. (1996). *Cultural Politics and Education.* New York: Teachers College Press.

Educators in the field of curriculum will recognize the name and writings of Michael Apple. This text is one of the most renowned. It emerged and evolved from the "John Dewey Society Invited Address by Michael Apple." Apple shows us how education is linked to the big picture as part of larger social processes and economics. Apple has written numerous books and articles on these themes. His lifework is an explanation of the politics and economics of education. The text is a collection of five major essays. The themes of these essays include:

1. Education and identity
2. The politics of official knowledge
3. Education and the conservative movement
4. Poverty and education
5. Taking the fun out of educational reform

Two of the essays are coauthored. Yet all share in the major realities of the efforts of conservative movements, big business, and economic connections to the curriculum. Apple argues strongly and persuasively about:

1. How the unresponsive nature of schools caused many to shift to the right to look for solutions
2. How the right has failed to enact any meaningful curriculum reform
3. How, more than ever, we must defend the social gains earned in schools from the 1960s to the present

Aronowitz, Stanley, and Henry A. Giroux. (1991). *Postmodern Education*. Minneapolis: University of Minnesota Press.

This text is a summary of the political issues involved in school reform, from a postmodern perspective. The authors critique institutionalized racism, gender issues, funding, and a variety of social issues. Basically, they expose how, since the Reagan era, schooling and school reform have been linked to the agenda of big business. The politics of literacy is basically the politics of big business. A key and profound chapter of the text is on teachers as pubic intellectuals. The authors clearly explain how curriculum issues are sites of struggle—for example, the struggle for control of the curriculum; the struggle involved in organizing knowledge; the struggle over values in the school; and the struggle for language and domination, or at least the language of domination. Finally, this text describes how "voice"—how students and teachers produce meaning—is a problem. It is another site of struggle. If one purpose of education is to help students reclaim and find their voice, teachers as public intellectuals need to engage students in meaningful dialogue and critique. Through the approach presented in this work, a genuine reform can be realized. The authors end the text with a chapter on working-class displacements. Thus, they focus throughout the text on postmodern issues of race, class, and gender in schools and society.

Ayers, William. (1993). *To Teach: The Journey of a Teacher.* New York: Teachers College Press.

Ayers is a reflective teacher. In this text, he authentically reflects on what it means to teach. His own journey is chronicled, and the result is a thoughtful, deep, and passionate narrative on being a student, a parent, and a teacher. This is a sensitive book about what really happens in classrooms. In addition, it is a model for any prospective teacher. Ayers covers what it means to be a teacher in all its complexities, nuances, difficulties, and triumphs. He uses his imagination and creativity, things that are nearly erased in technocratic systems of teacher training. Anyone who wishes to understand teaching should read this book.

Eisner, Elliot W. (1994). *The Educational Imagination: On the Design and Evaluation of School Programs.* 3rd ed. New York: Macmillan.

Eisner's text is a critique of those aspects of the traditionalist paradigm that erase imagination, creativity, the arts, and life history. He furthermore does a fine job of providing a concise history of the field of curriculum studies. In addition, he introduces the critical notion of "connoisseurship" as a viable way to understand curriculum. Like a wine connoisseur who samples and experiences wine, in a developmental path to judgment of excellence educators may become connoisseurs. In the case of education, experience, time spent in the classroom, and solving problems enables one to distinguish what is significant. If educators use the connoisseurship model, reform may ensue based on realistic, actual situations in the classroom. Eisner then distinguishes criticism as the art of disclosure. Connoisseurship is a private act whereas criticism, like art criticism, for example, is public. Educational criticism should be based on connoisseurship. Still further, Eisner argues for the place of art and aesthetics in curriculum as key ingredients to the educational imagination.

Fishman, Stephen M., and Lucille McCarthy. (1998). *John Dewey and the Challenge of Classroom Practice.* New York: Teachers College Press.

This book is a gem. It is the story of a teacher who is willing to examine his own practice in the light of John Dewey's pedagogy. Through the clear and vivid examples of daily classroom life, we come to appreciate Dewey's work. Both writers of the text model the collaboration Dewey writes about so precisely. Dewey's concepts of integration of the curriculum, interest and effort, continuity of the curriculum, and restoring a sense of community are put into practice. The final chapter on Dewey's relevance to contemporary education is the strongest and most compelling argument for a sense of community. The sense of community in a school is Dewey's balance to guard against the fakery of independence. Dewey and these authors warn about excessive emphasis on individual independence, since every individual is part of some community. They warn against falling into dualisms such as:

Competition versus cooperation

Independence versus dependence
Mobility versus community

In fact, the authors argue that Dewey would say the notion of individuality so popular today has outlived its time. That was fine for frontier America. In today's world, it is inappropriate given the high technology and interdependence of nations, businesses, and people. More than ever, building a sense of community in the school would serve as the most useful curriculum reform.

Freire, Paulo. (1994). *Pedagogy of Hope: Reliving* Pedagogy of the Oppressed. New York: Continuum.

Of the many texts written by the Brazilian educator Paulo Freire, this one is most provocative. As an educator, Freire explains how hope is required in order to advance the purposes of education and curriculum. Hope is a need that must be anchored in practice—an active agency, if you will. Freire argues that the progressive educator must unveil opportunities for hope, no matter what the obstacles. He adds that hopelessness and despair are the consequence of inaction. Freire offers examples of cynicism usually put forth by politicians as scare tactics. Hope in action counteracts these scare tactics, among other things. The most intriguing thread running through the text is a call for reawakening imagination, creativity, and spirituality, in the sense of going deeply into the tumult of the soul. His deep love and appreciation of history and how we all feel the imprints of our own history is another key theme. We are soaked in our history and thus must realize its meaning in order to advance our educational ends. Freire calls for a critical literacy for the purpose of arriving at freedom from oppression of any sort. He also calls for serious intellectual discipline, especially when speaking of educational matters.

This text also revisits his first book, *The Pedagogy of the Oppressed,* a landmark work. In the original text, Freire decried the banking system of education, which is basically used in most schools. Students come in and make a deposit by reciting pat answers, or they make a withdrawal by getting something to memorize. The teacher is like a banker rather than a critical, reflective practitioner. In addition, Freire argues that one who is oppressed cannot become free if the oppressed person uses the models of the oppressor. This single idea has changed many educators' thinking on the purposes of education. This text is a classic, and *The Pedagogy of Hope* is a reshaping of that classic work.

Giroux, Henry A. (1997). *Pedagogy and the Politics of Hope.* Boulder, CO: Westview Press.

Henry Giroux has written numerous books and is a key figure in curriculum writing. This text continues his lifelong theme of teachers as public intellectuals who are able to identify the ongoing struggle in schools. This struggle, however, is paired with movement toward emancipation, rather than defeat and domination. Giroux focuses on human agency. He values the experiences of teachers, administrators, and students as part of the process of schooling. This is in contrast to the technocratic approaches that are distilled down to rules and bureaucratic edicts that make little sense in schools filled with class reproduction, gender bias, violence, and racism. Giroux argues that human agency and hope are the vehicles to address the social problems in the curriculum. Perhaps the strongest chapter in the text is the discussion of multiculturalism as a key issue in curriculum. Giroux views multiculturalism as connected to the construction of historical memory, the purpose of schooling, and the meaning of democracy. Again, his theme emphasizes that we need a language of hope and possibility. He also sees multiculturalism as a broader attempt to engage the world of public and global politics.

Jackson, Philip W. (1998). *John Dewey and the Lessons of Art.* New Haven, CT: Yale University Press.

Philip Jackson, a well-known expert in curriculum studies and a professor of curriculum, has written a text where he describes John Dewey's thinking about the arts and their place in education. Jackson, who also was president of the John Dewey Society, has spent a lifetime in studying Dewey and the applications of Dewey's work to the classroom. In this text, Jackson deals with what the arts teach us about how to live our lives. He discusses Dewey's aesthetic theory as well as the power of the arts to transform our lives. In particular, Jackson argues that Dewey's view of the arts would improve learning experiences in all classrooms. John Dewey wrote his text *Art as Experience* in 1934, when he was seventy-five years of age. Yet the text is often regarded as the most valuable text on aesthetics. Jackson does a superb job of interpreting Dewey's critical text for educators. He aims his text at teachers, too. Again, by taking the best ideas of John Dewey on experience, art, and art-centered experiences, Jackson really forces the reader to think about how critical the arts are in the educative process. In addition, this text highlights Dewey's contribution in terms of his attempt to bring the arts into the curriculum.

Pinar, William, ed. (1975). *Curriculum Theorizing:*
The Reconceptualists. Berkeley, CA: McCutcheon.

Pinar's text is composed of twenty-six essays describing and explaining
the trends toward reconceptualizing curriculum. In a sense, this text is
the next step in a natural evolution away from the traditionalist approaches. Key writers in the field of curriculum such as the historian
Herbert Kliebard and social critics such as Michael Apple, Maxine
Greene, and Pinar himself clearly explain the major shifts away from the
traditional approaches and how this outcome was inevitable. The efficiency model is laid to rest as the writers cover a variety of topics in
chapters such as:

> Persistent Curriculum Issues
> Hidden Curriculum and Conflict
> Curriculum Criticism
> Curriculum and Consciousness

To say this text is a classic in the field would be an understate-
ment. Its importance rests on the opening up of our vision of what curriculum trends might be concerned with over future decades. Further,
all writers in this text relate the topic to the major changes in society following World War II. Some of these trends include the failure of the factory model of education and the authentic interest in personal growth
and development.

Sadker, David, and Myra Sadker. (1994). *Failing at Fairness: How Our*
Schools Cheat Girls. New York: Touchstone.

The subtitle of this text says it all. The Sadkers report on over twenty-
five years of study of inequity in schools. Their lifework was the research that led to this text. All parents, teachers, and educators should
read this volume. It documents the behaviors going on in schools that
cheat our daughters. For example, the authors systematically show how
feedback is given by teachers to males rather than females. Most fright-
ening are the data that show how standardized texts historically and
deliberately have been designed to exclude girls. There is a noticeable
gender gap in standardized tests even in the highest-achieving female
cases. Likewise, a huge gap exists in achievement in science and math.
Still further, the Sadkers have videotaped classroom activities that
show teachers calling on boys even when girls have their hands up for
recognition first. This text is a classic on the topic and directly relates to
all school curricula.

Schubert, William H. (1986). *Curriculum: Perspective, Paradigm, and Possibility.* New York: Macmillan.

Without a doubt, Schubert's text is a classic in the field of curriculum. In fact, many (including myself) believe it to be the quintessential text on curriculum. Schubert makes us understand the historical precedents for three major trends in curriculum. He uses all three to address critical issues and ideas in curriculum. The three paradigms he identifies are: (1) the intellectual traditionalist, (2) the social behaviorist, and (3) the experientialist. These three approaches are framed as commentaries at the end of each chapter to help readers understand the complexity of curriculum questions and to acknowledge that there is no one way to view curriculum problems. Throughout the text, Schubert embeds the two basic questions in the field: (1) What do we teach? and (2) How do we teach it? This applies for all levels, from prekindergarten to adults. By organizing this nearly five-hundred-page text into paradigm, perspective, and possibility, Schubert makes us understand various viewpoints, under the three lenses of tradition, behaviorism, and experience. Thus, the reader is immediately involved in an awareness and respect for the work of teachers, administrators, and educators in general. This text should be required for anyone who wants to understand the past century of schooling in America.

Tanner, Laurel N. (1997). *Dewey's Laboratory School: Lessons for Today.* New York: Teachers College Press.

Laurel Tanner has done something wonderful in this text. She goes back to the beginnings of John Dewey's Laboratory School at the University of Chicago (1896–1904) and finds that many of his issues are the very ones we speak of today. She examines the policies, procedures, and practice of Dewey's Lab School from their origins to the present day. As one reads this text, it is clear that Dewey was at least a century ahead of his time. The book traces major concepts then that are curriculum issues today. Specifically:

1. The school as a social and learning community
2. School-community relationships
3. The artificial distinctions between teachers and supervisors
4. Empowerment of teachers

In fact, each chapter covers problems and issues that are very relevant today. The book is a history lesson embedded in the still standing Lab School. Dewey in the late 1890s saw this school as a potential model for others nationwide. It is clear, as Tanner argues, that educational reform efforts in the present day could be stronger and more successful if we paid more attention to the work of John Dewey.

SELECTED ARTICLES REGARDING CURRICULUM TRENDS

There are literally over a million articles that address issues, problems, practices, trends, and changes regarding curriculum in schools. In this section, you will find some recent articles from well-regarded journals in the field. These articles capture the breadth, depth, and complexity of all the issues that fall under the two age-old questions: "What do we teach" and "How do we teach it?"

Allinder, R. M. (1996). "When Some Is Not Better than None: Effects of Differential Implementation of Curriculum-Based Measurement." *Exceptional Children* 62, no. 6: 525–535.

This piece discusses the effects of curriculum-based measurement (CBM) on math computation achievement of students with mild disabilities. The results of this study suggest that partial implementation of CBM may not be enough to yield greater academic progress in these students. The author also stresses the importance of teacher planning time and school organization as major factors in considering implementing new instructional or new assessment techniques. What is important here is that with a national preoccupation with math and memorization, the author looks at political and social factors as related to learning.

Beane, J. A. (1995). "Curriculum Integration and the Disciples of Knowledge." *Phi Delta Kappan* 76, no. 8: 616–622.

Curriculum integration is not simply an organizational device requiring cosmetic changes or realignments in lesson plans across various subject matters. Rather, it is a way of thinking about what schools are for, about the sources of curriculum, and about the uses of knowledge. The author is an advocate for curriculum integration and addresses the role the disciples of knowledge play in curriculum integration. The integration of curriculum is one of the trends that began with the reconceptualists and that continues to the present time with the postmodernists. This trend aims at a holistic approach to curriculum.

Beilke, P. F. (2000). "Implementing Multicultural and Global Studies: Selected Resources about Materials and Their Uses by Teacher Educators, In-Service Providers, and K–12 Educators." *The Teacher Educator* 36, no. 1: 70–84.

The numbers of multicultural materials, bibliographies, and indexes have increased in recent years. Original materials developed by persons from cultural groups whose heritage and imaginative works have traditionally been underrepresented are still underrepresented. This article contains an annotated bibliography representative of the variety of materials that may be useful for those who plan, develop, and implement multicultural and global studies; infuse them throughout curricula; and strive to develop personnel with the attitudes and skills to collaborate and empathize with youth.

Blackwell, Peggy J., Mary Futrell, and David C. Imig. (2003). "Burnt Water Paradoxes of Schools of Education." *Phi Delta Kappan* 6 (January): 356–361.

Basically, the authors argue that the way teacher education is conducted in schools and colleges of education today presents us with a paradox. On the one hand, we all clamor for high quality and professionalism. On the other hand, teachers work in a system that does not reward or recognize them for their efforts, compared to other professions. They note that the history of teacher education has totally been a part of the efficiency movement since the turn of the twentieth century. In order to survive, teacher education centers often started new programs without the personnel or resources needed to deliver quality teacher training. This contributed to the paradox of professionalism. How can teachers be considered professionals when licensing standards are waived by many states to offer alternative teacher certification? The programs are short and empty and have a watered-down knowledge base—all this to meet the so-called teacher shortage. The authors mention as well the historical root of behaviorism that fashioned teacher education programs for efficiency, which appealed to the business community. Problems will only persist if people expect high-quality programs on the cheap or have mind-sets focused on quantity and efficiency, all of which work against efforts for quality. The authors point out that quick fixes don't make sense. Policymakers want quick fixes that have never worked.

Goodlad, John I. (2002). "Kudzu, Rabbits and School Reform." *Phi Delta Kappan* 5 (September): 16–23.

In this article, Goodlad uses two examples to illustrate the folly of narrow approaches to school reform. The first example is the kudzu vine introduced in the United States in 1876 to give shade to the porches of southern mansions. Unfortunately, no one bothered to find out that the *uber* fast-growing vine also kills forests by covering trees and vines. Today, the kudzu vine covers millions of acres of forest in the South. The cost is around $50 million per year in lost timber. The initial purpose of introducing the vine seems to be forgotten. Goodlad uses a second, similar example of twenty-four rabbits introduced in Australia in 1859 to provide prey for hunters. After seven years, the rabbits had multiplied so rapidly that even shooting over 14,000 of them did not make a dent in the rabbit population. A century later, the rabbit calicivirus was introduced to kill the rabbit population. Unfortunately, this created a deadly disease that affects crops, people, and animals. The Australian government estimates that the cost is hundreds of millions of dollars per year in lost crops and land erosion and degradation.

Thus, Goodlad compares the kudzu vine and the rabbits with the current "eduvirus." The eduvirus is the school reform disease that politicians and some careless educators introduce when they conveniently name even the most shallow and mindless school reform as being "for the children." Goodlad reminds us that given the limited resources of schools, the low priority for change, and endless bureaucratic impediments to change, we should stop to consider how the narrow view of schooling as testing may harm us in the long run. As with the kudzu vine, we may be paying for a narrow view of school reform for many decades. Goodlad also points out that all data indicate a shortage of teachers ahead, continuing early retirement of current school personnel, and active parents fighting high-stakes testing as factors that will raise serious questions related to curriculum. More seriously, Goodlad exposes the preoccupation with simplistic prescriptions and reveals those prescriptions for what they are. In addition, these prescriptions are missing diagnosis and purpose. Thus, they can only fall flat. Goodlad calls for a reevaluation of the purposes of schooling and the relationship of education and democracy. He ends his article with a call for presidents and governors to cheer on successful educators rather than mislead the public with empty promises and the mythology of school reform.

Grace, M. (1999). "When Students Create Curriculum." *Educational Leadership* 57, no. 3: 49–52.

In an era of prepackaged curricula and state-approved standards, teachers can help their students generate their own curricula. This article discusses a student-generated curriculum project involving university pre-service teachers and an elementary school. The premise behind the project is that learning how to learn is much more important than learning what to learn. The belief is in direct contrast to rigid curriculum programs and other structured reading programs, in which ideas and skills are predetermined and sequenced by outside authorities. Authorities in this program are the students and their teachers. Students use reading, writing, and thinking skills and build content knowledge into a social constructivist set of teaching and learning beliefs that value process over product.

Hargreaves, A., and S. Moore. (2000). "Curriculum Integration and Classroom Relevance: A Study of Teachers' Practice." *Journal of Curriculum and Supervision* 15, no. 2: 89–112.

The integrated or interdisciplinary curriculum is an ambitious yet also contentious aspect of current approaches to educational reform that try to connect classroom learning to the lives and understandings of all students. Advocates of integration argue that it provides opportunities for information exchange among teachers about commonly held interests and talents as well as about the teaching goals, themes, and organizing concepts in their subject areas. Most important, curriculum integration is said to benefit all students by making learning more relevant to students' diverse lives and experiences. This article addresses the relationship between curriculum integration and classroom relevance in the practices of a group of seventh- and eighth-grade teachers who were actively committed to curriculum integration. It examines what sense a group of teachers made of curriculum integration in their own practice. It analyzes what curriculum integration actually looked like in their classes and sets out to build an understanding of what integration might mean, from the bottom up, in a teacher's own classroom context.

Hatch, T. (1999). "Dilemmas of Theory, Design, and Practice in Curriculum and School Improvement: Editor's Introduction." *Peabody Journal of Education* 74, no. 1: 61–72.

The struggles over the curriculum in America are legion. From debates among colleges and employers over the appropriate preparation for life after high school to the daily negotiations between teachers and students over the learning activities in which they engage, curriculum is in question. But what exactly is the question? Often, discussions revolve around what courses should be offered and required. Yet, as so many historians and educators have shown, curriculum cannot be contained in a course catalog. The curriculum is reflected not only in the explicit offerings of an institution but also in the structures, modes of operation, and interactions that shape both formal and informal learning opportunities. This article discusses dilemmas posed in curriculum discussion, including basic questions of the nature of schooling and the values embedded in educational activities.

Johnson, M. J., C. Janisch, and B. Morgan-Fleming. (2001). "Cultural Literacy in Settings: Teachers and Students Adapt the Core Knowledge Curriculum." *Journal of Curriculum and Supervision* 16, no. 3: 259–272.

Core knowledge has been the subject of much commentary in educational literature and the popular press. Although some practitioners who have implemented a core knowledge curriculum assert its benefits, critics have raised serious concerns. This article presents a study that explored the effect of core knowledge content on the curriculum development work of a group of teachers in an elementary school in a high-poverty neighborhood. The report offers a description and analysis of the outcomes of one group of teachers who used the Hirsch curriculum in real classrooms in one school.

Mettetal, G., C. Jordan, and S. Harper. (1997). "Attitudes toward a Multiple Intelligences Curriculum." *Journal of Education Research* 91, no. 2: 115–122.

In this article, attitudes toward the implementation of a multiple intelligences curriculum are described. The study presented investigated the impact of one school's multiple intelligences curriculum on teachers, students, and parents. The research question addressed was: What are the attitudes of teachers, students, and parents toward multiple intelligences in general and toward this curriculum in particular?

Mojkowski, C. (2000). "The Essential Role of Principals in Monitoring Curriculum Implementation." *NASSP (National Association of Secondary School Principals) Bulletin* 76–8384, no. 613: 76–83.

This article postulates that if the curriculum is to serve as a dynamic tool for creating high-quality opportunities for student learning, it will require a dynamic, real-time process for learning about its implementation. Shifting the focus to curriculum implementation monitoring will help districts and schools achieve that goal and give a special focus to the principal's instructional leadership responsibilities. Research reveals that when the curriculum development is completed and the committee disbanded, the task of watching curriculum implementation falls to principals in their role as instructional leaders. However, few principals collect information about implementation. The author states that research is clear that implementation does not inevitably follow from even exemplary curriculum development. Yet districts spend a disproportionate percentage of their resources on developing the curriculum, and they allocate few resources to ensuring its successful implementation.

Muller, J. (1998). "The Well-Tempered Learner: Self-Regulation Pedagogical Models and Teacher Education Policy." *Comparative Education* 34, no. 2: 177–194.

The author considers curriculum reforms and outcomes-based education within South Africa and New Zealand. There is an analysis of self-regulation as a widely prescribed social and pedagogic goal, as well as a civic ideal. The writer also reflects on the model of the self-regulating learner and suggests that the learner-centered approach empowers students to take control of their learning while they take control of their future. The implications for curriculum are closely related, then, to the ends John Dewey advocated for active engagement by the learner in the curriculum. It is interesting that New Zealand and South Africa are implementing and discussing reforms that the United States has yet to install.

Noddings, N. (2001). "The Care Tradition: Beyond 'Add Men and Stir.'" *Theory into Practice* 40, no. 1: 29–34.

For the past few decades, educators have been concerned with inclusion in a variety of forms. This article concentrates on problems of curricular inclusion and, in particular, on ways of including the interests and contributions of women in the social studies curriculum. First, Noddings comments on the "add women and stir" approach to inclusion that most view as inadequate. The discussion is then followed by a look at the tradition of care that has long been identified with female life. Finally, the author explores ways in which this tradition may be preserved and extended through a universal caregiver model.

Piirto, J. (1999). "Implications of Postmodern Curriculum Theory for the Education of the Talented." *Journal for the Education of the Gifted* 22, no. 4: 324–353.

This article views the field of education of the gifted and talented through a postmodernist lens. Concepts such as critical thinking, higher-order thinking, and creative-thinking processes were taught in curriculum models adapted for the gifted and talented long before they became part of the regular curriculum. The postmodern theorists go beyond the development and elaboration of curriculum models. They ask educators to engage in understanding what they are doing, why they are doing it, and whether they should continue to do it. This article indicates some areas for thought that may be pertinent to the field of the education of the gifted and talented.

Reid, W. A. (1998). "'Reconceptualist' and 'Dominant' Perspectives in Curriculum Theory: What Do They Have to Say to Each Other?" *Journal of Curriculum and Supervision* 13, no. 3: 287–296.

The field of curriculum is complex, ramified, multifaceted, and full of idiosyncrasy. This article is not about the field of curriculum as a whole. It is about two major perspectives that—in books, papers, and conferences—have tended to dominate the field over the last twenty years: the reconceptualist perspective and the dominant perspective. The author raises the questions: Do these perspectives actually have something to say to each other? Or are they pursuing incompatible agendas?

Rogers, Bethany. (1999). "Conflicting Approaches to Curriculum: Recognizing How Fundamental Beliefs Can Sustain or Sabotage School Reform." *Peabody Journal of Education* 74, no. 1: 29–67.

The author observes how curriculum reform can be derailed by conflicts among reformers, based on their various beliefs about education. She examines several critical variables for differing perspectives regarding classroom authority, and she offers recommendations for dealing with the differences in order to exact effective school reform.

Smith, Matthew W. (1999). "Teaching the 'Third World': Unsettling Discourses of Difference in the School Curriculum." *Oxford Review of Education* 25, no. 4: 485–499.

This is an examination of how the concepts of "self" and "other" are being taught in schools. Suggestions about perceptions of difference intercepting with the patronizing notion of the Third World are called to the forefront in this article. The author is writing as a postmodernist and calling into question the very notion of the labeling of the Third World altogether. As a trend, global issues will definitely be part of any future discussion on curriculum. In fact, an entire book could be written on this topic, and some author should tackle this critical topic. Recommendations are made regarding further curriculum research and changes in the area of understanding and teaching about the people and nations labeled as the Third World. As the technology of the day appears to be moving us closer to each other, we should definitely discuss issues pertinent to power and be clear about definitions, intentions, and indeed the use of language.

Thornton, S. J. (2001). "Educating the Educators: Rethinking Subject Matter and Methods." *Theory into Practice* 40, no. 1: 72–80.

The ideals laid out for social studies education in this article will be realized only, of course, if teachers embrace them. Teachers are curricular-instructional gatekeepers. But how should teachers be educated to tend to the curricular-instructional gate? This article discusses questions such as: What specifically do social studies teachers need to know and be able to do? What in particular do they need to study in the subject matters of the social sciences? What should they learn about its effective direction to desired results, that is, method?

The subject matter knowledge of teachers has become a central concern in both education research and in teacher licensing policies in recent years. Fueling this popular and scholarly concern is the belief that too many teachers are inadequately versed in the subject matters they teach. How to remedy this problem raises a host of questions that are described and explained in this article.

Van Scoy, I. (1995). "Trading the Three R's for the Four E's: Transforming Curriculum." *Childhood Education* 72 (Fall): 19–23.

This writer suggests that "reading, 'riting, and 'rithmetic" is an antiquated core curriculum that should be replaced by a new curriculum model of "experience, extension, expression, and evaluation," consistent with normal child development. The author proposes that teachers may use the four Es model selectively for appropriate curriculum activities or to integrate an entire program. Overall, this would make a stronger curriculum and allow students to take part in and engage in that curriculum. Obviously, school is more than the learning of subject matter, and the child's development is on equal footing at least with all that occurs in school.

Windschitl, Mark. (1999). "The Challenges of Sustaining a Constructivist Classroom Culture." *Phi Delta Kappan* 80, no. 10: 751–755.

Recommendations for a new vision of learning, aimed at helping educators create a culture of constructivism in the classroom with new roles for both teachers and students, lie at the heart of this piece. The author argues for keeping a constructivist mind-set and tries to remind teachers of the importance of constructivism for today's learners.

Wraga, W. G. (1998). "Interesting, If True: Historical Perspectives on the 'Reconceptualization' of Curriculum Studies." *Journal of Curriculum and Supervision* 14, no. 1: 5–28.

Since the early 1980s, a variety of new theories have appeared in the curriculum literature. A focus on understanding curriculum from the vantage points of disciplines such as political science, philosophy, psychology, and theology has often eclipsed practical matters of curriculum development in scholarly and even professional journals. This shift in emphasis from curriculum development to curriculum understanding is attributed to a "reconceptualization" of the curriculum field that began in the 1970s. Since that time, a particular historical account of reconceptualization has prevailed. This article proposes that new understandings of the reconceptualization of the curriculum field during the 1970s can be attained by examining it from alternative historical perspectives.

JOURNALS IN THE FIELD

Of the great many journals in this field, I will list only the eight that are most often referred to in the literature, for the reader's convenience and peace of mind.

American Educational Research Association (AERA) Journals

> *Educational Researcher (ER)*
> *American Educational Research Journal (AERJ)*
> *Educational Evaluation and Policy Analysis (EEPA)*
> *Journal of Educational and Behavioral Statistics (JEBS)*
> *Review of Educational Research (RER)*
> *Review of Research in Education (RRE)*

American Educational Research Association
1230 17th Street, NW
Washington, DC 20036
202-223-9485

Fax: 202-775-1824
http://www.aera.net/pubs/aerj
E-mail: webmaster@aera.net

Curriculum Inquiry (Ontario Institute for Studies in Education [OISE]—
University of Toronto)
Ontario Institute for Studies in Education
252 Bloor Street West
Toronto, Ontario
M5S 1V6
416-923-6641, ext. 2619
http://fcis.oise.utoronto.ca/~ci/
Blackwell Publishing
350 Main Street
Malden, MA 02148
1-800-835-6770
http://www.blackwellpublishing.com

Educational Leadership
Association for Supervision and Curriculum Development
ASCD Online Store
1703 North Beauregard Street
Alexandria, VA 22311-1714
1-800-933-2723
Fax: 703-575-5400
http://www.ascd.org/frameedlead.html

Elementary School Journal
The University of Chicago Press
Journals Division
PO Box 37005
Chicago, IL 60637
773-753-3347 or 877-705-1878
Fax: 773-753-0811 or 877-705-1879
http://www.journals.uchicago.edu/ESJ/home.html
E-mail: subscriptions@press.uchicago.edu

Harvard Educational Review
Harvard Graduate School of Education
Harvard University
8 Story Street

5th Floor
Cambridge, MA 02138
617-495-3432
Fax: 617-496-3584
http://gseweb.harvard.edu/%7Ehepg/her.html
E-mail: hepg@harvard.edu

Journal of Curriculum Studies
University of Illinois
341 Armory Building
505 East Armory Avenue
Champaign, IL 61820
Taylor & Francis Group
325 Chestnut Street
Suite 800
Philadelphia, PA 19106
800-354-1420
Fax: 215-625-8914
http://www.taylorandfrancis.com

Phi Delta Kappan
PDK
PO Box 789
Bloomington, IN 47402
800-766-1156
Fax: 812-339-0018
E-mail: kappan@ kiva.net

Teachers College Record
Teachers College
Box 103
Columbia University
525 West 120th Street
New York, NY 10027
Fax: 212-678-3790
http://www.tcrecord.org
Blackwell Publishing
350 Main Street
Malden, MA 02148
1-800-835-6770
http://www.blackwellpublishing.com

VIDEOTAPES RELATED TO CURRICULUM TRENDS

ASCD 1998 Assessment Conference on Teaching and Learning Set

Type: Audiocassette
Length: Not available
Cost: ASCD member price: $64.00
Nonmember price: $80.00
Date: 1998
Source: Association for Supervision and Curriculum
Development (ASCD)
1703 North Beauregard Street
Alexandria, VA 22311-1714
800-933-ASCD or 703-578-9600
Fax: 703-575-5400
http://www.ascd.org

This is a complete set of audiotaped live recordings from the 1998 Assessment Conference on Teaching and Learning.

Assessment and Grading: What's the Relationship

Type: VHS format
Length: Not available
Cost: ASCD member price: $79.95
Nonmember price: $95.95
Date: 1996
Source: Association for Supervision and Curriculum
Development (ASCD)
1703 North Beauregard Street
Alexandria, VA 22311-1714
800-933-ASCD or 703-578-9600
Fax: 703-575-5400
http://www.ascd.org

This tape offers a panel discussion exploring how assessment reforms will change current approaches to grading and reporting of student achievement. It is part of the ASCD Conference on Teaching & Learning Assessment.

Assessment in Elementary Science Video Series 3 Tapes with Facilitator's Guide

Type: VHS format

Length: Three 35- to 20-minute videotapes
Cost: ASCD member price: $680.00
Nonmember price: $780.00
Date: 1997
Source: Association for Supervision and Curriculum
Development (ASCD)
1703 North Beauregard Street
Alexandria, VA 22311-1714
800-933-ASCD or 703-578-9600
Fax: 703-575-5400
http://www.ascd.org

This ASCD video series takes you to classrooms where you see teachers using performance-based assessments to guide classroom practice, providing more opportunities for learning, and evaluating student and school performance. Video scenes from elementary classrooms show hands-on approaches to teaching science. Teachers in this series explain how they use authentic assessments to improve instruction.

Tape 1: Guiding Student Learning, 35 minutes. Tape 1 features classrooms where the teachers use journals, discussions, experiments, and hands-on activities to help students understand science. You will see how these activities improve the science learning experience for students and provide teachers opportunities to embed assessment in instruction by asking open-ended questions, listening to students, and observing their behavior.

Tape 2: Developing and Using Rubrics, 35 minutes. Tape 2 explains ways to evaluate student achievement objectives based on hands-on performance. You will see how teachers define the criteria for evaluating student performance by developing and using rubrics, understand how benchmarks from state and national standards can help define learning objectives, and explore practical ways to collect and record observations of student performance.

Tape 3: Evaluating Programs, 20 minutes. Tape 3 helps you look at your entire science education program and understand how state and science standards can guide reform efforts. You will see how feedback from large-scale assessment can provide information about problem areas in the curriculum and help teachers implement hands-on learning. This program explores three successful approaches to large-scale, performance-based assessment, and it offers examples of how state and national content standards provide guidelines for educators who want to improve their approach to science education.

Assessment in Math & Science—What's the Point?

Type: VHS format
Length: 22 minutes
Cost: $15.00
Date: 1998
Source: http://www.learner.org
Annenburg/CPB Fall 2000 Video Catalog

Individual programs include the following:

1. Will This Be on Test? Knowing vs. Understanding
2. What'd I'd Get? Scoring Tools
3. Is This Going to Count? Embedded Assessment
4. Didn't Know This Was an English Class! Connections across the Discipline
5. You WILL Be Tested on This: Standardized Testing
6. That Would Never Work Here! Seeing Assessment Reform in Action I
7. That Would Never Work Here Either! Seeing Assessment Reform in Action II
8. When I Was in School . . . Implementing Assessment Reform

Assessment Interactive Training Multimedia Package

Type: VHS Format
Length: Four 60-minute videotapes
Cost: $799 for all four
Date: 1997
Source: Phi Delta Kappa International
408 North Union Street
PO Box 789
Bloomington, IN 47402-0789
800-766-1156
Fax: 812-399-0018
http://www.pdkintl.org
E-mail: WEBMASTER@pdkintl.org

This package, created by Richard J. Stiggins of the Assessment Training Institute, is designed to introduce educators to sound classroom assessment. The four 60-minute videos cover all the bases on practical exercises for authentic performance assessment. The videos are:

1. Creating Sound Classroom Assessments

2. Assessing Reasoning in Classrooms
3. Student Involved Classrooms
4. Common Sense Paper and Pencil Assessments

Becoming a Multiple Intelligences School—Books in Action Video Series

Type: VHS format
Length: 15 minutes
Cost: ASCD member price: $79.95
           Nonmember price: $95.00
Date: 2000
Source: Association for Supervision and Curriculum
           Development (ASCD)
           1703 North Beauregard Street
           Alexandria, VA 22311-1714
           800-933-ASCD or 703-578-9600
           Fax: 703-575-5400
           http://www.ascd.org

Visit an innovative school where multiple intelligences theory guides curriculum, instruction, assessment, the parent-teacher relationship, and teacher collaboration.

Becoming a Multiple Intelligences School Package
(Ten Books and One Video from the Books in Action Series)

Type: VHS format
Length: Not available
Cost: ASCD member price: $229.00
           Nonmember price: $279.00
Date: 2000
Source: Association for Supervision and Curriculum
           Development (ASCD)
           1703 North Beauregard Street
           Alexandria, VA 22311-1714
           800-933-ASCD or 703-578-9600
           Fax: 703-575-5400
           http://www.ascd.org

This package includes ten copies of the book *Becoming a Multiple Intelligences School* by Thomas R. Hoerr and the related *Books-in-Action* video.

Challenging the Gifted in the Regular Classroom

Type: VHS format
Length: 50 minutes
Cost: ASCD member price: $378.00
Nonmember price: $448.00
Date: 1994
Source: Association for Supervision and Curriculum
Development (ASCD)
1703 North Beauregard Street
Alexandria, VA 22311-1714
800-933-ASCD or 703-578-9600
Fax: 703-575-5400
http://www.ascd.org

Rather than always excluding or segregating academically gifted students, learn how to meet their needs in the regular classroom with this videotape. Scenes from a variety of schools explain and demonstrate seven instructional techniques, including questioning tiered assignments, and learning and interest centers. See how you can meet the needs of gifted students through schoolwide strategies and with specialists, parents, and mentors from the business community. The package also includes a 108-page facilitator's guide.

Constructivism Series 2 Videos with Facilitator's Guide and Book

Type: VHS format
Length: Two 30- to 40-minute videotapes
Cost: ASCD member price: $396.00
Nonmember price: $466.00
Date: 1995
Source: Association for Supervision and Curriculum
Development (ASCD)
1703 North Beauregard Street
Alexandria, VA 22311-1714
800-933-ASCD or 703-578-9600
Fax: 703-575-5400
http://www.ascd.org

Two videotapes and a facilitator's guide explain the guiding principles of constructivism, showing elementary, middle, and secondary school classrooms where teachers use a constructivist approach to science, mathematics, English, fine arts, and social studies.

Tape 1: Putting the Learner First. Jacqueline Grennon Brooks presents five basic principles of constructivism; classroom teachers show how this approach improves learning and achievement.

Tape 2: Case Studies in Constructivist Teaching. Viewers explore four profiles of educational settings where constructivism helps shape instruction and assessment strategies that foster lifelong learning.

The 126-page facilitator's guide includes outlines for 1-hour, 2-hour, 6-hour, and 2-day workshops, along with handouts, overheads, and background readings.

Cooperative Learning (five-tape set)

Type:	VHS format
Length:	Not available
Cost:	ASCD member price: $980.00
	Nonmember price: $1,180.00
Date:	1995
Source:	Association for Supervision and Curriculum Development (ASCD)
	1703 North Beauregard Street
	Alexandria, VA 22311-1714
	800-933-ASCD or 703-578-9600
	Fax: 703-575-5400
	http://www.ascd.org

This training series explains and demonstrates what cooperative learning is and how to implement it in the classroom. The series includes examples from the elementary, middle, and high school levels.

Tape 1: Learning to Work Together
Tape 2: Planning and Implementing Cooperative Lessons
Tape 3: Teaching Social Skills
Tape 4: Three Frameworks
Tape 5: A Sample Lesson

Effective Schools for Children at Risk

Type:	VHS format
Length:	25 minutes
Cost:	ASCD member price: $228.00
	Nonmember price: $278.00
Date:	1991
Source:	Association for Supervision and Curriculum Development (ASCD)

1703 North Beauregard Street
Alexandria, VA 22311-1714
800-933-ASCD or 703-578-9600
Fax: 703-575-5400
http://www.ascd.org

This program shows how the characteristics of effective schools can be used as guidelines to improve learning. It includes a 25-minute video-tape, a leader's guide, and the ASCD book *Readings from Educational Leadership: Effective Schools and School Improvement.*

Part 1 explains how Ronald Edmonds observed schools that were effective with students from disadvantaged backgrounds and discovered characteristics that all effective schools shared.

Part 2 shows scenes from inner-city elementary schools in Kansas City, Missouri, and Baltimore, Maryland, to illustrate how educators work with the characteristics of effective schools every day.

Examining Student Work

Type: VHS format
Length: 25- to 30-minutes
Cost: ASCD member price: $420.00 (entire series) or $180.00 per tape
    Nonmember price: $540.00 (entire series) or $220.00 per tape
Date: 2002
Source: Association for Supervision and Curriculum Development (ASCD)
    1703 North Beauregard Street
    Alexandria, VA 22311-1714
    800-933-ASCD or 703-578-9600
    Fax: 703-575-5400
    http://www.ascd.org

This video series allows you to go behind the scenes of innovative schools to see how educators are using actual student work as data information to build a rich picture of student learning, improve classroom instruction, and provide teachers with opportunities for ongoing, job-embedded professional development. Scenes from actual classrooms and teacher work sessions reveal how to look at student work through a collaborative process. Interviews with educators explain how critical review of student assignments benefits classrooms and schools. Three tapes in the series provide in-depth demonstrations of three proven approaches.

An accompanying facilitator's guide helps you create a powerful workshop that gets teachers and other audiences started in the process.

Use Tape 1 in the series, *Improving Student Learning,* to give audiences an overview of why and how analyzing student work can improve teaching and learning. Then use Tapes 2, 3, and 4 to give audiences an in-depth understanding of three proven approaches to examining student work through collaborative teams. Scenes and interviews from actual schools demonstrate the steps in each process and how to follow up after student work is submitted.

Tape 1: Improving Student Learning
Tape 2: The Tuning Protocol
Tape 3: Standards in Practice
Tape 4: Collaborative Analysis of Student Learning

How to Effectively Involve Parents in the Classroom

Type: VHS format
Length: 15 minutes
Cost: ASCD member price: $79.00
Nonmember price: $95.00
Date: 2002
Source: Association for Supervision and Curriculum
Development (ASCD)
1703 North Beauregard Street
Alexandria, VA 22311-1714
800-933-ASCD or 703-578-9600
Fax: 703-575-5400
http://www.ascd.org

This video offers practical and proven strategies for effectively using parent volunteers in elementary classrooms. Topics include:

Enlisting parent volunteers for different types of jobs
Training parent volunteers and organizing work schedules
Organizing materials so volunteers can work independently
Putting parents to work preparing materials, working with
students, editing newsletters, and organizing events
Monitoring parent volunteers and matching them to tasks that
meet their skills

Performance Assessment in the Classroom:
A Video Journal of Education

Type: VHS format

> *Length:* Includes two videotapes: Program 1 is 29 minutes,
> Program 2 is 31 minutes
> *Cost:* $315.00 for both
> *Date:* 1993
> *Source:* Teach Stream, Inc.
> 8686 South 13th Street
> East Sandy, UT 84094
> 800-572-1153
> Fax: 888-566-6888
> http://www.videojournal.com

These tapes by Jay McTighe, director of the Maryland Assessment Consortium, include a performance-based assessment, an instruction video, and a "Creating Tasks" video.

Performance-Based Assessment in Quality Elementary and Middle Schools

> *Type:* VHS format
> *Length:* 30 minutes
> *Cost:* $189.00 for members
> *Date:* 1996
> *Source:* The National Association of Elementary School
> Principals (NAESP)
> 1615 Duke Street
> Alexandria, VA 22314-3483
> 800-386-2377 or 703-684-3345
> http://www.naesp.org
> E-mail: naesp@naesp.org

This video provides information on performance-based assessment, sample rubrics, and teacher testimonials.

Redesigning Assessment

> *Type:* VHS format
> *Length:* 98 minutes
> *Cost:* ASCD member price: $680.00
> Nonmember price: $780.00
> *Date:* 1991
> *Source:* Association for Supervision and Curriculum
> Development (ASCD)
> 1703 North Beauregard Street
> Alexandria, VA 22311-1714

800-933-ASCD or 703-578-9600
Fax: 703-575-5400
http://www.ascd.org

This "classic" three-part series includes an introduction video, a more in-depth treatment of performance assessment and its impact on classrooms and learning, and a video on portfolios. Featured educators include Grant Wiggins, Richard Stiggins, Monte Moses, and Paul LeMahieu.

A Safe Place to Learn: Crisis Response and School Safety Planning

Type: VHS format
Length: 35 minutes
Cost: ASCD member price: $328.00
Nonmember price: $398.00
Date: 1996
Source: Association for Supervision and Curriculum
Development (ASCD)
1703 North Beauregard Street
Alexandria, VA 22311-1714
800-933-ASCD or 703-578-9600
Fax: 703-575-5400
http://www.ascd.org

Feel the impact of a school emergency in this hard-hitting video program. While watching a principal deal with the realities of a school disaster, you'll learn what to do to minimize the physical and emotional trauma that the students, staff, and parents experience in a crisis situation. Scenes from the video and interviews with educators and consultants explain basic measures every school should take to protect children. Complete set includes one 35-minute videotape with a facilitator's guide and the book *How to Prepare for and Respond to a Crisis.*

A Visit to a Differentiated Classroom

Type: VHS format
Length: 60 minutes
Cost: ASCD member price: $145.00
Nonmember price: $170.00
Date: 2001
Source: Association for Supervision and Curriculum
Development (ASCD)
1703 North Beauregard Street

Alexandria, VA 22311-1714
800-933-ASCD or 703-578-9600
Fax: 703-575-5400
http://www.ascd.org

Here's a different style of ASCD video that takes you on an in-depth field trip to a differentiated classroom. Classroom sequences reveal many ways that teachers in every grade level can create and manage an active and engaging learning environment where instructional decisions are based on students' varied readiness levels and interests. While viewing the whole-class morning message meeting, language arts center time, a small-group portfolio session, a social studies lesson, and end-of-day activities, you will discover many tips that make a differentiated classroom work.

What's New in Schools: A Parent's Guide to Performance Assessment

Type: VHS format
Length: 14 minutes
Cost: Member price: $65.00
Nonmember price: $95.00
Date: 1996
Source: Association for Supervision and Curriculum Development (ASCD)
1703 North Beauregard Street
Alexandria, VA 22311-1714
800-933-ASCD or 703-578-9600
Fax: 703-575-5400
http://www.ascd.org

This video includes examples of tasks, projects, and portfolios with comments by students, teachers, and parents. It also comes with a leader's guide.

WEB SITES

About Alternative Assessments
Internet address: http://www.aubach.com/alt_assess.html

Materials presented on this site provide definitions and characteristics of various samples of alternative assessment modes. The site also has an excellent listing of resources through hyperlinks to provide additional information, especially on curriculum issues and trends.

Academy One
Internet address: http://www.nptn.org/cyber.serv/AoneP/

This is billed as "the premier site" for finding Internet projects to integrate into the curriculum.

Alternative Assessment for Adult Learners
Internet address: http://www2.nu.edu/nuri/llconf/conf1995/reif.html

Note: You must be a student to access this site.
This site contains materials aimed at adult learners and illustrates the importance of making goals clear for effective instruction and assessment.

American Association for Higher Education (AAHE)
Internet address: http://www.aahe.org

The Assessment Forum on this site has the "Nine Principles of Good Practice for Assessing Student Learning." The AAHE has selected four campus assessment sites as being particularly useful. They are listed here with AAHE's annotations:

1. *Eastern New Mexico University Assessment Resource Office.*
   This site includes 10 surveys used at Eastern New Mexico
   University, links to the New Mexico Higher Education Assessment Directors Association, and includes a section under the
   use of CYBER CATS: Classroom Assessment Techniques administered and reported via the Internet. Maintained by the
   Assessment Resource Office.
2. *Student Outcomes Assessment at Montana State University.*
   This site includes a list of suggested assessment techniques,
   and assessment information for general education and capstone courses. Maintained by Cel Johnson.
3. *Undergraduate Assessment & Program Review at Southern Illinois University, Edwardsville.* This site offers extensive assessment information, including an essay entitled "Why do assessment," an annotated bibliography of assessment
   resources, and thorough descriptions of Primary Trait Analysis and of Classroom Assessment Techniques that can be
   used via the WWW. Maintained by Doug Eder.
4. *University of Colorado at Boulder, Undergraduate Outcomes Assessment.* This well-known site contains an extraordinarily
   comprehensive list of on-line resources. Browse down the
   page and click on "Higher Education Outcomes Assessment

on the Web." This site was designed by Ephraim Schecter, of Student Affairs Research Services.

Students Outcomes Assessment Page and Internet Resources for Higher Education Outcomes Assessment are two additional comprehensive sites.

Apple's Youth Central
Internet address: http://www.youthcentral.apple.com

This site provides members with the opportunity to gain a new perspective and understanding from contributions made by children and teens around the world.

Assessment
Internet address: http://www.interactiveclassroom.com

This site provides information on outcomes, assessment, and materials for practicing in-service teachers. This is for K–12 teachers, regarding subjects in the curriculum.

Assessment-Related Sites, Index
Internet address: http://tiger.coe.missouri.edu

The University of Missouri maintains a site to provide links to information on state standards, accountability, and rubrics used by teachers.

Assessment, Accountability, and Standards
Internet address: http://www.serve.org/assessment/

This site provides information on accountability of teachers as related to state standards.

Assessment and Accountability
Internet address: http://www.nwrel.org/eval/index.html

This is a site by the Northwest Regional Lab (NWREL) and includes bibliographies of assessment information, a model writing assessment, and information about NWREL's "Alternative Assessment Toolkit," which is focused on the National Council of Teachers of Math (NCTM) standards implementation.

Authentic Assessment Samples
Internet address: http://www.miamisci.org/ph/deault.html

The Miami Museum of Science provides rubrics, lessons, and materials.

The site includes other assessment help and a "constructivist" approach to helping students learn.

Authentic Portfolio Assessment
Internet address: http://www.teachersworkshop.com/twshop

This site provides many models of portfolio assessment in all forms for prekindergarten through high school levels, again having to do with curriculum content.

Automating Authentic Assessment with Rubrics
Internet address: http://stone.web.brevard.k12.fl.us/html/comprubric

This site is maintained by educators for the prekindergarten through twelfth grade levels and supplies multiple models of assessment.

Behavior Home Page
Internet address:
http://www.state.ky.us/agencies/behave/homepage.html

Presented by the Kentucky Department of Education, this site offers job postings, teacher discussion forums, lots of intervention ideas, and links to educational resources.

BEST
Internet address: http://eyecatchers.com/eyecat/BEST/

This site serves as an archive of the best educational sites on the World Wide Web.

Bob's Little Corner of the Web
Internet address: http://ruralnet.net~bobseay/homepage.html

This site is an attention deficit disorder (ADD) page from someone who is ADD himself. It features wonderful material with exhaustive links and a chat room.

Born to Explore!
Internet address: http://borntoexplore.org/

This site presents the positive achievements of those with attention deficit/hyperactivity disorder (ADHD), with a special look at ADHD and creativity. Other parts of the site are titled "ADD Temperament," "Intelligence," and "Moodiness," and there is an opportunity for interaction.

Classroom Connect
Internet address: http://www.classroom.net/

This site provides information on Internet searching, educational conferences, school Web sites, and Web resources.

EDWeb
Internet address: http://K12.cnidr.org:90/

The site incorporates on-line educational resources and information about trends in education.

ERIC Clearinghouse on Assessment and Evaluation
Internet address: http://ericae.net/ftlib.html

The ERIC Clearinghouse on Assessment and Evaluation has opened the Text Internet Library at this site. Here, you will find links for full-text books, reports, journal articles, newsletter articles, and papers on the topics of educational measurement, evaluation, and learning theory. These materials include documents based upon criteria that are widely accepted in the library and in the community, and a framework is provided so that you can easily browse.

IMMEX Home Page
Internet address: http://night.immex.ucla.edu/

This site provides educators with multiple examples of how to assess problem-solving skills and critical-thinking skills.

Influence of Performance-Based and Authentic Assessment
Internet address:
http://www.eduplace.com/rdg/res/literacy/assess2.html

This site provides educators and parents with clear information on performance-based assessment. Many fine examples are used from the arts and physical education.

An Introduction to Science Portfolios
Internet address: http://www.accessexcellence.org

This is mostly a biology Web site that explains the why and how of portfolios and provides guidelines from the California State Department of Education for portfolio use. It also has some Web links and a chat room in which parents, students, and educators communicate.

Learning Resources and Technology
Internet address: http://www.library.ns.ca.lrt/

This site contains the Technology Demonstration Centre, Classroom Education Media Library, Software Evaluation Reports, Curriculum Related Links & Strategies, LRT—Update List Service, and Technology Recycling Program.

The National Center for Research Evaluation, Standards, and Student Testing (CRESST)
Internet address: http://cresst96.cse.ucla.edu/index.html

This site has helpful reports and a database of assessment samples. The site emphasizes rubrics and assessment techniques.

National Center to Improve Practice (NCIP)
Internet address: http://www.edc.org/FSC/NCIP/

NCIP, funded by the U.S. Department of Education, Office of Special Education Programs, seeks to promote the effective use of technology to enhance educational outcomes for students with sensory, cognitive, physical, and social/emotional disabilities.

The Pragmatism Cybrary's Dewey Page
Internet address:
http://www.pragmatism.org/genealogy/dewey/dewey.htm

This Web site offers a useful synopsis of John Dewey's life and work. It provides a list of recent editions of his writings, along with a chronological list of secondary works regarding Dewey. There are also Web-based links to related resources and e-texts, together with an on-line version of Dewey's "My Pedagogic Creed."

Special Education through Technology
Internet address: http://www.edu.org/FSC/NCIP

Developed by the National Center to Improve Practice (NCIP), this site provides a medium where you can learn and share with educators interested in technology as it relates to students with disabilities.

webCATS
Internet address: http://library.usask.ca/hywebcat/

This site provides a page of library catalogs that can be searched via the Web. webCATS is arranged for searching geographically, by type of library, and by library catalog vendor.

DISCUSSION LISTS

Classroom Connect
Internet address: crc-request@lisyserv.classroom.com

This is a moderated, general discussion list for K–12 teachers.

DEWEY-L
Internet address: listserv@ganges.csd.sc.edu

DEWEY-L is an international electronic forum devoted to the interpretation of John Dewey's philosophy. The list is open to anyone with an interest in any facet of Dewey's philosophy, including aspects of curriculum.

Educator's Guide to E-Mail Lists
Internet address:
http://www.gov.pe.ca/educ/resources/listservs/listserv.asp

This page has information on hundreds of educational lists organized under about thirty topics.

E-Mail Discussion Lists and Educational Journals
Internet address: http://sunsite.unc.edu/edweb/lists.html

Well-known Internet educator Andy Carvin provides a discussion list for educators.

Liszt, the Mailing List Directory
Internet address: http://www.liszt.com/

This is a searchable database of over 55,000 mailing lists of all kinds.

Pitsco's Launch to Educational Mailing Lists
Internet address: http://www.pitsco.com/p/listinfo.html

This page features an alphabetical listing of education-related mailing lists.

Tile.Net

Internet address: http://www.tile.net/tile/listserv/index.html

This searchable reference to Internet discussion lists is organized by name, subject, description, host country, and sponsoring organization.

Chapter Five

●◆ Curriculum Trends for the Future: Hope and Possibility

In reviewing the many trends influencing curriculum decisions, what is taught, and how it is taught, it appears there are five recurring trends to explore more fully as we look toward the future. These trends keep coming up in our history and won't go away. They are here to stay and give us great hope, and they offer us a serious space in which to make schools more effective. These five trends that continually appear in one form or another include: (1) multiculturalism and diversity in the curriculum, (2) integrating the arts into the curriculum, (3) critical thinking, critical pedagogy, and popular culture, (4) writing in all of its forms, particularly writing across the curriculum, and (5) authentic assessment in the curriculum. Here, I would like to briefly take up the issues surrounding these themes.

MULTICULTURALISM AND DIVERSITY IN THE CURRICULUM

Without a doubt, multiculturalism, sometimes decoded as diversity, has been a part of the discourse on curriculum development since the 1960s. Since then, the issues evolving from multiculturalism and diversity, to name a few, have included:

- ●◆ Bilingual education
- ●◆ English as a second language (ESL)
- ●◆ Special education referrals
- ●◆ Literacy issues
- ●◆ Teaching tolerance
- ●◆ Cultural awareness
- ●◆ Poverty and other minority issues
- ●◆ Social stratification

- Myths and stereotypes that are about minorities and that support the status quo
- Beliefs and behaviors of teachers and administrators about minorities in the system
- Attitudes of minority students toward dominant whites, affecting achievement and dropout rates
- Exclusion of minorities from the rewards of education, as promised
- Short-term, Band-Aid approaches that are used to deal with minority students rather than tackling the root causes of poverty, for example

As you can see, each of these issues will take decades to address and remediate. Nonetheless, as we continue to be a nation that is multilingual, multiethnic, and multicultural, these issues will persist. In addition, as long as we turn away from the root causes of poverty and continue to have underachievement in predominantly minority population schools, this trend of multiculturalism and diversity will be here to stay. In our multicultural society, the school is a complex institution. It reflects a strong commitment to the egalitarian ideal of providing each and every student an equal educational opportunity. In the long run, this will ensure social, political, and economic equality. But at the same time, there are many contradictions in its implementation, considering that blacks and other subordinate minority groups consistently do less well in school than their white counterparts. They also are more likely to drop out of school or to be placed in special education programs. Obviously, race is an issue here. Moreover, poverty and the overall economic inequities experienced by minorities are somehow related to performance in school.

Minority students and their parents have adapted to unequal opportunity, and, as a result, the students achieve less in school. Consequently, they are less economically successful. More blacks, for example, fall below the poverty level than any other group in our society. Even worse, statistics and ethnographic studies indicate that blacks and other minorities experience fewer rewards altogether in the economic, social, and political arenas than do their white counterparts. Still worse, serious and profound problems are associated with overrepresentation of minorities in special education. And even though Public Law 94-142 was to remedy these problems by eliminating overrepresentation, the situation remains, at best, a serious problem in some states and school districts. At worst, overrepresentation of minority students in special education continues to be a national phenomenon.

Furthermore, educational researchers have begun to study the achievement gap between blacks and other minorities and whites. This has provided us with data related to the discrepancy between the egalitarian ideal and its real-world implementation, and it has implications not only for racial minorities such as blacks and Hispanics but also for other ethnic minority groups arising from our immigration flow.

Teachers in general need to understand the economic, political, and social context of minority groups in our schools. And special education teachers in particular need to know about the issues related to overrepresentation of minorities in special education. Until we are aware of the ramifications, we will not be able to restructure and refine the current diagnosis and classification system of special students to benefit those students and meet the challenge of the egalitarian ideal.

In sum, these realities and concerns are as follows:

- Educators need to understand the complexities of minority status for children in school and to what extent this affects their achievement.
- Educators need to realize the significance of the discrepancy between the egalitarian ideal and its real-world implementation.
- Minority students have adapted to unequal opportunity and consequently achieve less in school. They also have the potential of dropping out of school and may never realize the economic rewards that may be available to them.
- Teachers often behave in a manner that indicates they may not understand the educational problems of minority students. Teacher training programs should address this and provide opportunities for teachers in training to redirect their behavior.
- When the egalitarian ideal makes sense to minorities in practice—when they realize both equal educational opportunity and equal rewards for their education—we should see changes in the status quo.

According to the Census 2000 Supplementary Survey Summary Tables of the Profile of Selected Social Characteristics, retrieved on-line from http://factfinder.census.gov, it is estimated that 30,271,370 persons living in the United States are foreign-born. Of that foreign-born population, 4,758,215 came from Europe, 8,263,012 were born in Asia, 853,636 originated from Africa, and 15,390,419 derived from Latin America; the remainder came from Oceania and other parts of North

America. Nativity and citizenship data show that 9,464,851 foreign-born individuals entered the United States prior to 1980, compared to 8,464,762 who entered the United States between 1980 and 1989 and 13,178,276 who entered between 1990 and 2000. Clearly, the trend of multiculturalism is escalating. A glance at the Profile of Selected Economic Characteristics for the Census 2000 Summary File 3 Sample Data, distributed by the U.S. Census Bureau, indicates that 13.6 percent of families with children under eighteen years of age lived below the poverty level in 1999. In terms of the time line, this trend began with the reconceptualists and continues in the postmodern era. For further demographic data, please go to the following two resources for a more elaborate description of the information presented here.

References

U.S. Census Bureau. (2000). "Census 2000 Summary File 3." Retrieved on January 9, 2003, from U.S. Census Bureau Web site at http://factifinder.census.gov.

———.(2000). "Census 2000 Supplementary Survey Summary Tables." Retrieved on January 9, 2003, from U.S. Census Bureau Web site at http://factifinder.census.gov.

INTEGRATING THE ARTS INTO THE CURRICULUM

Every child has the capacity for artistic self-expression and creative thinking. The use of art in cross-discipline curriculum promotes active exploration of core subject areas and reinforces academic achievement in core subjects. If artistic self-expression and creative thinking are encouraged through the use of the arts in core curriculum, the student gleans several enduring benefits:

1. Classes become more interactive and lively as student-initiated participation is increased through the engagement of art-based activities that engender enthusiasm and consequently motivate the student to attend class.
2. The arts encourage self-discipline, self-confidence, and hard work and provide concrete rewards for sustained effort.
3. The process of creating art in studying core subjects promotes imagination, originality, and creative thinking.
4. Learners recognize and analyze relationships through use of

cross-discipline arts-based curricula that provide a greater
understanding and ways of knowing fundamental material.

5. The arts permit learners to experience the world around
them in new ways, by connecting the arts to core disciplines
such as math, science, reading, and writing.

This trend has been with us since the beginning of the traditionalist period and continues to this day.

CRITICAL THINKING, CRITICAL PEDAGOGY, AND CULTURAL STUDIES AND WRITING IN THE CURRICULUM

These key trends are combined here because they are so totally related
and connected to each other. One of the most important techniques to
sharpen critical thinking skills is writing. Earlier in the text, I discussed
writing across the curriculum as well as journal writing. What follows is
my own example of journal writing about critical thinking skills and the
importance of journal writing. Because autobiography is a technique
evolving from postmodernism, reflective writing, though always present
in the curriculum, is being taken seriously today specifically through
journal writing. Following this example, I will take up the subject of critical pedagogy and its connection to cultural studies.

An Example of a Reflection on Using a Journal to Develop Reflective and Critical Thinking Skills in Classroom Settings

Beneath the rule of men entirely great
The pen is mightier than the sword
   —Edward Bulwer-Lytton
   Richelieu, 1839, Act II, Sc. 2

I write this as a teacher of over twenty years who has found that the best
way to teach my students to be critical thinkers is to model those skills,
which will help them in their quest to be critical thinkers. One such skill
I like to teach about and indeed to model, is journal writing. I would like
to describe and explain how a classroom practitioner might develop
critical thinking skills by keeping a journal, either as a written journal in
a notebook or on the computer in an electronic file. There are many
types of journals. I would like to focus on keeping a classroom journal.

A classroom journal is a journal that individual learners, as well as the teacher, construct and create on a daily basis. I have used this approach with adult learners who are student teachers, intern teachers, and with doctoral students who wish to improve their classroom practice. My doctoral students who themselves teach, in turn, use this with their students who range in age from elementary to postsecondary student ages. I invite the reader to adapt any of these ideas to the level appropriate to their own needs.

Keeping a classroom journal can be a tool for deepening critical thinking about classroom practice. I focus on the teacher in order to begin the journey. The next step of the journey would then be to work on journal writing with learners, the topic for another paper. In the meantime, although journal writing has its seeds in psychology, sociology, and history, I will rely on understanding the use of the journal from Social Psychology and the Symbolic Interactionists. In addition, what the sociologist Norman Denzin calls "Interpretive Interactionism" will inform and frame this discussion. Symbolic Interactionists have historically argued that we all give meaning to the symbols we encounter in interacting with one another. Interpretive Interactionists go a step further in that the act of interpretation is a communication act with one or more interactors. Basically, the art of journal writing and subsequent interpretations of journal writing produces meaning and understanding that are shaped by genre, the narrative form used, and personal cultural and paradigmatic conventions of the writer who is either the researcher, participant, and or coresearcher. As Progoff notes, journal writing is ultimately a way of getting feedback from ourselves and in so doing, it enables us to experience in a full and open-ended way the movement of our lives as a whole and the meaning that follows from reflecting on that movement.

Why Journal Writing?

Students and colleagues have often asked me, Why should one invest the time in journal writing? To this, I can only reply that journal writing allows one to reflect, to dig deeper, if you will, into the heart of the words, beliefs, and behaviors we describe in our journals. The clarity of writing down one's thoughts will allow for stepping into one's inner mind and reaching further into interpretations of the behaviors, beliefs, and words we write.

For example, a student conducting a ministudy in a qualitative methods class wrote in her journal and described some of her inner thoughts:

I am a bit wary of this research. Am I really a researcher because I am taking a class? Can I ever hope to portray what someone else believes or at least says she believes? How will I know if I am being fair? Will I be able to trust this person? Will she trust me? Why should she trust me? Am I being too critical of myself? I am waiting here and she is already 20 minutes late. I hope she gets here soon. . . . Here she comes. Now I try to capture this person's thoughts on why she is an administrator.

K. S. 97

As we look at this journal entry, one can easily see the learner/researcher in training, asking questions that cause reflection on various issues about the research process. She is beginning to know more about herself and her strengths and weaknesses. To continue with examples of journal writing to illustrate my point on reflection, I would like to present most of the rest of this chapter in the form of my own journal about writing this topic.

Monday

I am trying to decide if I should write this reflection with a section on describing the various uses of journal writing like keeping a journal of one's dreams, a journal in the form of a dialogue like Ira Progoff suggests. . . . Or, should I write about only keeping a classroom journal? If I do that will I be limiting the options for readers of this paper? Of course, I have had great success with classroom journals with two simple prompts for the teacher to write about. One is: POSITIVE ELEMENTS IN THE CLASSROOM TODAY, and the other is, FRUSTRATING ELEMENTS IN THE CLASSROOM TODAY. I wish I could find the examples I saved from one of my students, who did keep a journal based specifically on these two questions each day. I think I will try to find these . . .

Tuesday

In my quest to find examples, I was most fortunate. Here is an example from J. D., an experienced teacher of some 15 years who teaches middle school in a metropolitan area. What an amazing example of her thoughts on the classroom:

I love these kids . . . most from broken homes, most thinking I am their parent, advisor, guardian, good cop, teacher, analyst, and coach. I am trying to get them to read more . . . comic books, novels, go to the library, and then get them to write about this. I think I will go for the two page report idea again. It gives me something to reinforce their understanding

of what they read and to give them some feedback. I am worried about P.
He is always skipping class these days and although I know his brother is
home from prison, I wish he would come back to school. I will talk to the
principal about this today if I don't forget. I also want to design a new
way of evaluating my class without the letter grades we are stuck with.
I am reading about the use of portfolios in classroom assessment and
I think I will try it this month and get the kids to plan it with me.

J. D. 4-96

If this isn't a good example of what I myself am trying to achieve as a
teacher/professor, I don't know what is.

Wednesday

Back to this reflection, should I write about the fact that the teacher who
decides to keep a journal is a researcher in effect? The teacher is documenting her life history or at least a portion of it. She opens herself up
for redirecting her teaching or reshaping it upon reflection of some of
her practices and feelings about that practice. Also, the teacher is a kind
of historian, documenting life on a daily basis providing a continuous
written record. Then, the students who elect to keep a journal are also in
that same situation. Should I mention that not everyone can keep up
with the demands of journal writing? The discipline and desire involved
nearly outweigh some individuals' ability and time. On the other hand,
can this not be for all who are interested in becoming better writers,
thinkers, scholars? How does one set time apart for journal writing? I recall the teacher who said she only had twenty minutes after school to
write in her journal and that was it. Then, as she ultimately decided she
needed keep a journal at home as well since once she started to write,
she found she was staying at school and writing for at least an hour each
day. She got up an hour earlier than anyone in her house and started
writing in the early morning hours, a technique advocated by many
writers. It seems she had to write about her problems in the class from
day to day. I will ask her about this tomorrow and see if she will let me
use her examples from her journal.

Thursday

I am so happy H. H. let me see her journal entries. I am going to use only
one of her examples regarding a problem in her classroom.

Once again I have to deal with M. Why is he refusing to write in class
and why is he afraid to tell me what is bothering him? He has done this

before but we could always talk this out before. . . . I am taking a class right now that relates to this directly. . . . None of the books or papers is helping me so I am just going ahead and going to try a home visit to talk to his Mom and see if she can help. . . . Since I started visiting parents who were unable to come to teacher conferences, I am humbled by what I am learning. . . . M's mother is working three jobs to keep the family of three children and herself together. . . . I wonder if I would have her courage at this point? She has told me that M. is getting in with the "wrong crowd" and has been involved in questionable activities which is why he is skipping school so often. Even sending someone to check on this has not yielded any positive results. She said she thought this was due to more than "being a teenager" but felt that there were no strong role models for him at home. No relatives live nearby. I brought some of M's work to show her and she felt a bit reassured that at least he was doing something, though she added that "he could do better." I decided I would talk to him tomorrow and ask him to help me organize the class project on voting in the November elections. I felt conflicted upon leaving the house, for I feared that M's Mom needed to talk to someone about her kids and that I wasn't very much of a help at all. I do feel more inspired to be better at letting the kids take over more of the responsibility for class projects. Actually it was M. who taught me this month when he volunteered to lead the book circle discussion.

H. H. 96

When I look at this entry I can see someone still alive and thinking about teaching in a way that makes the basic questions of what and how to teach take on a renewed meaning. Is this a good time to talk about how journal writing can assist one in developing creativity? I am reminded about creativity by Ira Progoff's text, *At a Journal Workshop: Writing to Access the Power of the Unconscious and Evoke Creative Ability*. I am also reminded that Anais Nin didn't like Progoff's method; it was too methodical for her. Yet every time I read that text, I see something new in it. Even reading the publicity blurbs about it, like Joseph Campbell saying "Progoff's Intensive Journal Process is one of the great inventions of our time," makes me rethink my own writing. Tomorrow, I will describe a bit about Progoff's method.

Friday

When did I first hear about Ira Progoff? Now I recall. It was nineteen eighty–something and I was giving a talk at the University of Alberta in

Edmonton on Qualitative Research Methods. In the audience was a former high school teacher of mine who happened to be working on her doctorate and she mentioned it to me in passing. Since that day, I have tried to put into practice much of what Progoff describes. His intensive Journal Workshop teaches us to be reflective and aware of our unconscious self. He advocates writing a journal as a dialogue with oneself. Can you imagine? I thought I could never be able to do this; then, step by step I started. He began his journal workshops in 1966 and has been refining them ever since. He talks about keeping a daily log. Yes, there is no getting around it—you need to write in this journal every day!!! No resting! There is only movement forward. He suggests keeping dialogues with key persons in our lives, with our body, with our works, with our roads not taken, with events that were critical in our lives with society, and with our dreams. In other words, we write our journals in dialogue form that prompts us to think in new ways.

Sunday

Last night I couldn't sleep as I thought about all the examples of journal writing in popular culture. First, I recalled *Doogie Howser.* The television show of a few years ago chronicled a youthful doctor who was a sort of Leonardo DiCaprio type. Younger than his peers in the medical profession, Doogie opened and closed each show writing in his journal that he kept on his laptop. His struggles as a gifted teenager among cynical colleagues and his struggle to know himself were the focus of the journal writing moments in the show. Then, I remembered Bob Packwood's diaries. The Senator actually wrote about his extracurricular sexual activities away from home and family which ultimately was used to force his resignation from the US Senate due to his sexual harassment of young office workers. And of course, who can forget the O. J. Simpson trial? The mass media circus that surrounded this bizarre case was highlighted for me by the fact that the murdered woman's diary was not allowed as evidence even though it described in great detail circumstances directly related to the case. All this makes me wonder what would be most helpful to the reader of this paper. Since the audience is an audience of practitioners in educational settings, I think I need to mention one more resource about journal writing. It is Tristine Rainer's (1978) text, *The New Diary.* Rainer co-taught with Anais Nin a course on journal writing to students at a Los Angeles college. She wrote this book, which contains superb examples of journal writing. She, as I, uses the terms journal and diary interchangeably. She describes seven techniques for journal writing, some very similar to Progoff's technique. Here is her list: portraits, lists, maps of consciousness, guided imagery, altered points of view, unsent letters, and dialogues.

The dialogues come from Gestalt therapies and of course Jungian therapy. In Rainier's text (pp. 104–111), she offers examples of dialogues with the self, the body and works. These examples are fine models for anyone attempting a dialogue. She highlights a Progoff idea, "dialogues with the body," which suggest conversations with the body as a whole. Here is a portion of that example:

ME: Well body, how do you feel?
BODY: Weak, shaky, a bit hurt. I feel open and vulnerable. I can't trust my environment yet.
ME: But you'll mend?
BODY: Yes, I'll mend. I don't know how soon . . .
ME: Maybe when you are feeling better, it won't sound so awful.
BODY: Maybe. . . . I'm strong, and I can take it . . .

Obviously, something like this helps the journal writer relate to the body's messages. In this particular case, the writer was a person who felt disengaged from her body. I recall how many of my students who keep a journal in class resonate with this dialogue technique, though I myself have not tried it yet.

Later on Sunday

I am trying to think about the best way to summarize all the ideas of this paper so far. Especially the reader who is a classroom practitioner may be more interested in the two prompts I wrote of earlier: Positive Elements in the Classroom, and Frustrating Elements in the Classroom. I found this example of a Frustrating day from a teacher who just taught music classes all day:

> Oh dear, I am fed up again with everything. And I am particularly fed up with this journal today. Why am I writing about my failures? Are they really failures? Am I not seeing progress with my students because I am So burnt up? Yes that's right—burnt up not burned out. I love teaching so much and my kids ... but all the endless bureaucratic Snafus are killing me. I am trying to get my choral group to perform around town at all the schools to raise awareness of violence in our schools and once again, the principal says "forget it" because he doesn't want parents to think we have violence in the school. Yesterday when the two gangs had a fight across the street, he called the police but would not even go

outside and lead. Am I only going to work at schools where there is no leadership? Of course I have to keep focusing on the good kids—the breakthroughs like T. who sang her heart out today in her solo and who really wants to go on and study music on a scholarship next year. What's wrong with me that I am getting beaten down by the negative stuff? How can I pull myself to higher ground?

K. L. L. 1-96

This entry shows the teacher's self-reflection, of course; but now look at this same teacher just four months later.

I looked over my journal from this year and I see a pattern in it. All my complaints and big headaches seem to come from situations where I have no power. Usually, no—make that, ALL the critical incidents I describe in my journal are about the principal, the state regulations, the characters who have some power. But then I see I am playing their game too—I am avoiding confrontations, I am running away from letting myself take control and be Empowered. I have been a wimp. And somehow, I have to deal with my principal. I usually go around him altogether. I also feel like I may need to find a better place to work at this my beloved music.

K. L. L. 5-96

The example goes on at length with this soul searching and although at this point it is not resolved, the writer certainly is thinking through major issues about teaching and learning. Now let us turn to an example from a teacher, therapist, and educator who uses journaling as a means of personal discovery.

Journal Writing as a Means of Personal Discovery
Lorna R. Elam

Journaling was not a new concept to me when I began my doctoral studies, but I have since gained a new respect for its powerful benefits to mind, body, and spirit. For years I had been using journal writing as a therapy technique in providing mental health treatment to patients and clients who desired to understand their behaviors, thoughts, and feelings at a more meaningful level. As a marriage and family therapist, I had long discovered the power of this type of intimate writing as a means of purging deeply painful secrets that only serve to clog one's mind and soul. I had worked with countless individuals who had reported problems with sleeping or eating disorders, or who had complained of difficulties in maintaining healthy relationships. Many of them had pervasive fears or intrusive memories that seemed to haunt them daily, prohibiting them from moving on to enjoy life. Most of them also reported high levels of stress and difficulty with concentration. More often than not, however, they didn't know why they behaved and felt the way that they did. They couldn't identify antecedents to their albeit self-destructive behaviors. They didn't recognize patterns of events or behaviors that seemed glaringly obvious to the others around them. But once they began freely expressing their thoughts and feelings on paper, they inevitably gained a level of self-awareness and insight that helped them discover new strategies and solutions for their problems. Through their journaling, they were actually beginning to understand more about *themselves*; and in doing so, they had also begun reshaping their future.

Journaling is frequently used in the mental healthcare field by practitioners (i.e., therapists and psychologists) who are interested in helping people recover from the effects of stress, anxiety, anger, trauma, and a myriad of other emotional problems. Both the American Association for Marriage and Family Therapy (2003) and the American Psychological Association (2003) provide several online books, journal articles, and audiotape resources (including information on the usefulness of journaling in doing research and treatment) for therapists and psychologists who are interested in improving their practices. For example, Granvold (1998) suggests that journaling should be an integral part of the therapy intervention process in working with a separated couple that has not yet divorced. But journaling is also a commonly recommended practice for working with individuals who may have problems in other sorts of interpersonal relationships, because writing can bring insight to an individual regarding the way he or she has been treated by other people. Conversely, journaling can also bring insight regarding the way an individual cares for (and behaves toward) others. Writing can be a handy way to track one's behavioral patterns, identify and sort through problems, and even process harmful emotions that may not necessarily be visible on the surface, due to elements of denial and other ways that we protect ourselves from facing painful realities.

Shortly after the September 11th attack on the Pentagon and World Trade Center, Jordan (2001) wrote an article that appeared in *Family Therapy News* urging therapists to encourage journaling in working with persons who had either lost a loved one; had a loved one who was unaccounted for; had themselves been injured; had somebody in their family, a friend, or a neighbor injured; had personally witnessed the terrorist act; or had witnessed the devastation through exposure to television, radio, and internet coverage of the tragedy—in order to bring emotional healing to these individuals who were consequently suffering emotional pain from being victimized (either directly or indirectly) by the terrorism. Indeed, journaling can help people process negative events in order to find hope and emotional healing. But recent research also indicates that in addition to the emotional benefits derived from the journaling process, individuals can also gain physical benefits as well. Journaling has been shown to strengthen the immune systems of individuals when they write about their emotions and stress (Murray 2002). Writing apparently permits individuals to release pent-up negative emotions regarding the unhappy events and circumstances in their lives that have consequently compromised the functioning of their immune systems. So, through expressive writing, individuals are able to vent their emotions to relieve their stress, thereby improving the way that they feel while simultaneously reducing the stress that exacerbates physical illness and disease. Thus journaling can be an important and effective tool in the therapeutic process because it may bring with it the added value of improving physical health as well as improving mental/emotional health.

Like any good practitioner, those of us who are trained as therapists are charged with the responsibility to "practice what we preach." As such, in addition to taking care of others, we also have the onus to take care of ourselves. Thus, experts in the field are encouraging mental health professionals to facilitate their *own* self-awareness and self-care in balancing their personal and professional lives by building a relationship with *themselves* via the use of journaling, in order to tend to their emotional, physical, and spiritual needs (Baker 2002). I've learned firsthand how journaling can connect me to how I am feeling about myself, my goals, my job, my etc. In essence, I've learned a lot about *me* through my personal writing. It has become an important part of my daily life in my desire to take good care of myself. Moreover, upon entering doctoral studies, I also learned how journaling can be a beneficial and practical tool in my journey as a learner because it provides me with a method through which I can deconstruct and analyze key concepts in a way that gives meaning to the information I receive as a student/researcher.

The use of journaling to connect course content in a more intimately meaningful way for higher education students is gaining credence in the field of psychology (Murray 1999). Undeniably, there is tremendous value in adding this type of personal relevance to course information and research data, so that students genuinely gain even more knowledge about what they have experienced, read, or researched. Journaling is also being utilized in conducting qualitative research to track the thoughts, assumptions, biases, and interpretations of the family therapy researcher (Gehart, Ratliff, and Lyle 2001). Therefore, many professionals in my field are finding that journaling has educational benefits, in addition to its well-established physical and emotional benefits. But as Murray suggests in "Writing to Heal" (2002), journaling's power to heal does not lie in the pen or paper, but rather in the mind of the writer. Likewise, I surmise that journaling's power to enhance the *learning process* is also greatly dependent upon the mind of the writer. And this is where I have gained a new respect for the way that journaling has personally transformed me as doctoral level learner.

Although I had utilized journaling, in one way or another, for many years before I returned to school as a doctoral student, oddly enough I had never used journaling as an approach to reflecting on what I was supposed to be learning in doing the coursework I was assigned. On retrospect, I dare say that my master's level work (and all the schoolwork that preceded it) would have been *so* much more meaningful to me if I had systematically utilized this technique to understand the curriculum I was reading. Of course, the mere act of writing is not where I've discovered the most benefit. On the contrary, words on paper that don't uncover the hidden personal relevance of how I can apply this information to my "real life" worldview and/or experiences are, in essence, simply useless words on paper. They have no personal meaning to me. They might as well be in a foreign language because I cannot usefully apply them, as I haven't yet made sense of them! At best, they are a regurgitation of what I have read—but nothing more. In contrast, I've discovered that I reap the greatest benefits from my reflective journaling process when I focus on how the information fits or challenges my personal values, beliefs, and perceptions . . . and I put *that* on paper. As a result, I *understand* more about what I am reading in the curriculum when I use reflective journaling to deconstruct what I have read in order to make sense of it from *my* perspective.

I've been very pleased with how my journaling efforts have transformed me as a learner. I acknowledge that there is a practical side of my journaling, in that my professors can monitor my understanding of both content and process during my journey as a student. Without a doubt, journaling helps me learn what I am supposed to be learning. But journaling alone hasn't been the critical factor. In truth, I've discovered that *how* I journal makes a big difference in how much I learn about a subject and how I apply the information that I glean. Furthermore, journaling has also brought me valuable insight about myself as a learner, university student, and cohort member. In my studies, by using reflective journaling to apply information in a relevant way that makes sense to me, I've discovered new strengths and new challenges that I had never been aware of before. Consequently, my self-esteem and self-efficacy levels have been boosted because I've become empowered to be more self-aware and in control of how I utilize the information I receive from curriculum, in any given day. All things considered, over the years I've witnessed how journaling can bring about self-discovery and self-awareness in many different aspects of life. And now I find that I've come full-circle in finding personal growth and a new level of *my own* self-awareness that has transformed me into a more confident and competent learner.

REFERENCES

American Association for Marriage and Family Therapy. (2003). Family Therapy Resources. Retrieved June 12, 2003, from http://www.aamft.org.

American Psychological Association. (2003). APA Online. Retrieved June 12, 2003, from http://www.apa.org.

Baker, E. K. (2002). *Caring for Ourselves: A Therapist's Guide to Personal and Professional Well-being.* Washington, DC: American Psychological Association.

Gehart, D. R., D. A. Ratliff, and R. R. Lyle. (2001). "Qualitative Research in Family Therapy: A Substantive and Methodological Review." *Journal of Marital and Family Therapy* 27, 2: 261–274.

Granvold, D. K. (1998). *Separated but not Divorced: Goals, Processes, and Outcomes.* (Audio tape). Alexandria, VA: American Association for Marriage and Family Therapy.

Jordan, K. (2001). "Anger Reactions to Terroristic Acts." *Family Therapy News* 32, 5: 8–9.

Murray, B. (1999). "Connecting Course Content with Students' Lives." *APA Monitor* 30, 11.

Murray, B. (2002). "Writing to Heal." *Monitor on Psychology* 33, 6.

Another Monday

As I try to conclude this piece on journal writing, the major ideas I want to punctuate have to do with journal writing and thought processes. Writing down what we think and feel helps in the journey to improve classroom practice. Some of the examples used in the body of this text may serve to illustrate the individual writer's thinking processes and the willingness to analyze, rethink, and go deeper into a critical stance about one's life and work. Progoff calls this the scope of personal renewal. Others call it reflection. Still others see journal writing, myself included, as a tangible way to evaluate our experience, improve and clarify one's thinking, and finally become a better writer and scholar, if you will. In my own experience of journal writing, and as I see what my students write, I find that we are writing to chronicle our profession. We are talking about examining our own thoughts, beliefs, and behaviors. Many will say that this helps only the writer. Still, if that were the only outcome of writing a journal, I would say that in itself it may help to ensure the continuing self-reflection each of us claims as a first step to modeling this for our students. Perhaps this quotation of Virginia Woolf's from her own diary will inspire the reader:

> Oh yes, I've enjoyed reading the past year's diary, and shall keep it up. I'm amused to find how it's grown a person, with almost a face of its own.

Summary

Thus, here we have an example of journal entries that are about writing and its importance and that also illustrate a format of journal writing. Now let us turn to critical pedagogy and cultural studies. One of the key writers is the well-published and versatile critic Henry Giroux. Earlier in the text, I spoke of his work and his contribution regarding pedagogy and hope. Now I want to reiterate the importance of his work in terms of critical pedagogy, that is, how we teach, and cultural studies. He has recently done a serious analysis of the Disney Corporation and its effect on popular culture, with a critical eye. In his book *The Mouse That Roared: Disney and the End of Innocence,* Giroux raises questions about the consumerism and entertainment turned mass culture message that is Disney at its best. Giroux does not deny that there is imagination, delight, and joy in many of the Disney products. But at what price, he asks? The consumerism of mass culture can be seen in, for example, an ad for Disney products based on any recent movie. Giroux is saying that this has cost our children their innocence, for they learn to be good little consumers from age two onward. What I am pointing out here is that as we become more critically aware of mass culture markers, we can only do our children and ourselves a service by being critical and by questioning the results of the imprint of mass culture. Thus, the field of cultural studies will only blossom. This is truly a postmodern era concept.

AUTHENTIC ASSESSMENT

I have written earlier of the importance of authentic assessment and quoted a passage from the philosopher Michel Foucault:

> People write the history of experiments on those born blind or wolf-children or those under hypnosis. But who will write the more general, more fluid, but also more determinant history of the examination—its rituals, its methods, its characters and their roles, its play of questions, and answers, its systems of marking and classification? For in this slender technique are to be found a whole domain of knowledge, a whole type of power.
>
> Michel Foucault (1970, 94)

As Foucault points out, how we classify people is about many things but mainly power. Authentic assessment is a valuable tool for showing what any student "can do." This flies in the face of some power structures, but imagine the possibilities if we were serious about talking about our students' achievements and what the students can accomplish.

The well-known evaluator and writer Grant Wiggins argues that there are equitable, fair, and authentic means of assessment. He offers us a new way to look at how we assess our students. Here are some of his major guidelines:

1. Assess the student's accomplishments and progress, not merely the total score that results from points subtracted from a collection of items. In other words, score longitudinally toward exemplary performance at exemplary tasks, not by subtraction from "perfection" on simplistic and isolated tests.
2. Devise a scheme that assigns degree-of-difficulty points to assignments and test questions, thus distinguishing the quality of the performance from the degree of difficulty of the task.
3. Give all students the "same" demanding work but differently scaffolded assessments based on equitable expectations.
4. Devise a sliding grading system wherein the proportions of

what is counted over time varies. Move toward increased emphasis on achievement, with a weight for effort and progress.

In other words, Wiggins has suggested that there are ways to test students, still maintain standards, and be fair and equitable in the process. His system of authentic assessment (1998) is based on the following premises:

1. Authentic tasks must be realistic. The task must match the real knowledge and abilities based in the real world of experience with that task.
2. Authentic assessment requires students to use their judgment and their imagination. The learner has to use knowledge, theory, and skills wisely and inventively in order to solve problems or pose problems.
3. Ask students to "do" rather than recite, memorize, replicate, or restate information. In other words, let students demonstrate what they have learned. Authentic assessments are related to the real-world context in which adults are tested in the workplace.
4. Assess the learner's ability to efficiently and effectively use a repertoire of skills and knowledge to negotiate complex tasks.
5. Allow appropriate opportunities to rehearse, practice, consult resources, and get feedback on and refine performance and products.

Teachers are always concerned about assessment. The reason authentic assessment is important is obvious. Every teacher is forced to assess the achievement and progress of students. Since teachers deal with assessment issues constantly, educators in every arena want to find a realistic, workable, authentic system of assessment. The reader can clearly see the difference between typical tests and authentic assessment as listed in the next section.

Characteristics of Typical Tests and Authentic Tasks

Requires correct answer	Requires quality performance or product
Is disconnected from the learner's environment	Is connected to the learner's world
Is simplified	Is complex and multilayered

Is one-shot	Is continuing with multiple tasks
Provides one score	Provides complex feedback continually recurring and the learner self-adjusts, perform-ance is improved
Looks for one level of thinking	Looks for higher-order skills with a demonstration of knowledge

Thus, an authentic assessment task is designed to provide a richer, stronger, more complex approach to understanding student progress. The actual performance or production not only tells us about what the student has been learning but also provides a way for students and teachers to keep track of the students' progress. When authentic assessment is used, the student must provide evidence of some growth and improvement. It is an approach to assessment whose time has come. It stands in contrast to typical tests. In typical testing, one cannot always be sure that growth has taken place. If a student crams for a test and memorizes facts to be recalled one time on a one-shot test, how can we know exactly what was learned? Since the typical test is usually test-ing some facts devoid of the learner's actual experience or social con-text, how can we assume the learner learned?

The Assessment Discussion

Practitioners in the field of assessment are engaged in a series of dia-logues and discussions on the following matters:

1. The nature of the use of assessment.
2. The need for displaying how students think, learn, and solve problems.
3. The need to focus on student achievements.
4. The correct balance, case by case, school by school, between performance-based and authentic assessment and the use of standardized testing.
5. Delineating the concerns and problems with standardized tests. For example:
   - Schools and districts may not be reporting data accurately. The literature is filled with examples on the way some school test reporters get around accurate reporting. Conse-quently, the data reported are used deceptively.

- Some teachers are pressured into teaching for the test only. Consequently, the regular curriculum is abandoned for drilling for the test.
- Pressure to report test scores publicly—in newspapers, for example—divides communities and individuals. Most often, poor, underfunded schools have lower test scores on standardized tests.
- Test bias exists against various ethnic groups, females, limited English proficiency students, and low-income students.
- Testing is extremely costly. Considerable school district resources go into the high cost of standardized testing. This takes money from other worthy budget categories such as teacher development or classroom materials. The testing industry has become a multibillion-dollar industry, which profits test makers.

Thus, the discussions that are raised and that continue on these critical points are at the heart and soul of assessment. Now, at this point in the text, you may be the judge on the status of this discussion by checking the sources for evidence listed in this text.

Some History on Assessment

Public schools in the United States have always been under scrutiny. However, since the 1950s, a number of writers have been concerned with measuring just what is learned. Calls for reforms in education began in the 1980s when students were described as illiterate. What is critical to remember here is that the public perception of our schools is affected by newspaper and popular media reports, whether or not there is evidence to support the negative reports. Educators consequently have gone on the offensive and taken up the reform agenda. They are seriously committed to:

- Making schools better for students
- Providing meaningful and appropriate instruction for each grade level
- Designing authentic assessment tasks, which truly show what students can do and what they learned from their studies
- Responding to critics of public schools with solid, demonstrable results

Thus, we need to imagine a new way to look at testing and assessment and a new way to help students learn and grow. If we follow these tenets, there is room to use information from authentic assessments in a way that is healthy, respectful, fair, and demanding for students, without reducing their work to one and only one indicator.

Although I have recounted some of the complexities of all those issues earlier, there remains an important and critical consideration about assessment that relates to language. I am speaking of the need to be careful with language not just because of political consequences of these words, as shown in the Texas case and others, but also because of the emotional consequences of these words. If we are to take seriously proposals about assessment of authentic tasks, we need to be aware of the social and political effects of language. Language is about power. How we use language is also about power. The skillful use of language that is not injurious is needed in the process of evaluating, assessing, setting standards, and measuring. This notion is also reinforced by the organization Fairtest, whose Web site is a delightful resource on any aspect of authentic assessment. One important notion is about an agreement to do what is best for children by agreeing on standards to be used in assessing their achievement. Fairtest has addressed this subject on its Web site, where the National Forum on Assessment listed "Principles and Indicators for Student Assessment Systems" in order to help guide assessment reform. Fairtest used surveys to gather data, along with follow-up interviews and selected document review.

Fairtest adapted the "Principles and Indicators" to create appropriate standards for large-scale assessment. As listed on the Web site, they are:

Standard 1: Assessment supports important student learning
Standard 2: Assessments are fair
Standard 3: Professional development
Standard 4: Public education, reporting, and parents' rights
Standard 5: System review and improvement

Thus, Fairtest uses the principles of authentic assessment to reassess where schools are going. There is a continuous loop of trying something, reviewing it, and then improving it.

Authentic Assessment in Today's World

The politics of schooling most often gets in the way of student progress. Bureaucrats want a score in most cases. They want to measure the progress of students with a one-shot score because it's easy to do so. It requires less time. And sad but true, time is indeed money. In the past, educators, researchers, and writers did not question typical tests. But from the social movements of the 1960s onward, all sectors of society began raising issues of civil rights, women's rights, gay rights, etc. When people on the macro level became concerned with issues of equality, it was not long before this trickled down to the micro level in the school-room. On a global level, people were asking for fairness.

In the schools, issues of fairness were applied to the most basic activity of learning, or how we assess what learners know. It takes much more time, effort, involvement, teacher training, and teacher profes-sional development to put authentic assessment techniques into prac-tice. Since the 1980s, in every state in the country, educators have been clamoring to know more about authentic assessment. Why? Put simply, because it makes sense. Do you want your children judged and graded by a typical one-shot test, which provides a simple score? Or would you rather have them assessed and graded with performance and product tasks that show not only what they learned but also what they can do? I go with the latter. The reasons for preferring authentic assessment are the following:

1. Authentic assessment overall is fair. No one racial or ethnic group is penalized with a one-shot score.
2. Authentic assessment overall tells us a great deal about how a learner connects content knowledge to a given problem un-der study, in the learner's world.
3. Authentic assessment overall provides us with feedback on a learner's progress on a continual basis.
4. Authentic assessment shows us how a learner constructs a product or performance so that we can see the learner's growth.
5. Authentic assessment overall provides for continual feedback, allowing the learner to adjust and improve performance.

These are not the only reasons to select authentic assessment as a solid evaluative technique. Obviously, in today's world, students are bombarded with media images and information technology and, one might say, a sophisticated information explosion. The needs of today's learner we know to be a bit more demanding, a bit more realistic, and a bit more challenging and competitive. This is all the more reason to give the learner the opportunity to display what he or she has learned through performance-based authentic assessment and actual products, which verify a student's progress.

How Authentic Assessment Is Suited for Today's World

The pace, complexity, and demands of today's world require much more when it comes to student learning. Yet it was years ago, in the early part of the twentieth century, that John Dewey, America's foremost philosopher of education, wrote prolifically on the topic of experience and education. He reasoned that students must have an actual experience with learning something or the meaning would be lost. For example, rather than read about how to bake a cake, a student should actually perform the activity of baking a cake. The preparation of material and ingredients, the putting together of the ingredients, baking, frosting, decorating, and so on all are part of the actual, real-world experience of the learner. At the time Dewey was writing, he encountered mixed reviews. Educators, of course, were intrigued and enthused about his work. Yet he worked in the realm of philosophy applied to the real world of education, earning him the title of pragmatist. He once said there is nothing so practical as a good theory. With an understanding of his work in experience and education, I see Dewey as the starting point for what we now call authentic assessment. It is important to understand our history in order to understand where we are now and where we are going. American pragmatism, the philosophical approach most often represented by America's own educational philosopher, John Dewey, provides us with the first seeds of what we now call authentic assessment. In essence, experience is one of the greatest teachers. Authentic assessment requires the learner to experience what is being learned, whether it is baking a cake or documenting a semester's work of writing assignments. Given our fast-paced, mass-media world, this is the only alternative that makes sense.

References

Foucault, M. (1970). *The Order of Things: An Archeology of the Human Sciences.* London: Tavistock.

SUMMARY

Of course, there will be additional trends as we evolve as a society and as our children grow and develop. And even by the time this piece is published, there may be new research findings that begin new trends or reiterate the meaning of the five key trends outlined in this chapter and others as well. Yet if our schools teach us anything about ourselves, we cannot look away from these critical trends of multiculturalism, integrating the arts in the curriculum, critical thinking and pedagogy and cultural studies, writing, and authentic assessment. They are part of the educational landscape where we live.

Appendix A

●◆ A Glossary of Terms Related to Curriculum Trends

Academic standards: These are the clearly written expectations of what every learner must learn at a specific grade level.

Arts-based curriculum: This is an interdisciplinary model integrating core academic curricula with art forms. It involves the use of visual and performing arts in the instruction of core disciplines, including math, reading, writing, science, and social studies.

Authentic assessment: This type of assessment requires authentic tasks of students that show what they can do. It assumes feedback and redirection for student growth.

Charter schools: Charter schools are public schools under a performance contract called a charter. They receive money as usual but are free from the bureaucratic red tape of regular public schools. Normally, the contract or charter is given for three to five years and there is active involvement with the parents and community who hold the charter.

Consumerism: This refers to the preoccupation and promotion of the consumer's interests; the inclination toward buying; and the acquisition and consumption of goods, services, and experiences. Consumerism affects environment, community development, education, and gender issues.

Curriculum: Many call this the race or course to be run, taken from the Latin word *currere.* It may also refer to the planned and unplanned experiences that take place in school.

Differentiated classroom: This term refers to differentiated plans, curricula, and activities in a given classroom, so that the teacher uses different techniques for each person in class. This enables teachers to match instructional approaches to each and every student.

Gender gap: This term usually refers to the gap reflected on test scores between boys and girls. A gender gap favors boys across all demographics, including family income, parents' education level, grade point average, rank in school, size of high school, size of district, etc.

High-stakes testing: This is a term referring to standardized tests that are used for high stakes, such as withdrawing money and support from a school or retaining a student in a grade level.

Home schooling: Home schooling is the current trend for students to be taught at home. Parents are usually the teachers. All fifty states have rules from the respective state departments of education for home schooling. All home-schooled children must still pass the required aptitude and achievement tests of regularly schooled children. One criticism of home schoolers is that they are disadvantaged by not having the social activities a school provides. Often, home schoolers' parents try to provide those social activities as well.

Inclusion: This term is associated with the reform movement that attempts to normalize the educational experiences of students with disabilities by "including" them in the regular classroom. This is the alternative to separating them in segregated special education classrooms.

Mass culture: This term refers to the viewpoint of popular culture as being a commercial culture and an aggregate group of isolated individuals who are behaviorally homogeneous and lacking in self-awareness.

Montessori Schools: These are the alternative schools begun by noted physician Maria Montessori (1870–1952), which focus on education of the whole child. Exploration, joy, creativity, and imagination are stressed as a means to learn content in all disciplines. Worldwide, there are over 5,000 Montessori Schools.

Multiculturalism: This term describes the ethnic, religious, and cultural diversity of the United States, and it is further defined by the trend away from assimilation. It embraces the premise of cultural tolerance and equality and encourages the ideal of the individual's right to cultural heritage, identity, beliefs, and expression. It is articulated through multicultural policies aimed at the removal of barriers of race, ethnicity, culture, language, religion, and gender. And it is symbolized by the movement toward expanding the awareness and study of the range of cultures being represented in the United States.

Responses to the nation's cultural diversity have included the "melting pot" concept as well as the more recent "tossed salad" and "stew" metaphors. The concept of the United States being a melting pot in which different cultures merge and blend together into one common concoction has given way to new metaphors of

American society. In these new metaphors, different cultures maintain their values, beliefs, and identities in coexistence, like vegetables in a tossed salad or stew that maintain their own distinct colors, shapes, and flavors. As such, members of various cultural groups exist separately and maintain their respective cultural heritages.

Multiple intelligences: This term refers to the theory of multiple intelligences formulated by Howard Gardner. This broadens the view of intelligence and how the mind works to include musical, bodily kinesthetic, mathematical-logical, visual-spatial, interpersonal, intrapersonal, linguistic, and naturalist intelligences.

Norm-referenced test (NRT):   This type of test compares a person's score against the scores of a group of people called the "norm group." NRTs are most often multiple-choice tests. Some examples of NRTs are the California Achievement Test (CAT), the Iowa Test of Basic Skills (ITBS), and intelligence quotient (IQ) tests.

Pedagogy: Pedagogy refers to the principles, practices, art, science, and profession of teaching. It also refers to the teaching skills that educators use to impart specialized knowledge to their students.

Performance-based assessment: This term is often used interchangeably with *authentic assessment.* It is assessment based on performance tasks to show what a student can do.

Pragmatism: This branch of philosophy is marked by the belief that the meaning of things is to be found in practical applications. In education, it is often associated with John Dewey, who urged a balance between theory and practice.

Proficiency level: This is a cutoff level that indicates that a student's performance is at minimal, basic, proficient, or advanced level. The levels are set against an absolute standard.

Progressivism: This term is used to describe the movement in educational philosophy that held that the goal of education is to support and advance progress. Social change was deemed critical to an informed democracy, and education was the key. John Dewey is most often named as the father of the progressive movement.

Retention: This term refers to nonpromotion of a student from one grade to another, or holding a student back in a grade. This is often done on the basis of standardized test scores.

Rubric: This is a set of scoring guidelines for evaluating a student's work. Rubrics provide criteria for judgment of performance. Usually, there is a scale, or range of possible points, assigned to a rubric. Each level of performance on the rubric must have specific descriptors that indicate what a student must do to achieve that level. Rubrics are often associated with standards and how those standards are met.

Social stratification: This term refers to the unequal distribution of desirable resources (i.e., social advantages) such as wealth, income, prestige, power, and status, often involving social factors concerning race, gender, and age. A central concept of social stratification is that of "class"—the division of individuals into different hierarchical levels with unequal social advantages—and the process and attainment of social class mobility from one level to another.

Waldorf Schools: Waldorf Schools are private schools with an innovative curriculum. Students construct their own textbooks, and one teacher stays with each class from kindergarten through eighth grade for the purposes of nurturing and caring and for fostering a community spirit. Founded on the beliefs of Rudolf Steiner (1861–1925), a philosopher, writer, and educator, the schools aim to educate the whole child and include movement, dance, the arts, and exercise as well as content subjects to educate the whole human being. Steiner's concept of "eurhythmy," the integration of movement and thought, revolutionized thinking about schooling. Noteworthy is the fact that experience is at the core of the Waldorf curriculum, similar to John Dewey's and Maria Montessori's work.

Appendix B

⚫⟳ Questions for Reflection on Curriculum as Ethical Text

Carolyn Stevenson

Periodically it is essential to reflect upon our beliefs and values regarding education. Questions for reflection include:

1. Can members of the educational community answer: What business is our business?
2. What does the school/college hope to become?
3. Is the vision widely shared and accepted?
4. What are my personal values, goals, mission, and vision?
5. Do informed groups and individuals make decisions?
6. How must members behave in order to make shared vision a reality?
7. Is there clarity on organizational values?
8. Are goals specific and measurable?
9. What attitudes, behaviors, and commitments must be made to create a professional learning community?
10. Does the college reward individuals for a job well done?
11. Does the college support continuous improvement?
12. Is the learning community action oriented?
13. Are the guiding principles of shared mission, vision, and values apparent in the college?
14. What is my role in the learning community?
15. How can I promote a positive school climate?
16. Does the college value cultural diversity?
17. Does the college value collective inquiry about its members?
18. Does the college promote collaborative curriculum development?
19. Do instructors evaluate individual learning styles when planning for instruction?
20. Is instruction student-centered?
21. Is collegiality and school culture connected?

22. What are the relationships among students, faculty, and administrators?
23. Are professional development seminars and workshops offered for faculty and staff?
24. Do I continually educate myself on best practices?
25. Are instructors and administrators evaluated in a timely manner?
26. Do teachers plan instruction around a diverse student body?
27. How do I continue to grow in my profession?

Appendix C

●◆ Reflections on Curriculum as Aesthetic Text

Hank Thiele

A CRITICAL REFLECTION UPON READING PINAR'S CHAPTER ON CURRICULUM AS AESTHETIC TEXT

As a music teacher I found this transformative. I felt as though the author went a long way toward validating the arts in the curriculum. It is important for educators to realize that the curriculum is no longer centered on the traditional core subjects. In the last ten years, Howard Gardner has anchored this idea further through the theory of multiple intelligences. Pinar makes some striking examples as to how aesthetics can help an individual see him or herself in a more autobiographical fashion and begin to open up to new experiences. This essay has made a strong case for the use of autobiographical reflection within the school curriculum. This is a technique that I have used in my teaching and have found to be a valuable resource for the teacher and the student. It should be a major goal of education for the student to discover the person that they truly are through experiences. This section points out that through the use of aesthetic experiences students may be able to find out who they are more easily.

The example that is used most prominently is theater. This is an interesting selection, for the arts serve to support Pinar's arguments very well. A major issue within this book is the hidden curriculum and in no other art is there hidden meaning like there is in theater. For example, many people love to go to the opera, even though many operas are not in their native language. How is it that the observer can understand what is going on? It's the other entire context going on in front of the viewer. They are able to grasp the meaning through things such as facial expression, tone of voice, and the music in the background, hand gestures, and a multitude of other things happening onstage. This can easily be compared to the classroom where there are many other things being learned. As established clearly the classroom contains many different forms of information. This information is being taught just as it was on stage. The teacher and class's mood, facial expressions, offhand remarks, the design and layout of the room, and a multitude of the other things going on teach lessons that are sometimes stronger and more memorable than the subject matter. As I made this connection it really stuck out in my mind the comparison to classrooms and plays that I have been part of in the past. When I think of classes I have taken in the past, most of the time I remember the setting and the people within the class before I think of the subject matter I learned. Just as I think back at the plays I have gone to see, I often remember the set, lighting, and how the actors carried themselves before I think of the storyline. I believe this is reflected in how anybody discusses the experiences that they have. When reading a movie review it is often how the actors presented themselves, how they were dressed, and the special effects that will be discussed before the plot line is. This is just one example that shows how people's experiences are not just focused on outcome, they are also wrapped up in the process.

Once Pinar establishes theater as a good example of autobiographical reflection he then does an excellent job of showing how it can be used within the classroom. As I continued to read I realized that the classroom was not just one stage. The classroom is a place where each person is on their own stage, with everyone else in the classroom acting as the audience. A good actor must think of how they are observed from the audience, a good student or teacher will evaluate how they are observed from their stage in the classroom. It is also important that students and teachers learn skills from observing what happens on the other stages in their classroom. Just because the curriculum is hidden does not mean it is not important to learn. It is up to the observers to take what is seen in the classroom and change it into their own experience and knowledge.

When the classroom setting is created that allows for an autobiographical experience it will sometimes be uncomfortable for the students. This is an opportunity for a strong form of self-discovery, which is not always a pleasant experience. Combining this with the fact that it may be a new experience it will be difficult for a teacher to keep the students going down this new and important path. Teachers must act as a driving force to keep students moving forward so that they may discover who they are and gain their own individual voice. An aesthetic experience can be one of many ways to achieve that goal.

✏ Curriculum as Autobiographical Text

This section reviews the examples of practicing educators, principals, and teachers on curriculum issues. In this case, the issue is curriculum as autobiographical text.

CRITICAL REFLECTION ON CURRICULUM THEORY
Brian Coleman

In studying, reading, writing, and discussing curriculum theory from the post-modern perspective over the last three months, I have probably learned more about my own thinking and pursuits than I have in any of my prior classes. Thus, instead of reflecting on a particular issue from the text, I am going to attempt to reflect on the changes that have occurred in my thinking, autobiographically so to speak, as I have participated in both of my curriculum courses this semester. My writing will also reflect a more candid and free-flowing style rather than my formal, customary style. This sounds very postmodern and at the beginning of the semester, you would have had to force me, tooth and nail, to write a reflective paper like this.

As an educator, my thinking has always been very sequential in nature, yearning for the bottom lines and always examining the "what" of education. Those who are close to me know that I am somewhat of a perfectionist, wanting everything level, square, and flush. I approach my job as an administrator in much the same way; very efficient, no loose ends, and highly organized. The several principals on our administrative team that are "global thinkers" always tend to get under my skin (and their desks are cluttered). They have come to mind several times this semester as we have studied a more "global minded" approach to curriculum rather than concrete. To top it off, I have limited, if any, artistic inclinations to speak of. My "global thinking" counterparts of course act and sing. To enroll in two courses that examine the value of reflection, relationships, connectiveness, community, and yes, a global perspective, was going to be challenging to say the least. I told myself at the beginning of the semester that I would not succumb to this "fluffiness."

As I mentioned earlier, Postmodernism and all of its theory at first seemed extreme and detached from the practicality of the classroom and my career as a principal. Being a principal, my day is full of practical and common sense decisions to resolve problems and manage people. Now, in the last few weeks of these courses I have evolved in my thinking, not quite full circle, but somewhere in the middle between the global thinker and the sequential thinker. I have come to realize that process is just as valuable as product and that the "why" is just as valid, if not more valid, than the "what."

After studying the spiritual aspects of children with the likes of current writers for my curriculum issue paper, I have begun to question the things that are truly important that we not only teach our children today, but cultivate within them. As so many writers ask, "Are we paying a great price for an educational system that fails to address the real issues of our lives—dispensing facts at the expense of meaning, information at the expense of wisdom." At this point in education, I believe the balance is weighing heavily on the side of facts and information. We have become a bottom line–driven educational system that has nearly forgotten the inner workings of a child's development. Being a half-way-converted-global-postmodern thinker, I have come to believe that as educators, we need to do a much better job of shepherding our students' hearts and spirits.

So where does this leave me now? It is practical and logical that schools prepare students with skills and abilities to be successful in the real world market. And we need sequential and concrete ways to do this. But we must not continue to ignore the responsibility we have as educators to nurture and foster the human spirit within our students. They need to understand that with becoming adults there is more than just freedom and a check at the end of the week. There is an expectation of responsibility, stewardship, and wisdom. If we run our lives driven by the bottom line, we lose out on the joys of the journey that gets us there.

I rarely get the chance or take the time to reflect on the big picture or even question why we are doing what we are doing. Both of these courses have challenged my thinking and my beliefs. I have not succumbed to the fluffy stuff, but have realized what appeared to be distant and disconnected from the practical (fluff) is really what we are all about as educators.

FROM SCIENCE TO LEADERSHIP: HOW DID I BECOME A SCHOOL PRINCIPAL

Cheryl Buck

Writing part of an autobiography is a scary thought for me. My thoughts should help and give direction in pursuing my future educational goals. It should also help define what I have done in the past and delineate present and future directions. By looking at the past, present, and future, we are able to juxtapose the past, present, and future and assess the relationships between them. Educators are able to begin with the individual experience and move to broader connections. The autobiography allows us to review what we enjoyed about our careers and treasure what we enjoy in the present. Through autobiography, we should come to a greater understanding of ourselves.

I was undecided as to which direction my schooling should take me prior to entering college. I did not know what my career path should be. Some people know when they are very young what they want to "be when they grow up." I am not one of those people. I came from a middle class background where my father was a factory supervisor and my mother a stay at home mom. Many of the men in my neighborhood during the 1960s were gas station owners, factory salesmen, or worked in the factories. The women were all stay at home moms. I worked part time in factories or the local department stores in order to raise money for college. My experience with careers was limited to the people whom I was in contact with on a daily basis, teachers and factory or store personnel. My limited experience in the factories and stores made me realize that I wanted to do something else with my life. But what? I was never sure and my parents did not have experience with colleges, so I was on my own.

In college, most of the women (we had all women dorms at that time) were pursuing educational careers and I thought about my education. I enjoyed science and wanted to continue with something that had to do with science. I also had good memories from my Junior High School experience. I preferred changing classes and the teachers had a great deal of influence on my development at that time. Science was my first passion, thus I found my niche. I loved my science classes and the education courses. I spent my last summer at the Life Science Station on a bluff overlooking the Mississippi River. What a great experience . . . a real outdoor education experience. We lived with and studied wildlife, plants, birds, and animals. We explored holes in the ground that opened into beautiful caves teaming with wildlife. We woke up in the morning before the birds trying to identify songs and took many hikes at various times of the day to identify plants and animals. There were approximately 10 of us who lived and studied at the site. After graduation, this memory stayed with me as I pursued teaching jobs in the field.

Since the fall of 1974 until 1988 I had worked as a science teacher. As a teacher, I saw many situations that could have been handled more efficiently and effectively. I also noticed that many veteran teachers seemed very unhappy in their work. I knew that I had more to offer education and that I could make positive differences in the educational environment.

Graduate Work

I enjoyed taking classes and went back to school for science class work. Early in my career I thought it would be best to get a master's degree. The district paid teachers a small sum as reimbursement for professional classes. I began work on an instructional leadership program at the University of Illinois at Chicago in 1978. I finished the program by 1980. I was able to move on the salary schedule, which at the time was my goal. As I studied and became involved with the outdoor education program, I found I took on more administrative responsibilities. I liked the administrative end of the program and as I observed other administrators, I knew I could administrate programs and schools better than what I saw happening. So I went to school to obtain administrative certification. The year 2000 began a new journey when I started an educational doctoral program at Roosevelt University in Chicago. I have been studying educational leadership and organizational change for the past two years. I remember quantitative, qualitative, and program evaluation courses as being the most relevant to me in that I was able to use information learned within my current work assignment.

Administrative Experience

From 1988–1993, I was gainfully employed within my district as an assistant principal. I became principal of an elementary building in 1993 where my responsibilities were staff evaluation, building management, curriculum and instructional leadership, student supervision, scheduling, and school and community relations as well as the school improvement processes. In addition I was responsible for district wide curricular review processes. In 1999, I was assigned to another elementary school within the district. The responsibilities remain basically the same. I enjoy the position of principal but find that I am unable to make the changes necessary for the organization that would be in the best interests of the students. Consequently, I am working on post-graduate level courses that will lead to an educational career change.

Five-Year Plan

I plan to complete my Doctoral work in 2004. During my dissertation writing time, I plan to continue working as a principal. I hope to be able to study and work at the same time. After completing my doctoral degree, I will send resumes to local colleges and universities in order to find a position in elementary education or educational administrative departments so that I may teach, at least on a part time basis. I would like to work at the university level with pre-service teachers. My goal is to make positive changes within the school district that will enhance student learning.

Reflections

I remembered what I loved about my schooling and my educational career. Themes emerged. They include relationships, experiential learning, and problem solving. The following paragraphs discuss those topics. The relationships I held were important to me even though the types of relationships changed through time. Relationships with teachers, students, friends, and family were influential during my adolescent period. I specifically remember kindness, closeness as well as times when I personally became emotionally detached from specific alliances. All of the relationships influenced my educational decisions and progress. I learned most effectively in all phases of schooling when I learned from hands-on experiences, discussions, activities, tasks, and fieldwork. Science classes are in my mind's eye as I reflect upon my past educational experiences. I liked organization, structure, and predictability as a teen-ager as well as the excitement of laboratory classes and exploring the unknown. My science classes were organized, structured, and routine.

Reflecting upon my teaching career, I find that in a short time I became a linear thinker. I taught science, the scientific method through hands-on learning as well as organization, structure, and routine (all of which I needed as an adolescent). My philosophy was to give students as many different experiences as possible. In a classroom environment that is not always possible.

No longer can I continue to be a linear thinker. The unexpected is the norm as a building principal and I must react to each situation. How best to react situationally and lead a professional community are questions building principals deal with daily. I have studied this question in an ELOC practicum/ internship and will continue with the question as my dissertation topic. Doctoral work identifies the same themes that have been important to me in my learning. Discussions with peers, relationships with my cohort and instructors, experiential learning and problem solving are themes I have found while reflecting on my educational autobiography. As I continue with my professional pursuits, I would like to have a position in which I can have meaningful discussions with others, study, work on tasks, and move beyond the routine. Currently, I believe I will find what I am looking for at the college level of teaching. The section above regarding my five-year plan outlines my plan of action for a short-term career goal.

Appendix E

⬤◗ Curriculum as Spiritual Text: An Example

AWAKENING THE SPIRIT IN STUDENT LEARNERS
Brian B. Coleman

Introduction: Turning toward the Human Spirit

Within the past decade, several national events have stimulated educators to re-evaluate and re-think the importance of what they are teaching. From the questionable character and integrity of our national leaders and society's temptation to look the other way, to the school shootings and hate crimes committed by our youth, educators have begun to examine the importance of teaching character, empathy, compassion, service, and even spirituality within the classroom.

Many children psychiatrists and educational psychologists believe that some of our troubled children don't fully grasp the value of life. Many child psychiatrists believe that the troubled students involved in the school shootings never developed the ability to empathize with others. They could not place themselves into another's feelings or situations. In our competitive need as educators to have our students measure up academically, have we ignored the need to nurture the human spirit found in our students today? Teachers and educational leaders have just recently begun to look seriously at the broader implications of teaching the whole child by examining Gardner's intrapersonal intelligence for example.

The term "spirit" has been considered taboo within the public school arena for some time and because of the separation of church and state is often feared by teachers and educational leaders. Many suggest that we are paying a terrible price for a school system that is so fearful of things spiritual that it fails to address the real issues of our students' lives. He believes that as educators, we are dispensing facts at the expense of meaning and information at the expense of wisdom. Is there a place within the modern day academia-driven classroom to grow the human spirit of our students?

This paper will explore ways in which educators can seek out the human spirit found in all of our students in an effort to teach to the whole child, and not just to the intellectual child. The use of the term "human spirit" or "spirit" in this article is not referring to the spiritual dimension of our lives that is fed and cultivated through traditional faith, even though this writer is a strong believer in and highly respectful of the faith. Rather, the "human spirit" or "spirit" refers to the quality of being fully human that ignites our potential. The purpose of this paper is to examine ways educators can begin to link their teaching to ways that awaken the human spirit that is desperately needing direction in the lives of many of our young people today. The three areas that will be addressed are awakening the spirit through experience, awakening the spirit through holistic learning, and awakening the spirit through teaching.

Awakening the Spirit through Experience

Parker Palmer (1999) suggests that, "spirituality—the human quest for connectiveness—is not something that needs to be 'brought into' or 'added onto' the curriculum. It is at the heart of every subject we teach, where it waits to be brought forth" (p. 8). The key to bringing forth the human spirit in children is connecting the current content that is being taught with meaningful experiences found in the life of the learner. Palmer (1999) explains that we can awaken the spirituality of any discipline by teaching in ways that allow the "big story" told by the discipline to cross with the "little story" of the student's life. Connecting learning to the meaningful experiences students have will deepen their understanding of the subject matter and enhance the students' ability to internalize the concepts and retrieve the knowledge in the future. Charles Suhor (1999) suggests that personal experience, of the teacher and the student, are key to the internalization of the content by the learner. This suggest that the sharing of human experiences within the classroom in relation to the curriculum being taught not only cultivates and grows a child's spirit, but improves their learning as well.

Palmer (1999) provides a wonderful example from his own life of how his history teacher was less than adequate in connecting the "big story" of the Holocaust with the "little story" of his own life. Palmer explains that because he was taught only the "big story" of the Holocaust, with no application to his own life, he grew up believing that this tragic event happened on some other planet, to people completely different from himself. How many of our own students today are thinking the same thing? Because Palmer's own life experience was not connected to the Holocaust, he failed to realize that not only did the city he lived in at the time coerce Jews into their own ghetto, but more importantly, he failed to realize the "little Hitler" lurking inside of himself (Palmer, 1999). As educators, can we afford not to open up this window into the inner worlds of our students in an effort to connect past tragedies, and victories, with the present realities our students live in? If we are to awaken the human spirit within our classrooms, we must strive to link the curriculum to the life experiences of our students so that not only the mind is challenged, but also the heart.

It is reasonable to expect schools to give students the skills and abilities necessary for them to be successful and competitive when they enter the work place. At the same time though, along with the skills and abilities, there needs to be a fostering of critical thinking, empathy for others, and community. It is difficult to be given a skill, yet lack the judgment and wisdom needed to use it in a way that contributes rather than destroys.

In John Miller's (1999) article entitled "Making Connections Through Holistic Learning," he suggest three key elements that nurture the human spirit within the learner: balance, inclusion, and connection. In today's schools, educators seem more concerned with measuring what students have learned rather than fostering a love for the learning process itself. Our educational system should not be solely outcome-driven to the point where the focus on the process of learning is vacated. The journey should be just as important as the finish line. As educators we need to maintain the balance between preparing students and nurturing students.

Inclusion is Miller's (1999) second element of holistic learning. The holistic learning process includes learners of diverse backgrounds, races, and abilities. To accommodate the diverse learners we need a wide range of teaching and learning techniques (Miller, 1999). Miller suggests that teachers use a combination of three kinds of methods: teacher-directed learning, student-teacher interactive learning, and a multiple-intelligence approach that focuses on nurturing the student's inner life. This third element seems to primarily focus on the nurturing of the human spirit. Miller (1999) identifies these approaches as transmission, transaction, and transformational and believes all three approaches can be woven into a teaching style that meets the needs of all the students in the holistic classroom.

Connection is Miller's (1999) third element in the holistic learning approach. He views the holistic classroom as a learning community and one that students should feel connected to the people around them. He suggests that not only should there be connections made between subjects at multiple levels using various themes, but students should see the classroom and school as a learning community where they can work collaboratively with each other. Students should have some connection to the community by either having volunteers come in to the classroom or by sending students out to do service learning for example.

Awakening the Spirit through Teaching

"Spiritual teaching is about helping children find questions that are worth asking because they are worth living, questions worth wrapping one's life around" (Palmer, 1999, p. 8). The human spirit grows in the classroom when teachers see themselves not as coaches or promoters of measurable gain, but as agents of joy and transcendence.

It is clear in the literature reviewed that it is the teacher that is the cornerstone in the development of students' spirits. Second only to a child's parents, the teacher is probably the most influential adult in a child's life. Several authors, including the ones cited above, have suggested ways in which teachers can be the "transformational agent" within the classroom, cultivating the human spirit in their students. Two areas of teaching seem to be more prevalent in the literature than others: questioning techniques and classroom climate.

Spiritual questions are the kind of questions we ask and our students ask every day, as we long to connect with the largeness of life. Palmer suggests these questions include, but are not limited to: What is the meaning of my life? Does my life have a purpose? Do I have gifts and abilities that people need or enjoy? Whom and what can I trust? How do I deal with my own suffering and that of my family and friends? Many of these questions fail to be verbalized, but they are still present in the inner worlds found in the hearts and minds of our students. "Our real questions are too risky to ask in front of one another" (Palmer, 1999, p. 8). The real art to teaching is not to have all the right answers, but to ask all the right questions.

When we fail as educators to honor the deepest questions in the lives of our students, education remains mired in technical triviality, cultural banality, and worse: It continues to be dragged down by the sadness one feels in too many schools where teachers spend their days on things unworthy of the human heart (p. 11).

The classroom climate developed by the teacher is just as critical in the nurturing of a student. Developing activities that foster critical thinking and reflection stimulate students to think about those inner questions they never ask. A teacher needs to craft his or her classroom into an environment that nurtures insight and inquiry.

Recently, this writer observed a gifted teacher teaching a group of students. The teacher read a short story about a thief stealing a small amount of grain each week from his employer to feed his family, knowing that he would one day repay the merchant. The teacher posed the question if what he was doing was right or wrong. She even extended the question by asking students whether stealing a few grains of rice was the same as stealing a full bag of rice? Students really had to reflect on their own sense of right and wrong and ask the question of what determines right from wrong. The students initially probed the teacher for her answer, but she refused to give in. The students wrestled with the question for some time, taking sides, debating, and even questioning what they initially thought.

With this exercise, the teacher not only was able to connect meaning to the content of the story and ask the right questions, she had developed an inquiring atmosphere within this group of students that gave them the freedom to wrestle with and contemplate some of life's most difficult questions. Here the teacher was more interested in the path students took to arrive at their own understanding.

In Conclusion

Educators are now realizing that education and learning are multi-goal in nature and not just driven by the goal of achievement. As Wesley suggests, "The education of the spirit is like a circle game that goes round and round from teacher to students and back again." A student's "something special" may be little more than a healthy dose of potential, but educators can choose to awaken it and to cultivate it rather than ignore it.

REFERENCES

Palmer, P. (1999). Evoking the spirit in public education. *Educational Leadership,* 56(4),6–11.

Suhor, C. (1999). Spirituality—Letting it grow in the classroom. *Educational Leadership,* 56(4), 12–16.

Halford, J. (1999). Longing for the sacred in schools: A conversation with Nel Noddings. *Educational Leadership,* 56(4), 28–32.

Wesley, D. (1999). Believing in our students. *Educational Leadership,* 56(4), 42–45.

Miller, J. (1999). Making connections through holistic learning. *Educational Leadership,* 56(4), 46–48.

🕮 Sample of a Reflective Journal Entry

REFLECTIONS OF A TEACHER/GRANDMOTHER
Susan Hill, Ph.D.

My seven-year-old granddaughter is reading *Dr. De Soto* to me. At a point of increasing excitement and tension in the plot, she turns to me in a voice that drops down several octaves and takes on a maturity that is not her own, and says, "Bubby, what do you think happens next?" I feign ignorance, and she says, "Now think, Bubby. Dr. De Soto told the fox he would never have to see him again. What did he mean?" And there is a pregnant pause as she waits for me to respond. I answer, and she says, again in a voice that I know she has borrowed from her second grade teacher, "That is very good, Bubby. Should we take a picture walk through the rest of the book to see if you predicted right?"

I suppress the impulse to laugh out loud, because you see I have been teaching since I was nine years old, and I picture this precious little girl following in my footsteps and entering the teaching profession. I suspect that my earliest attempt to "teach" also closely resembled the work that I saw my teachers doing in the classroom. I liked the sound of their voices and had a fascination with the words, the language they used.

When I was nine—and I know that because we had just moved into a house that a new baby brother made necessary—I labored for hours to construct book cases out of tomato crates, and desks and chairs out of my brother's blocks as I readied the corner of our basement for the arrival of my new friend's Ginny dolls. (Ginny preceded Barbie, and had a much more realistic body shape and more childlike accessories.) I used a set of Golden Book Encyclopedias my mother had purchased one a week at the local grocery store to research the contents of my doll students' textbooks. I made sets of ten books for each subject that I felt was important to teach. Even then, I had a heavy humanities orientation. There was lots of history and literature and foreign language, because the same year my doll school opened up my Aunt Luz Maria, who had been born in Puerto Rico, became our babysitter. Luz introduced me to Spanish and consequently my students learned Spanish. There was no science, and math was taught only sporadically because I had difficulty in the subject.

That summer, almost daily I sat in front of my doll students and mimicked the intonation of my teachers, worked to have the same degree of authority that they seemed to me to have. I mediated arguments, soothed wounded spirits, and I suspect did additional work with the slower students, because by that time my brother David had entered kindergarten and begun encountering serious difficulties with prereading and writing. My Aunt Luz's son Andreas, who had been born deaf, blind, and with cerebral palsy and mental retardation, had become part of my small world. Luz brought Andreas to our home with her each day, and when I was not playing school or riding my bike, I helped with the many teams of workers who came to our home to do what Doman and Delcado then called "patterning." It involved moving Andreas' limbs in certain ways for hours and hours each day, and it was done in order to reprogram the neurological pathways of the brain. That year I became my brother David's protector and tutor and my cousin's physical therapist. And I began work that I believe eventually led me to the field of education, and special education in particular.

I was the oldest of five children. David was the third in line. He was born with what they were then calling minimal brain dysfunction and what was first called mild retardation but eventually renamed a learning disability. He walked and talked very late. He was very shy and awkward with other children because he had difficulty expressing himself. I often had to intercede on his behalf with neighborhood children.

Kindergarten created a crisis for David. School was such a struggle. Letters and sounds eluded him. Writing was laborious. We walked to the nearby elementary school, and we returned each day at noon for lunch. That was frequently when my problems began, because often David would hide in the bushes or escape over the fence behind our house to the woods rather than return to a place that created so much pressure for him. David repeated kindergarten with the hope that the extra year would give him an edge. But reading and written and expressive language would remain a challenge for David throughout the years. Eventually he was diagnosed as dyslexic, but the school he attended didn't have any specific help for students with dyslexia. It was really up to our family to help him. My parents were busy trying to run a family owned business and gone all the time. It became my job to help David with his school work. This is a job that I apparently took on voluntarily and actually enjoyed. I know that I kept track of the methods that worked with my brother and began to understand the importance of carefully observing your student.

When David entered first grade, we faced a new challenge; he had to pass all the class work required to make his first holy communion. He couldn't read the catechism and had difficulty memorizing. So for the six months of catechism classes, I set up a study routine. I had to walk to the elementary school from my middle school and pick David up. As we walked a third of a mile to the

Catholic church, we practiced reciting the catechism. We repeated sections over and over until David could take pride in answering the nun's questions. Somewhere along the way, I acquired another student, a classmate of David's who also struggled with the catechism. One day he quietly joined us and began reciting along with us. While David and his friend took part in catechism class, I sat outside the door and listened in order to know what still remained a challenge for my brother. I also worked on my homework. My own school work was very important to me. My mother says that I always had my own sense of momentum when it came to academics. I never needed to be pushed.

I may not have needed a push, but I got one just the same from my father. I'm not sure how old I was when the dinner table discussions began, but they were firmly institutionalized by the time I entered high school. My father would introduce a topic or introduce a dilemma, often a moral dilemma, and tell me to prepare to discuss and debate it at an upcoming meal. At first I did not prepare very much for these discussions, so I would receive what amounted to a lesson on history or politics or ethics. Often he brought a globe to the dinner table and pointed out the location of certain political hot spots or places where World War II battles took place.

Eventually I began to research in the library and read news magazines and newspapers in preparation for these events. I felt enormous pressure, but also pride, when I delivered my response to my father's question. I gradually learned to choose words carefully and accurately, to never say anything that I could not back up with facts. I was encouraged to challenge things, to develop my own independent position on issues. I got caught up in the love of learning and ideas that was so evident in my father's eyes and his voice. Years later, when I became the principal of a Jewish day school, I learned about Mishnah and the Jewish tradition of questioning, interpreting and reinterpreting holy or sacred text over and over, and I realized that my experience had been very much like that of a young yeshiva student. Of course, like Yentl, the female character in an Isaac Bashevis Singer short story, I would not have been allowed to study in a yeshiva, but I like to picture myself there, sitting on a wooden bench, arguing and debating until the daylight faded. Because I am my father's daughter, I like to think I too would have challenged the prohibition against young women studying Torah.

My knowledge of Isaac Bashevis Singer and Shalom Aleichem comes from my mother, who had an enormous collection of Yiddish and Jewish literature in our den. I loved our den. It was loaded with books, at that time all hardbound, many of them very old and inherited from grandparents. The pages of these books were discolored and musty, the bindings often stiff but made of beautiful embossed leather. I spent many hours looking through them. I read myself through the family den—my father's collection on Western civilization,

World War II, twentieth century politics, and historical biography, my mother's collection of American and British and Jewish literature, and on art. When I went off to college as a freshmen, I secreted some of my favorite books away to my dorm room. I still have some of those books today in my own study. They make me feel connected to the past and to my family.

From my mother I inherited not only this love of beautiful books but of reading. My mother has always been a voracious reader. She belongs to several book clubs and literary societies, and as a woman in her mid-seventies still attends open enrollment college courses on American and comparative literature because she loves to talk about and interpret literature. She encouraged me to stay away from the television and to spend my time reading. By the time I was in the fifth grade, I was spending two or three hours a day reading. I became interested in vocabulary and the precision of language. How marvelous it seemed to me that changing a few words changed the meaning conveyed. I began keeping journals and notebooks full of vocabulary words I encountered in my reading and then looked up in a dictionary or thesaurus. I found the dictionary and thesaurus frustrating at times and learned that the best way to grasp the nuance of words was to listen carefully to the way people spoke and conveyed meaning. I was famous as a little girl for making the adults around me explain the meaning of the words they were using. I find my granddaughter has the same habit. She does not know that it is a gift from me.

Once I began baby sitting in middle school, I had the money to begin acquiring my own library. I took great pains researching which books to spend my hard-earned money on. I got into the habit of frequenting the local library and a nearby independent bookstore, sitting on the floor with piles of books around me, reading the first chapter of various books to determine an author's style. I targeted different sections of the library or book store each week and scanned the shelves for new authors. This is how I first found the anthropologists Margaret Mead and Ruth Benedict, the work of Freud and Jung, Ayn Rand, John Steinbeck, Ernest Hemingway, Edith Wharton, Faulkner, Elie Weisel. And this is how I met Mary Pritchard.

Mary was a schoolmate of mine who had been born blind. She had never been in my homeroom, and we lived in different parts of our town, but one day I found her scanning a large, oversized book written in braille while tucked away in a private corner of the public library. I asked her to tell me something about how braille works and where she got her book. I ended up walking her home that day and going into her room to see how much room a volume of an encyclopedia written in braille takes up! I found Mary to be bright and funny and amazingly brave. She walked all the way to school on her own and maneuvered around our school on her own. She took karate and self defense classes. And she was an artist and creative writer. We became very close friends over the next few years. I asked for and was given permission to dictate her tests out loud to her. I learned how to write and read braille. Mary helped me to understand that being blind did not have to be a disability, that a disability in one area did not mean that you were not intelligent and capable. Mary was a whiz on her brailler, and I'm sure that by now she has become a whiz on a computer. Although I lost touch with her when my family moved to a neighboring town, I have never forgotten her or the impact she had on me. Working with Mary on schoolwork and on tests made me begin to think seriously about teaching as a profession. Although there was nothing like special education at that time, I knew that I had a special interest in working with people who had disabilities of different kinds.

But there was a problem. I couldn't imagine myself being an education major in college once I found out what they were asked to study, and I didn't really believe that you went to college in order to prepare for a specific career or job. I thought—because that was what I had been told at home—you went to college to find out who you were, to deal with identity issues, and to become well-educated and learn how to think. The important thing to me was to have some control over what I got to learn and to be well steeped in the humanities. I wanted the broadest exposure that I could get through my course work or experience.

I also had some religious issues I needed to settle once and for all. I had been raised Catholic because my father was Catholic and would have been excommunicated if my Jewish mother had not agreed in writing to raise all of us as Catholics. But I didn't feel like a Catholic and was drawn toward the Judaism that everyone tried so hard to keep me away from. So I became a Religion and Humanities major, and that meant that I had a heavy concentration of literature, history, religion and foreign language. I found a mentor in my Old Testament professor and began studying with him privately outside of class. I studied the Kabbalah, or Jewish mysticism, I studied all the major religions of the world. I took courses in ethics, the holocaust, esoteric courses like Myth and Ritual. And what I learned from all of this was to put things into the widest possible conceptual frame, to think broadly, to think about integration, connection, relatedness. I learned to respect culture. And I learned to think critically and not accept taken for granted truths. I began to think like a critical theorist. I even began to challenge the way in which I was being taught.

The last trimester of my freshman year I took a course with my mentor in the religion department, and he assigned a paper to be written. I had been reading—on my own—the work of the existentialists and I began to challenge the meaning of my schoolwork. My mentor had a favorite expression, when he had explained and explained a difficult point about sacred text and there was no more to be said. He would say, "He who understands understands," and then throw up his hands and leave the classroom. When it was time to turn in my final paper, I turned in instead a piece of paper with the quote, "He who understands

understands." Instead of a grade, I received a sheet of paper with a series of biblical quotations. I almost left college for good that semester because I felt so strongly that I should be in charge of my own learning and my own curriculum.

My roommates wisely talked me out of leaving school. In my senior year, I had an elective credit I needed to fulfill, and my advisor suggested I take a certain psychology course. Part of the requirement of the course was a field placement. I chose a placement in a resource class for emotionally disturbed adolescents. After a few months, the teacher who was supervising me asked if I would stop by for a talk. She told me that I had a special knack for these kids and asked if I had ever considered going into the field of education. I told her I had always wanted to teach but couldn't see me fitting into a school system with rigid requirements for curriculum. Nevertheless, she suggested that I speak to her principal about an opening they had for the upcoming year. I was interviewed by the principal and hired as a teacher of emotionally disturbed elementary students. I would come to this job with a degree in religion and with no course background in teaching methodology or curriculum. I accepted the job because I needed employment, and because my instincts told me that I should be there. I had no idea what I was getting myself into.

The first year, I spent 16 hours a day either teaching or looking at curriculum and trying to figure out what I should be teaching my students. The truth is that that first year all I figured out was how to teach reading and language arts; math and science was barely touched. I spent the next two summers commuting 200 miles round trip to a site where courses for certification in special education were being offered. I taught for four years before I ever had certification or went through student teaching. I essentially taught myself, my students taught me, about pedagogy and curriculum. I determined what I needed to know and what course of study would help lead me toward answers. I relished the time I spent researching curriculum theory and learning how to develop curriculum for my difficult students. I still do.

Three education degrees later, I can tell you that I am a constructivist and a critical theorist. The college of education I teach for has included constructivism in its conceptual framework, and my students assume that is why I teach it to them. But I explain that I became a constructivist many years ago, many years before I even knew of Piaget and Montessori. Constructivism is just a fancy word for a world view that I arrived at many years ago after having observed my students carefully and thinking about how learning progresses. Constructivism is what I know to be true as a result of examining my own adult learning experience, and going back and thinking about the nine year old me constructing curriculum for my doll school. And I have certain notions about curriculum that come out of my thoughts on constructivism.

I believe that students must construct their own meaning. They should have an opportunity to say what it is they want to learn. The "what" of learning, the actual content, is not as important as the opportunity to learn how to think independently, to be critical about what one reads, to be able to make important connections. Students must learn how to read and to write, and that can be facilitated by a study of moths or World War ll, or genetics, or baseball. Learning is not a linear process. There is no absolute core of knowledge that, once taught, makes one literate. We learn what we want to learn, what we feel is important to us to learn, what we need to learn, we learn what we choose to actively engage in. We cannot, as Freire has pointed out, just deposit knowledge in our students, make one-way transactions. Students must struggle with things, chew on things, notice that there is discontinuity, experience cognitive dissonance, and then choose to resolve the conflict.

When I watch my granddaughter, this little girl who, like me, is showing at a young age an interest in teaching, what I wish for her is that she will find her own voice, move beyond the mere mimicry of her elementary teachers, begin developing her own theory of learning and curriculum. In a real sense, her course of study will be her "self," for as Parker says we teach who we are. She will, of course, also learn math and English and literature and science, so that she has certain content knowledge necessary to make judgments about curriculum development. And if we keep reading together, talking together, maybe she will also learn from me to trust her own ability to construct meaning, establish a path for learning, and to later trust her own students in the same way.

✒ Samples of Reflective Journal Writing as a Performance Task

REFLECTIONS ON RETURNING TO HIGHER EDUCATION
Lorna R. Elam

I was somewhat apprehensive about being an older student in a classroom of twenty-something persons, when I returned to college to get my master's degree. I was almost forty years old at the time and had been out of school for nearly two decades. I was nervous about doing schoolwork again. I cringed at the thought of being in a class with much younger students who were fresh from being undergraduates and therefore much more capable of keeping up with assignments. Although I had already managed to negotiate my way through the career and family track that many of my fellow students were just beginning to consider, I was not sure that I could handle master's level curriculum. At the time, I viewed myself as being a successful Mom and a successful businessperson, but I did not view myself as being all that "scholarly." I had met my responsibilities at home and in the office with flying colors, but I was not sure if I would be able to keep up with the other students in my classroom. Furthermore, I felt that I had all but missed the Technology Age, as I didn't own a personal computer and had never surfed on the internet. The last time I was in school we were still using huge stacks of color-coded 80-column keypunch cards to batch run data through giant mainframe computers that filled the dreary basement of the college science building. Back then, when I was a young college student just out of high school and raring to learn about data processing, there was no Microsoft and I had never heard of Bill Gates. Since then I had only had minimal contact with computers at work for the limited purpose of writing memoranda and maintaining the company's internal data files of customer contact information. Thus there were several reasons why I was overwhelmed with anxiety about returning to school.

Indeed much had changed since I was last a student. On a very intimate level I had found myself reevaluating individual relationships and reexamining my personal goals. My deep introspection happened to be accompanied by the onset of the so-called *empty nest syndrome*. I had become dissatisfied with my career, my home, and my hobbies. I was restless and therefore eager to make some sort of significant change in my life in an effort to suppress my internal discontentment. For years I had been promising myself that one day when the time was right I would return to college to earn a graduate degree. For several years I had focused my energy and attention almost exclusively on family and career, putting my personal dream of attending graduate school on the back burner. But now I found myself in the perfect position to fulfill that dream and to keep that promise to myself, despite the angst I was currently feeling about my being so much older than the other students and a tad out of touch with the latest technology.

I was convinced that I was headed for an enormous struggle to learn how to catch up with the other students who were half my age. Oddly enough, although I routinely learned new things during my everyday life, I told myself that perhaps too many years had passed since I had last been a student, making it even harder for me to learn what I needed to know in order to meet academic requirements. I was intimidated about pending coursework, and I envisioned thick texts and dry lectures full of ten-dollar words that I wouldn't understand. Regardless of my sense of personal and professional accomplishment, returning to college initially brought fear and trepidation to my life.

It took me awhile to figure out how to relax in my new college environment. My sense of purpose and determination helped me get through the first few weeks of classes. I was a resilient and motivated student, committed to reaching my academic goals. In time I became accustomed to the campus pace and even found myself enjoying my interaction with the younger students. I began to recognize some value in my previous life experiences that I could appropriately integrate into participation in class discussions. I also recognized how certain sociopolitical values and beliefs had changed for me over the past twenty years, as I had become a more tolerant and passive adult as a result of my diverse contact and experiences with others over the years. I even recognized that I had become a much more conscientious student than I had been in my early twenties, now giving serious attention to class lectures with more interest in the subject matter. But it wasn't until one of my course instructors assigned reflective journaling as part of the course requirement, that I recognized just how much I was actually learning in school.

I had purchased an Apple Macintosh computer the month before the semester began. Within a few hours of getting the hardware connected and the software installed, I had learned how to access the worldwide web. Within days I had become quite proficient at sending and receiving email. I soon knew how to download information and perform simple word processing tasks with ease. In a matter of just a few weeks of ownership I had declared that I could not imagine how I had managed to get along without a computer in my home for so long.

After all, I was now spending hours in front of that computer screen typing letters, searching for lost friends and relatives, comparing recipes, and bidding in online auctions. I was becoming, according to my son, a "computer junkie." He was right—I was hooked. I was enchanted by the new technology at my fingertips. For the first time in my life I was printing mailing labels for the purpose of addressing Christmas cards; cataloguing gift ideas for birthdays and anniversaries; searching for online medical advice for my neighbor; "chatting" with people across the globe; and catching up on correspondence with old high school chums whom I hadn't contacted in years. I felt organized and efficient, with a renewed vigor and hopefulness for school success, thanks to my new Mac. So by the time classes began that first semester of my graduate studies, I had already discovered I was competent at completing the technology-driven course requirements for my first graduate class.

According to the syllabus for my first master's level course, my final grade in the class would be heavily dependent upon my ability to retrieve and transmit information over the internet. Internet access was a necessary component of the class because students were required to perform online research and email a weekly reflective journal to the instructor. At that time, I had not yet purchased my computer. I had read this technology requirement in the syllabus long before the semester began which, on reflection, had probably only served to heighten my anxiety level concerning returning to school. I could tell from the syllabus that in order to access the internet and to transmit emails to my instructor, I would first need to purchase a computer. So I purchased the Macintosh knowing full well that I would have to quickly master some basic computer skills before the semester began, in order to succeed in the class. When I first read the syllabus I was panicked a bit at the thought of using a computer, but by the time I actually had to go online to do research for the course I felt delightfully adept at it.

The reflective journal was a major key to my being able to overcome the initial apprehension and fear I had concerning my returning to school. I hadn't noticed it at first, but I was retaining quite a bit of the information. Somehow I had managed to hold onto important concepts that had been given to me via course lectures and required reading materials that could be utilized in other areas of my daily life. Each week I would sit down at the computer and recall the information I had gleaned from the lectures and doing coursework, then I would type up some thoughts about what I had learned and how I had applied the knowledge. Many times I found myself asking more questions about the concepts, pondering the utility of those concepts, or making connections between concepts that hadn't been brought up during class. Ultimately the journaling permitted me to challenge some assumptions I had made about myself prior to the semester beginning. As a result of my reflection, I began to critically reevaluate the way that I was seeing myself. In doing so, I reconstructed my self-perceptions. No more could I accept my negative self-talk regarding my ability to learn. To me, being able to reflect on the learning process was evidence enough that I had somehow recaptured my belief in my ability to once again be a good student. The reflective journal provided me with ample evidence that I was a critical thinker, capable of reaching my academic goals. Sure, the journal was also proof to my instructor that I had completed the reading assignments and had taken lecture notes during class, but on a personal level the journaling helped me change some important fundamental beliefs about myself that permitted me to succeed in that class and in the classes that followed.

I eventually graduated Summa Cum Laude with a Master's of Science degree in Marriage and Family Therapy. Graduating with honors meant a lot to me, as it reinforced my renewed positive self-esteem concerning myself as a student. During the course of my therapy studies I had learned about creating paradigm shifts and reframing events in order to effect cognitive and behavioral change. I was now prepared to help individuals learn how to change the way they viewed the world around them, by first changing the way they viewed themselves in that world. In a powerful way, I had experienced these steps firsthand. I had effected a personal change through self-reflection and overcoming barriers, and had consequently discovered a new *me* along the way. By the time I graduated with my master's degree, I no longer viewed myself as an outmoded student, destined to struggle in school. On the contrary, I had proved myself capable of scholastic excellence. Moreover, I was elated about the possibilities for reaching further goals in my life.

I had surprised myself several times during the course of my journey to earn a master's degree. I had learned so much about myself as a student and had grown more confident in the classroom. I had also been able to apply my new knowledge and self-confidence to other areas of my life. I made significant changes in my career and personal relationships that brought me new satisfaction. I discovered a gift for teaching and began developing new clinical instruction resources at the agency where I worked. I was excited about the potential for personal and professional growth. I felt empowered and strong, and capable of conquering just about anything that could come my way. So I wasn't that surprised to find myself searching for new learning opportunities to experience.

I had been encouraged by a number of my instructors to apply for the doctoral program at the university where I had received my master's degree. After all, it seemed logical for me to continue the academic momentum by returning to school shortly after having just graduated. The instructors seemed to want me back in their classes and I certainly enjoyed myself in that arena. Thus the decision to go back to school to get my doctorate degree carried with it relatively little anxiety. Indeed, in comparison to the feelings I had experienced during the months prior to entering graduate school to earn the master's degree, I was clearly feeling confidently secure about succeeding at the doctoral level. I knew that the doctoral level brought with it increased competition and much more work, but I felt self-assured and quite capable of meeting course expectations. So I began my search for an appropriate doctoral program, and within a few months I was packing up my household belongings in order to move 2000 miles from home so that I could attend the university that I chose.

I weighed several factors in deciding which doctoral program to choose. I was interested in leadership, policy-making, and teaching, as well as mental health administration and ethnic studies. I had been involved in conducting multicultural and ethnic diversity training through my job, and had always enjoyed working with people to enhance their understanding and acceptance of others. I had also been a business manager or administrator in some capacity for most of my adult life. Furthermore, within a year of becoming internet-savvy I had developed a thriving web-based business, and I was currently enjoying being a dot-com entrepreneur. In sum, I had a wide spectrum of interests and possibilities for a career track. Although I had a basic idea of what direction I wanted my career to take, I was flexible and open to alternative career paths. So I considered several universities and various doctoral programs that might offer me a diverse and enriching educational environment. I established a set of criteria that I used to narrow my search down to two choices. I applied for admission at both schools and was accepted at each. Both universities were located outside of my state, so I knew that I would have to leave family and friends behind in order to pursue my doctoral degree in the way that I wanted to. I made my final decision on which university to attend based on subsequent interviews that I had with each of the relative department chairpersons for the programs where I had applied.

I noticed a tremendous change in the way I interacted with the department chairs during my doctoral-level interviews, as opposed to my interactions with the department chair who interviewed me years prior for the master's program. Sure, they were different people, in different programs, and at different universities. Their interviewing styles were marginally different as well. But the most significant difference was noticeably in my level of confidence and participation during the interviewing process. Back when I applied for entrance into the master's program, I wasn't sure that I belonged there; I lacked confidence about my academic abilities; and I was worried about whether or not I could meet the program's requirements. Conversely, when I interviewed for both of the doctoral programs where I applied, I found myself less concerned about whether or not I could meet the *program's* needs and more concerned about whether or not the program could meet *mine*. In other words, over the years my self-assuredness had progressed in a way that permitted me to focus on meeting my needs like never before. My dreams and goals would no longer be placed on a back burner. My vision of myself as a doctoral student clearly contrasted my previous self-perceptions as an entry level student in the master's program.

For some reason I had begun to see myself as a valuable *consumer of education*. And as such, I had a belief that the instructors and support personnel at whatever university I would ultimately choose to attend had the onus to meet my needs as a consumer. I had a clear understanding of what I wanted in an institution of higher learning. I saw myself as being worthy of a high quality and innovative doctoral program with national recognition. I wanted to be in a program that "meant something" to me; I wanted to be part of a university that was committed to social justice; and I wanted to graduate with a degree of which I could be proud. I was not afraid of hard work and purposely sought a program that was committed to maintaining high standards of academic excellence and positive interaction with its students and the community surrounding it. So during the interviews, I was assertive in asking questions and relaxed in giving responses to the persons who interviewed me. It was relatively easy for me to make my final decision as to which university to attend, and within a few weeks of the interview I was settling into my new home and my new life as doctoral student at that university.

Today I am part of a doctoral cohort group at that university, where I continue to study and grow as a member of the university's diverse community of learners. I am an empowered and active participant in my learning process. I don't worry about my age and I don't fret about the ages of the students who surround me. I continue to enjoy learning about new technology and new means by which to access information. I embrace new experiences and glean knowledge wherever I can. I am growing as a leader and as a professional committed to making positive social changes in my community. Overall, mine continues to be a fruitful journey, and I am most grateful for the route I have taken in discovering some truths about *me*.

REFLECTIONS ON BECOMING AN EDUCATOR
Susan Katz, Ph.D.
December 2002

When I am asked to write about my motivation to become an educator, I have to reflect upon my background, and how I became interested in children. The interest in children stems from a belief that there is much to learn from children, and that by nature they are producers (rather than consumers) of knowledge. My experiences growing up in a small midwestern town are relevant; experiences as a child amidst a large immediate and extended family with lots of aunts, uncles, and cousins. Cousins at each generation led to big gatherings at birthday parties, holiday celebrations, and family events. All that sense of togetherness was probably the biggest precursor to my ability to be at ease with and relate to children of all ages.

The best teachers, those who I remember well, seemed to be the eccentric ones. Ms. Monahan had orange hair, dressed in a Bohemian style and liked to brew tea and knit in her seventh grade speech class. Students were routinely sent to the store across from the junior high school to get the special tea our teacher required. Ms. Monahan introduced the class to the concept of extemporaneous speech making. This was the assignment that showed me I had talent for speaking about virtually anything for an extended period of time while seemingly holding the interest of my audience. Was this an important prerequisite to an academic teaching career? Possibly.

As an undergraduate at the University of Texas, Austin, I had to declare a major. My mother said, "Be a teacher because if your husband dies, you can always have something to fall back on to support yourself." In my family and in my mother's generation women were housewives. In the mid 1960s their daughters went to college. Why? To find a husband, mainly: that was the subliminal message. So that is exactly what I did. I married after my college sophomore year and since my husband was enrolled in his freshman year in medical school, I had to go to work. What kind of job could I get after only two years of college, and as a woman? The jobs I was able to find were menial—clerical, secretarial jobs. After four years of working in jobs I disliked, I happily went back to school and earned both the Bachelor's and the Master's degrees in Communication Disorders: Speech/Language Pathology. My education was empowering. I found a fit with this field, excelled in the academics and the clinical practicum, and had good feedback from my supervisors. My first job as a Speech and Language Clinician was at a residential treatment center for children in grades K–12 with emotional/behavioral disabilities. That was definitely trial by fire. After that year, I knew I could be comfortable and interested in any child, any disability, and of any age. After working in private clinics, public and parochial schools, and rehab centers, I transitioned from clinician to administrator and spent several years directing and supervising staff in special education. Time went by, my children graduated from college and became independent adults, and we survived several years away from the Chicago we loved, only to return again very recently.

Before moving back to Chicago, I entered a doctoral program in Educational Administration at Indiana State University. Coursework was stimulating; working in a cohort was a special experience, somewhat like my experience with extended family. When it came time to think about a topic for my dissertation, I had to think through a dilemma. As an administrator in special education, I wasn't sure if I wanted to confine my research to that field or broaden my scope to educational administration as a whole. I found my topic through a workshop given by two women school superintendents geared toward encouraging women to enter leadership positions in schools. It was powerful to hear these women talk about the success they were having in their positions particularly in view of the fact that only about 10 percent of superintendents in the U.S. are women. I had encountered gender discrimination in applying for administrative positions in my career and this topic "spoke to me"! My research with women school superintendents taught me about the resiliency of women, how they approach the top job in education and how well they are doing in a typically male-dominated position.

My current position as assistant professor in a department of educational leadership at a small private nondenominational university has given me the opportunity to reflect on my wide range of experiences in education. How can I bring it all together to make some meaning out of where I have been and what it can bring to my "new" career? Because of the diverse urban student population at my university, I have been able to embrace the university's mission of social justice and infuse that purpose throughout my courses. I have been able to rekindle my interest in special education. Teaching a course in special education for school leaders, I am not only a strong advocate for students with disabilities, I strive to teach future school leaders that they need to embrace the principles of inclusion in providing an effective and caring education for students of all abilities. From my research, I am able to integrate into my courses what I have learned about how powerful women are leading their school districts, since most of my students are women. I teach about the problem of gender discrimination in schools and how it begins early and how it impedes women from believing that they can become leaders in the nation's schools. Also from my research I learned that aspiring women leaders need women mentors, there are not many in the world of educational administration. I do my part to mentor women leaders. I encourage women students I teach, counsel, and advise to believe in themselves as leaders and to seek those top leadership jobs in education. Through my teaching, I try to walk the walk, not just talk the talk.

Through my teaching, I am continually evolving as an educator. Each class changes me. How are learners approaching the content of my courses and using the knowledge they gain to inform and transform their practice as educators and future school leaders? Through my teaching, I am also evolving as a researcher. What needs to change in programs of educational leadership so that women in the pipeline do go on to aspire to the superintendency and experience success in that position? These are just a few questions that I have recently begun asking. I look forward to asking and finding answers to these and more overarching questions. So I am excited to say that I firmly believe I have found that "good fit" for me as an educator, at this stage of my life. And it might have all begun with Ms. Monahan's extemporaneous speaking assignment.

Appendix H

•• Examples of Reflection on Curriculum as Racial Text

A REFLECTION ON CRITICAL RACE THEORY AND CURRICULUM
Eva Smith

The racialization of curriculum manifests itself in content, materials, instructional activities, relationships between adults, and between teachers and students in schools. The influence of race in curriculum mirrors its influence in society, powerful, complex, and devisive, yet is minimized in discourse. As a determinant of power, privilege and opportunity race is embedded in the sociopolitical and socioeconomic structures of the United States. Civil rights legislation and executive actions have caused some improvements in the most outward expressions of discrimination. However, these initiatives have not permeated societal beliefs and practices enough to reduce the forces of marginalization in favor of inclusive practices in hiring, business, housing, or education that would create redistribution of power and wealth. The existence of haves and have nots continues and prevents social change while contributing to frustration, resentment, and racial isolation between African-Americans and Caucasian-Americans. The unheard voices of all marginalized people hinder the collective depth of our knowledge (Pinar, 2000). The voices from the bottom theorize differently the standards conceptualized in a "raced" world.

Black curriculum development has been conceived to promote views and purposes within the black experience and those imposed from without, including colonialism, American apartheid, and discriminatory exclusion (Watkins, 1993). Ogbu (1994) and Watkins (1993) suggest racial and structural stratification as imposed socio-educational ideologies in black curriculum development. Both forces are concerned with the physical (restriction to neighborhoods and locations) and sociopolitical (short-circuiting of radical activity) containment of blacks. Within the black experience differing views regarding response to dominant culture attitudes about race, African-American responses to domination and marginalization, and literary versus utilitarian education for African-Americans shape curriculum debate. Black curriculum development as a force for changing educational inequity and inequality is informed by the history of the black experience in the United States. Socially oppressive and politically repressive systems impose adverse effects on black education through societal educational policies and practices, non-representation in textbooks and curriculum, and community forces or African-American perceptions and responses to schooling (Ogbu, 1994, Watkins, 1993). These factors have resulted in deep distrust in the public schools and the white or minority representatives who control them, within the African-American community.

The implications of critical race theory, borrowed from legal scholarship and Ladson-Billings' (1994) culturally relevant pedagogy, on black curriculum development will be discussed. Critical race theory "challenges the experiences of whites as the normative standard and grounds its conceptual framework in the distinctive experiences of people of color." Through the use of storytelling, the negative experiences of people affected by racism are used "to confront beliefs held about them by whites" (Taylor, 1998, p. 122). Culturally relevant pedagogy considers cultural competence (firm grounding in the culture of origin), sociopolitical consciousness and critique, and academic achievement to be foundational concepts of successful teachers of African-American students (Ladson-Billings, 1994). Critical race theory and culturally relevant pedagogy are concerned with the educational needs of African-Americans in a non-assimilationist context emphasizing pedagogy and practice that support black cultural identity.

Introduced by Derrick Bell and others in the legal community dissatisfied with civil rights progress given the increasingly conservative leanings of the judiciary, critical race theory seeks to include the issue of racial oppression in the discourse about legal issues and society. It provides an analysis "by and about people of color" as it questions the dominant group's assertions of its own standards of neutrality and colorblindness (Lynn, 1999, p. 2, Taylor, 1998). Historically, black interest in racial equality has been given little consideration unless presented and implemented in ways that served the power and economic self-interests of whites. As the foundation of the white power structure, the legal system has been instrumental in the maintenance of white privilege. The history of the legal system's service to African-Americans places in question the courts' commitment to racial equality. For analysis of the philosophies and processes of existing systems, critical race theory:

1. Offers a sound and systematic critique of the legal system in the United States;
2. Recognizes the centrality of race and intransigence of racism in contemporary American Society;
3. Rejects West-European/Modernist claims of neutrality, objectivity, rationality, and universality;

4. Historizes its analysis by relying heavily on the experiential, situated, and "subjugated" knowledge of people of color;
5. Is interdisciplinary in its focus because of its roots in philosophical, historical, and sociological thought, such as Postmodernism, Marxism, Black Nationalism, and Black Feminist thought; and
6. Seeks to eliminate racial oppression in the United States by linking it to other forms of oppression, such as sexism and classism/elitism.

(Lynn, 1999, p. 2)

The tenets of critical race theory inform educational curriculum theory by giving voice to those traditionally at the bottom in the determination of the philosophy and knowledge worthy to be studied. It critiques research and interpretation that minimizes the influence of racial oppression in educational decision-making. It redefines educational best practice for African-American students to require the centering of African-American culture, worldview, and history in pedagogy and practice. Ladson-Billings and Tate (1995) use the notion of education as a property right and curriculum as representative of "a form of intellectual property," in their interpretation of critical race theory in education. "The quality and quantity of the curriculum varies with the property values of the school." Inequitable facilities are violations of students' civil rights when "standards" are unsupported by the resources and materials necessary for learning related to the standards. Critical race theory, in their thesis, respectfully notes the shortcomings of Thurgood Marshall and the NAACP in arguing the Brown case. The benefit of "forty years of hindsight" provides that anti-discrimination arguments were and are dependent on the nonexistent meritocracy of the courts and the dominant social order in regard "to ending racial subordination." The "intransigence" of racism was not fully recognized. The reality of all that has happened since, particularly the present racialization of educational opportunity, rejects integration as the relief for racial oppression in school systems.

Resistance to critical race theory questions the extent to which race determines thought, action, and in the university, writing. The acceptance of racism as "normal activity in American society" is also resisted. It is criticized as "too cynical, nihilistic and hopeless" (Taylor, 1998, p. 124). However, the redistribution of power, privilege, influence, and wealth necessary for the next steps toward racial equality will not occur until the pervasive, negative forces of racial oppression are identified and addressed. Derrick Bell contends that the struggle against racism must be maintained and the quest for integration and "equality under law" should be pursued less vigorously, in favor of reform of the existing power structures, to avoid further erosion of black rights. In the application of this process to curriculum, critical race theory contributes to the discourse by including the lived experiences of African-Americans in and out of schools. It contributes further by providing a thoughtful explanation of power structures within the educational community and how those structures support oppressive pedagogy and practice within the educational community and in society.

> Culture is both the result and the consequence of the struggle; it is dynamic and ever changing, yet structured around collective memories and traditions. The cultural history of U.S. blacks is, in part, the struggle to maintain their own group's sense of identity, social cohesion and integrity, in the face of policies which have been designed to deny both their common humanity and particularity. (Marable, 1995, p. 6)

Culturally relevant pedagogy offers a framework for instruction of African-American students that includes academic achievement, competence in African and African-American history and culture, and consciousness raising critique of national and international sociopolitical structures and events. In common with critical pedagogy, culturally relevant pedagogy:

> refers to a deliberate attempt to influence how and what knowledge and identities are produced within and among particular sets of social relations. It can be understood as a practice through which people are incited to acquire a particular "moral character." As both a political and practical activity, it attempts to influence the occurrence and qualities of experiences. (Ladson-Billings, 1992, p. 382)

Both pedogically "strive to incorporate student experience as 'official' content" (Ladson-Billings, 1992, p. 382). They differ in the individual focus of critical pedagogy contrasting the collective action urged by culturally relevant pedagogy (Ladson-Billings, 1992). Resulting from research with teachers of African-American students, identified as successful by the students' parents (all mothers), for having "encouraged their children to *choose* academic excellence, while at the same time it allowed them to maintain a positive identification with their own heritage and background" (Ladson-Billings, 1992, p. 382). Working with eight teachers, common strands emerged. Strong sense of purpose, awareness of the position of African-Americans in society and of "how this played a part in the school's expectations for African-American students," a level of concern regarding the workings of U.S. society, and responsibility for helping students identify the existence of contradictions and inequities in their communities and the world, guided their practice (Ladson-Billings, 1992, p. 382). Compared to traditional or "assimilationist" teachers, instruction was intended to "prepare students to effect change in society, not merely fit into it" (Ladson-Billings, 1992, p. 382). Capitalizing on the home and community culture, culturally relevant teachers sought to empower students "intellectually, socially, emotionally and politically by using cultural referents to impart knowledge, skills and attitudes" (Ladson-Billings, 1992, p. 382). Culturally relevant teaching builds on the cultural capital of students as a means of creating student interest in and commitment to academic achievement. Achievement provides students with the skills to navigate racialized sociopolitical relationships and environments.

Opposition, ambivalence, and mistrust are responses of involuntary minority adults and children that schools and teachers must deal with to work effectively with African-American students. The development of trusting relationships is essential and such relationships evolve as parents and students come to believe that teachers have students' best interests at heart and students' identities and self-esteem are valued (Ogbu and Simons, 1998). The use of culturally relevant pedagogy and practice in teacher education programs would help to prepare teachers to use and teach the critique of existing social structures. Preservice teachers must also become proficiently culturally competent, given the diversity of student cultures, not only in the teacher's culture of origin but in other cultures as well. Preparation should extend to shared experiences and contexts for using informed cultural competence to improve learning. Though culturally relevant teaching is concerned with providing better-informed practice for teaching African-American students, cultural competence, sociopolitical consciousness and critique, and academic achievement would provide a sound theoretical foundation for the development of curriculum to address the learning needs of students across cultures. The tenets of culturally relevant teaching contribute to the discourse regarding learning styles, differentiated instruction, student-centered instruction, and afrocentric curriculum. It may also advance cultural communication, particularly when teachers and students are from different cultures of origin.

> The most effective and enduring black responses to invisibility and namelessness are those forms of individual and collective black resistance predicated on a deep and abiding black love. These responses take the shape of prophetic thought and action: bold, fearless, courageous attempts to tell the truth about and bear witness to black suffering and to keep faith with a vision of black redemption. (Gates and West, 1997, p. 90)

"Any comprehensive theory of curriculum must include race and its concepts—such as multiculturalism, identity, marginality, and difference as fundamental" (Pinar, Reynolds, Slattery, Taubman, 2000, p. 319). Color-blindness has become the notion used in existing power structures to justify moving away from affirmative action and other legally based remedies for addressing racial inequality. Teachers often relate "I don't see color, I just see children." The move away from acknowledging recognition of difference is more accurately identified as the failure to come to terms with the role that difference plays in our society in favor of white privilege. "What we should seek is not a color-blind society but a more democratic social order where race 'disappears' as a fundamental category for the distribution of power, material resources and privilege" (Marable, 1998, p. 3). Nearly one-hundred years ago The Reverend Alexander Crummell and W. E. B. DuBois introduced the idea that black ministers, civil servants, educators, and scholars would provide the necessary leadership for the resistance of black oppression in the United States (Watkins, 1993, Gates and West, 1997). Prepared for "significant societal participation," black intellectuals would commit themselves to the elevation of African-Americans through scholarship and action. Critical race theory and culturally relevant pedagogy are representative of African-American scholarship that honors the history, culture, and traditions of African-Americans, placing this knowledge as distinct and essential to sociopolitical, socioeconomic, and socioeducational advancement (Watkins, 1993, p. 328). Recognizing that all Americans, across races and cultures experience a "repressed American identity" from the loss of knowledge the curriculum has denied, consideration of theory from people of color engages previously hidden ideas and perspectives (Pinar, Reynolds, Slattery, Taubman, 2000). Curriculum development will reach a new level when black curriculum theories inform curricular decision-making and practice to restructure and redefine the knowledge base.

References

Brown, E. (1995). The Tower of Babel: Bridging the divide between critical race theory and "mainstream" civil rights scholarships. *Yale Law Journal* [On-Line serial], *105* (2). Available OCLC FirstSearch: Full Text.

Gates, H. and West, C. (1997). *The Future of the Race.* New York: Vintage Books.

Ladson-Billings, G. (Sum 1992). Liberatory Consequences of Literacy: A Case of Culturally Relevant Instruction for African American Students. *Journal of Negro Education* [On-Line serial], *61* (3).

Ladson-Billings, G. (1994). *The Dreamkeepers: Successful Teachers of African-American Children.* San Francisco: Jossey-Bass.

Ladson-Billings, G. and Tate, W. (Fall 1995). Toward a critical race theory of education. *Teachers College Record* [On-Line serial], *97* (1). Available OCLC FirstSearch: Full Text.

Lynn, M. (Jan. 1999). Toward a critical race pedagogy: A research note. *Urban Education* [On-Line serial], *33* (5). Available OCLC FirstSearch: Full Text.

Marable, M. (July 1995). History and black consciousness: The political culture of black America. *Monthly Review* [On-Line serial], *47* (3). Available OCLC FirstSearch: Full Text.

Marable, M. (Dec. 1998). Beyond color-blindness. *Nation* [On-Line serial], *267* (20). Available OCLC FirstSearch: Full Text.

Ogbu, J. (Winter 1994). Racial stratification and education in the United States: Why inequality persists. *Teachers College Record* [On-Line serial], *96* (2). Available OCLC FirstSearch: Full Text.

Ogbu, J. and Simons, H. (June 1998). Voluntary and involuntary minorities: A cultural-ecological theory of school performance with some implications for education. *Anthropology & Education Quarterly* [On-Line serial], *29* (2). Available OCLC FirstSearch: Full Text.

Pinar, W., Reynolds, W., Slattery, P., Taubman, P. (2000). *Understanding Curriculum* (Vol. 17). New York: Peter Lang.

Taylor, E. (Spring 1998). A Primer on Critical Race Theory. *The Journal of Blacks in Higher Education* [On-Line serial], *0* (19). Available JSTOR.org.

Watkins, W. (Fall 1993). Black Curriculum Orientations: A Preliminary Inquiry. *Harvard Educational Review, 63* (3).

THE IMPLICATIONS OF CRITICAL RACE THEORY AND CULTURALLY RELEVANT PEDAGOGY ON BLACK CURRICULUM DEVELOPMENT

Eva Smith
July 17, 2002

Critical race theory challenges the experience of whites as the normative standard and grounds its conceptual framework in the distinctive experiences of people of color. Culturally relevant pedagogy is concerned with the practice of successful teachers of African-American students. Cultural competence (in the culture of origin), sociopolitical consciousness and critique, and academic achievement provide the framework.

Critical race theory in education is borrowed from legal scholarship. The movement was founded by Derrick Bell, Charles Lawrence, Lani Guinier, Richard Delgado, Mari Matsuda, Patricia Williams, and Kimberle Crenshaw. The stories of the disenfranchised are used to place racial oppression in a social and experiential context. References to race, difference, marginalization, and oppression inform the dialogue for naming black reality.

Culturally relevant pedagogy is the work of Gloria Ladson-Billings. It places the history and culture of Africa and African-Americans at the center of the curriculum. Critique of the methods and motives of existing power structures, including the school, are encouraged and African-American students are motivated to use academic achievement as a form of empowerment for navigating racial oppression.

Both are examples of African-American scholarship for elevating black cultural identity to the center of curriculum, focused on the improvement of educational experiences of African-American students.

●◦ Index

⚭ About the Author

Valerie J. Janesick is professor of educational leadership and policy studies at the University of South Florida, Tampa. She teaches courses in qualitative research methods, program evaluation, and curriculum theory, development, and assessment. She has written books and articles in these areas, and her most recent text is *The Assessment Debate: A Reference Handbook* (2001), published by ABC-CLIO. She recently participated in the Oxford Roundtable 2002, at Lincoln College, University of Oxford. Her text *Stretching Exercises for Qualitative Researchers* (1998, second edition 2004) uses the metaphor of dance and the arts to teach interviewing, observation, and archival techniques. Her articles and book chapters on qualitative research methods argue for understanding the value of aesthetics in the research process. She looks forward to her next text on the work of John Dewey and her continuing study of Hatha yoga.